GLOBAL JOURNALISM ETHICS

Global Journalism Ethics

STEPHEN J.A. WARD

McGill-Queen's University Press
Montreal & Kingston · London · Ithaca

© McGill-Queen's University Press 2010
ISBN 978-0-7735-3678-4 (cloth)
ISBN 978-0-7735-3693-7 (pbk)

Legal deposit second quarter 2010
Bibliothèque nationale du Québec

Printed in Canada on acid-free paper that is 100% ancient forest
free (100% post-consumer recycled), processed chlorine free

McGill-Queen's University Press acknowledges the support of the
Canada Council for the Arts for our publishing program. We also
acknowledge the financial support of the Government of Canada
through the Book Publishing Industry Development Program
(BPIDP) for our publishing activities.

Library and Archives Canada Cataloguing in Publication

Ward, Stephen J. A. (Stephen John Anthony), 1951–
    Global journalism ethics / Stephen J.A. Ward.

Includes bibliographical references and index.
ISBN 978-0-7735-3678-4 (bnd)
ISBN 978-0-7735-3693-7 (pbk)

1. Journalistic ethics. I. Title.

PN4756.W373 2010   174'.90704   C2009-906990-3

Typeset by Jay Tee Graphics Ltd. in 10.5/13 Sabon

Contents

To my parents

HAROLD and MACRENA

who taught me love without boundaries.

GLOBAL JOURNALISM ETHICS

The Importance of Philosophy

Journalism faces a crisis of ethics that threatens to lower its standards, demean its honorable history, and question its future as a democratic agent of the public sphere. Economic and social forces undermine the relevancy of journalism principles while technology creates a universe of new media that redefines the definition of journalist. These staggering changes occur as news organizations can now, more easily than ever before, reach people around the world.

Journalists struggle to maintain a credible ethical identity as they sail the roiling sea of wired and wireless media, a postmodern version of Heraclitus's world of flux where nothing can be known because nothing stays the same. What can ethics *mean* for a profession that must provide instant news and analysis, and where everyone can be a publisher, thanks to the internet? Rapid change has created confusion about existing goals and standards of journalism. This confusion runs deep, going even deeper than debates about specific problems of practice, such as the use of confidential sources. The confusion extends to how journalists should serve the public good and what journalists are "for."[1] No wonder the ship of journalism lacks direction.

Three convictions motivate the writing of this book. The first conviction is that journalism ethics is in the midst of a difficult transition that cannot be adequately addressed by traditional principles and concepts. There is no turning back. We need to reinvent journalism ethics for a new age, from the ground up. The second conviction is that, to achieve this reinvention, philosophical thought is essential. The third conviction is that philosophical thought will lead us to the

conclusion that any adequate ethic of journalism should be cosmopolitan in content, procedure, and aim.

MAIN TOPICS

The book's argument starts from the belief that, to do ethics systematically and critically, we need to gain a philosophical perspective on
three things: the nature of ethics, the nature of ethical thinking, and
the aims of ethics. First, we seek to understand why humans articulate and follow ethical norms. Second, we ask what forms of reasoning promote good ethical judgment and analysis. Ethical thinking
includes not only a consideration of method and practical reasoning.
It also includes the articulation of appropriate principles for spheres
of activity, from medicine to journalism, and the application of those
principles to concrete situations. Third, we ask about the purpose
of ethics and reasoning. In sum, to do ethics properly, we need (1) a
conception of ethics and its aims, (2) a set of principles and forms of
reasoning, and (3) an ability to apply these principles to situations
to determine correct action.

The same point holds for journalism ethics. It is difficult to determine what a journalist should do unless we have a conception of the
aims and principles of ethical journalism, and we are able to apply
principles to situations.

Our theories for the three topics are like three pieces of a puzzle
that must fit together smoothly, if we are to be in possession of a
coherent ethical philosophy. Consistency and coherence in theory
is required because our beliefs in these three areas influence each
other. My conception of the aims of ethics will be influenced by
my reflections on the nature of ethical activity; my conception of
ethical reasoning will be influenced by my conception of the aims
of ethics. Consider this: If you change your views on the aim of ethics, it is likely that you will feel pressure to modify your principles
and judgments about correct conduct. Imagine that I believe that
the aim of journalism is to aggressively hold the state to account
for its actions in order to benefit citizens. However, you hold that
the aim is to advance the interests of the state and social stability.
It is likely that you and I will differ on what principles and practices are ethically acceptable among journalists. Where I encourage
journalists to embarrass and criticize the state, you may see such
criticism as undermining public confidence in the state and causing
instability. The moral is that ethics needs to be systematic. It needs

a philosophical framework that links the three topics in a consistent manner.

STRUCTURE OF *GLOBAL JOURNALISM ETHICS*

The book is organized around three topics. Section 1 lays out my views on ethics – its nature, reasoning, and aims. Chapter 1 deals with the nature of ethics and journalism ethics. Chapter 2 outlines my view of ethical thinking in general and in journalism, and chapter 3 presents the ultimate aim of ethics as ethical flourishing.

With regard to the nature of ethics I advocate naturalism, which conceives of ethics as a rational, human invention. With regard to ethical reasoning, I advocate a holistic model of reasoning about situations, principles, and aims. With regard to aims, I put forward a theory of the "good in the right" – a theory that combines justice and the human good. I claim that the aim of ethics is the construction of a liberal democracy where citizens enjoy a relatively free pursuit of their goods within the bounds of justice. To construct this theory, I draw ideas from the philosopher John Rawls, theories of human development, and the tradition of perfectionism.

In section 2, I show how my philosophical positions redefine journalism ethics and provide a foundation for global journalism ethics. Across three chapters, the basic concepts of my naturalistic journalism ethics are extended and redefined to become the basic concepts of a global journalism ethics. Chapter 4 describes the project of a global journalism ethics. Chapter 5 shows how the political aim of global journalism ethics is to promote global democracy where nations (and other groups) pursue their good within the bounds of global justice. The aim of a cosmopolitan journalism ethics is the promotion of this global democratic world. Finally, in chapter 6, I show how this form of global journalism ethics addresses an important question in journalism: to what extent can a global journalist also be a patriot?

In this way, journalism ethics crosses borders. The journalist becomes a global citizen with a global social contract and a cosmopolitan set of ethical principles.

PHILOSOPHICAL RESPONSE

This book, then, is a philosophical response to the practical problems that beset journalism. Theoretically, philosophy should bring its intellectual resources to bear on the most important problems of the day. It can give us new aims while clarifying old assumptions. As Alasdair MacIntyre writes, one of the central tasks of the moral philosopher is "to articulate the convictions of the society in which he or she lives so that these convictions become available for rational scrutiny."[2] John Dewey argues that philosophy should offer "hypotheses" to "render men's minds more sensitive to the life about them."[3]

Philosophy is relevant because ideas and assumptions influence how individuals, institutions, and nations behave, and how they understand the problems they face. Philosophical analysis can have impact on practice via its influence on our conceptual schemes, values, and beliefs. Given the central role of journalism in society, a philosophy of journalism is no more unusual than a philosophy of science or a philosophy of mind.

A philosophical response is especially pertinent in journalism today because traditional values and established practices are under question. We need to step back from the confusion and obtain a general perspective that can once again place some conceptual order on journalistic values and beliefs. Only with the help of a philosophical theory of justice and goodness can we be clear about what it means for journalism to serve the public interest in a global age. Without philosophical grounding, journalists will be uncertain about their fundamental goals and allegiances.

Once journalists define what they stand for, they can proceed, with greater clarity, to redefine standards, improve institutions, and alter practices. To be in possession of clear bedrock notions is one way to keep one's head above Heraclitus's flux. My framework attempts to provide this sort of philosophical clarification. It steps back and asks about the nature of ethics – its reasoning and its aims – in a global world.

In *The Invention of Journalism Ethics,* I explored how journalism ethics evolved. In this book, I am not concerned with the history of journalism ethics. I am concerned with its future. This book is not another tirade about the evil forces at work in journalism. The sins of modern journalism have been documented and "deconstructed" for years. The time has come for reconstruction. We need a convergence of conceptual inventions and practical proposals.

This book offers some conceptual inventions for consideration. It is a book of ideas with an eye to how journalism is practiced on the ground. I hope these concepts provide signposts for the road ahead. I hope to assist journalism, conceptually, in its passage to a global journalism ethics.

SECTION ONE

Ethical Foundations

1

The Ethical Sphere

The good is, like nature, an immense landscape in which man advances through centuries of exploration.

José Ortega y Gasset[1]

The natural starting point for a philosophy of journalism ethics is the nature of ethics. In this chapter, I draw the contours of the ethical sphere, and then I explain how journalism ethics is part of that sphere.

The first half of the chapter explains how ethics is a distinct normative part of human experience defined by the attempt to live in goodness and right relations with others. I claim that serious engagement with ethical questions begins with doubt prompted by complex situations and a tension between our many values. Ethics responds by engaging in reflection that seeks to integrate basic values and guide conduct. This ethical response is distinctive because it adopts a caring yet impartial stance toward fundamental issues recognized as "ethical." Having described the ethical sphere in this manner, I recommend naturalism as a specific approach to ethics.

In the second half of the chapter, I describe journalism ethics as one form of naturalized ethics applied to an important domain of society – journalism. I explain the elements of journalism ethics, its history, and its characteristic problems. I conclude by explaining how a naturalistic perspective perceives journalism ethics.

NATURE OF ETHICS

"Ethics" comes from the Greek word, *ethos*, meaning "character" or "personal disposition." It refers to the manner in which people conduct themselves. "Morals" stems from the Latin "mores," the customs of a group. Morality as mores is close to the common idea of ethics as conduct according to the rules of a group.

The etymology of "ethics" and "morality" suggests that ethics is concerned about both internal things such as character, and external things such as the rules of society. Ethics is both individualistic and social. It is individualistic because individuals are asked to make the rules part of their character and set of values. It is social because ethics is not about every person formulating their own rules. Correct conduct is honouring rules that apply to all members of a group.

These preliminary reflections lead to an initial definition of ethics. Ethics is correct conduct, responsible practice, and fair human interactions according to certain principles and values. It consists of three elements. First, analysis: the articulation and justification of principles. Second, practical judgment: the application of principles to issues. Third, virtuous character: the development of ethical character so that people are disposed to follow principles. Ethics has three core concerns: appropriate ethical beliefs, correct application, and the disposition to act ethically.

Ethics has wide scope. It analyzes the practice of individuals, groups, institutions, professions, and countries. Ethics is demanding. It demands that we live in a specific manner, that is, in goodness and in right relation with each other. Ethics may require us to forgo personal benefits, to carry out duties, or to endure persecution. Through ethics, we articulate our deepest values. Ethics is fundamental and serious. It concerns rights, duties, human flourishing, and the reduction of harm. Through ethics, we find a way to live and to give ourselves an identity – who we are, at our best.

The principles of ethics are brought together to form moral systems, or codes of conduct, such as utilitarian ethics and Buddhist ethics. The Bible's Ten Commandments is one such code. In addition, there are codes for doctors, lawyers, and journalists. Consequently, "ethics" can refer to something singular or multiple. We can understand "ethics" as the proper name for a single ethical system. For example, one may believe that there is only one set of correct principles and that is what ethics *is*. Or, we can think of "ethics" as a general term that refers to many ethical systems. "Ethics" in this sense, resembles "language," which refers to many language systems.

Despite this emphasis on codes, ethics should not be identified with a set of rules, such as "Do not steal," "Do not lie," "Keep one's promises," "Do not kill or harm," "Help those in need," "Treat others as you would have them treat you." A set of principles is too static to capture the dynamic nature of ethics. Although ethics uses principles, ethics is best regarded as practical *activity*. It is something we do. We *do* ethics when we weigh values in making a decision. We *do* ethics when we modify practices in light of new facts, new technology. Moreover, the content and the boundaries of ethics change. In our time, ethics has come to include such issues as animal welfare, protecting the environment, and the rights of gay couples.

If ethics is dynamic and changing, ethics is not a set of rules to be followed blindly or defended dogmatically. In many cases, there will be legitimate debate as to *whether* and *how* rules should apply. Even principles we hold dear will have to be reinterpreted. For example, how should we apply the principle of respect for life to the issue of how long to keep a dying person alive medically, through new technology? Once-accepted practices, such as slavery, come to be rejected. Ethics is the critiquing of practices, and the development of better principles. The difference between living one's ethics and simply following social mores is that the former rejects the uncritical acceptance of rules and conventions. Ethics requires that we follow rules that we have critically examined for their justification and their consequences.

Ethics refers to the never-completed project of inventing, applying, and critiquing the principles that guide human interaction, define social roles, and justify institutional structures. Ethical deliberation is *reason in social practice* – the construction of fair ethical systems for society. Philosophy is crucial to ethics since philosophy is reflective engagement with the urgent issues of any era.

Ethical Experience

The starting point of ethics is lived experience. We discuss ethics philosophically *after* we have had some experience in living well or badly. Ethical experience encompasses learning norms, dealing with the consequences of ill-considered actions, of having the moral emotions of guilt and compassion. We know *directly* what ethics is when we are ashamed of our behaviour or when we are torn between conflicting values. We experience ethics internally as the tug of conscience. We experience ethics externally as the demands placed upon us by codes of ethics, backed by social sanction.

To anyone who asks "What is ethics?" we can reply: think about your most difficult decisions. Did you break a promise? Did you have to report improper behaviour by a colleague to authorities?

Did you promote your career by spreading rumours about a rival worker? Think about those actions where you had a sinking feeling that you let yourself and others down. Or, think about the most dehumanizing types of action, such as torture or child abuse. The heartbeat of ethics is felt wherever people contest judgments of good and bad, wherever people debate obligations and rights, wherever people disagree on what goods ought to be pursued.

Psychologically, ethics refers to a set of norms and capacities learned through family life, school, and social custom. One's ethical perspective consists largely of learned responses shaped by enculturation and the ethical "climate" of society.[2] Later, ethics as a critical activity may arise. Ethics is a sort of internal "normative control system" that mediates between my understanding of a situation and my response.[3] I consult these norms "within me" before I decide how to act. I exercise my capacity to judge things, actions, and traits of character as having or lacking ethical value – as good or bad, right or wrong, optional or obligatory, worthy of praise or condemnation. The ethical capacity includes the ability to make commitments and display character.

Sociologically, ethical norms have social origins. My ethical values and capacities are nurtured and exercised within groups. The subject matter of ethics is the values of social groups. Also, ethics requires that I adopt a social perspective that looks to the common good and transcends selfish individualism. That is why we teach ethics by asking children to take others into account. Ethics is not just about me; it is about us, whomever "us" happens to be. "How ought I to live?" cannot be asked in isolation from the question, "How ought *we* to live?"

While we experience ethical emotions and intuitively recognize ethical problems, we should not rest content with this surface understanding. Our intuitions about what is right may be the product of groups with discriminatory attitudes. Knowing ethics intuitively is an unsystematic affair. Intuitions don't always tell us how to sort out complex situations. We need to subject our intuitions to reflection and theorizing.

Ethical Reflection

Ethical experience is the origin of ethical reflection. Confronted with uncertainty, doubt, and conflict, we think.[4] We define our terms, generate principles, and clarify goals. As experience throws up new situations, we alter our principles. We construct codes of ethics for complex activities, like accounting or nursing. If philosophically inclined, we produce ethical theories. Then, as experience throws up new and perplexing situations, we alter our principles. We find ourselves in a circle of experience and reflection. Part of this reflection is theoretical. We inquire into the "logic" of ethical assertions. Another part is applied. We ask whether a practice, such as the use of hidden cameras, is ethical.

At least four experiences stimulate ethical thinking:

Inadequacies of current beliefs. We reflect on our beliefs when our norms lead to troubling consequences. For instance, we may question the value of patriotism when it leads to extreme nationalism. We may question our belief in a free press when reporting causes irreparable harm to someone's reputation. We take thought when new developments go beyond the reach of existing norms. Can ancient ethical philosophies deal with today's issue of human cloning? In journalism, is the ideal of news objectivity applicable to the new interactive media, with its emphasis on opinion?
Other ethical systems. We consider our beliefs when confronted with people and cultures with different beliefs.
Complexity of experience. Difficult situations present us with a "knot" of facts, potential consequences, options, and rival values. Moreover, the sheer variety of situations can overwhelm our ability to think clearly. We look for the guidance of general rules. In this way, we face the world with a manageable number of principles.
Pluralism and integration. As complex creatures, humans are conflicted between their desires and ethical norms. Life confronts humans with many values and obligations. How do my duties as a parent line up with my career ambitions? How can I integrate my desire to help the poor with a desire to retire to my garret to paint my masterpiece? The challenge is to integrate these values and capacities into a consistent and ethical form of life. Thinking is stirred by these "fault lines" that run through our ethical identity.

How Distinct?

We can now rephrase our initial definition of ethics. Ethics is the activity of critically constructing and adhering to norms, in a practical and social manner, starting from the experience of ethical doubt, conflict, and plurality. Yet this rephrasing does not explain how ethics is distinct from other activities in society.

There are many types of norms and many types of agencies that enforce norms. Some norms are not ethical, such as norms for greeting someone on the street. There are the norms of etiquette; the norms of behaviour in private clubs; the norms of fashion, aesthetics, law, and ethics. When we say that we "ought" to do some action we may not mean that we have an ethical duty. Instead, we may mean that we ought to be polite and gracious, as a matter of etiquette. Or we ought to buckle up our seat belts because it is required by law.

These different types of norms comprise society's "normative sphere" – those areas where behaviour falls under rules and standards. It is important to distinguish one normative system from another, say law from etiquette, because these systems ask different types of questions and require different types of answers. A failure to distinguish these normative perspectives may cause us to fail to recognize an ethical issue, or to confuse an ethical issue with a non-ethical issue.

Why are we persuaded that there *is* a distinction between ethical and non-ethical norms? One reason is the force of examples. In teaching ethics, instructors use examples of exceptional behaviour to distinguish between ethics and self-interest. For instance, they note how some Americans in the nineteenth century participated in the "underground railway." A group of people courageously helped blacks escape slavery. They allowed the blacks to use their houses and barns as safe places, as these slaves travelled northward to states that had banned slavery. Many of the people who assisted the slaves did not act out of self-interest. Self-interest dictated that they avoid such assistance which, if detected by authorities, would have led to severe penalties. They acted out of an ethical concern for others in distress.

Other examples contrast ethics with desire or inclination. For example, I ethically ought to repay a loan to John even if I will never see John again and even if I am inclined to avoid repayment. Further, students are asked to consider examples where ethics and the law differ. Some acts that strike us as ethically wrong, like child slavery, are legally permitted in some societies. Protesting against a country's human rights record is correct but may be legally forbidden.

These examples persuade us that there is a distinction between ethics and other kinds of norms. But, although we "get" the contrast, we may still not be able to say what features explain the distinction. Saying how ethics is distinctive is surprisingly difficult. The sociologist Steven Lukes explained it as such:

> Moral norms cover matters of importance in people's lives. They are directed at promoting good and avoiding evil, at encouraging virtue and discouraging vice, at avoiding harm to others and promoting their well being or welfare. They are concerned with the interests of others or the common interest rather than just the individual's self-interest, and they are distinct from the rules of etiquette, law, and religion – though the conduct they enjoin may overlap with what these enjoin.[5]

Examples of "overlap" are theft and murder, which are illegal and unethical.

Philosopher Thomas Scanlon thinks that ethics is distinctive because people think of moral requirements as extremely important. They feel guilt or self-reproach when they violate them, and the victims of ethical actions feel resentment and indignation.[6] Such moral emotions are not usually caused by the violation of etiquette or minor traffic regulations.

These writers capture essential points. Put more formally, ethics is distinguished by a combination of four features: (1) a specific subject matter defined by a family of identifiable concerns and familiar principles that (2) is approached through an impartial, "caring" stance. These concerns and principles (3) are serious and (4) justify other norms. Ethics is distinguished by its concerns and how it reasons about those concerns. Let's examine each of these four criteria.

IDENTIFIABLE CONCERNS

Ethics has an identifiable subject matter, even if the boundaries are not precise. So far, this chapter has appealed to our implicit understanding of this subject matter. We said that ethics was about treating others rightly and about fundamental questions of rights and duties. We named familiar ethical rules such as the prohibition against murder and theft and the virtues of honesty and kindness.

One way to summarize these concerns is to regard all ethical discussions as falling under one of three themes: the good, the right, and the virtuous. A discussion is ethical when it considers which action promotes the good. A discussion is ethical when we debate what is just and right, as opposed to what is convenient or in someone's interest. A discussion is ethical if it is about the virtues. A discussion or a moral system that did not address any of these questions would not be "ethics." It would not engage the subject matter of the ethical sphere.

SERIOUSNESS

These three themes make ethics a serious enterprise. Lukes and Scanlon underline the fundamental importance of ethical questions.[7] Ethics is about the most significant issues in our lives: rights, freedoms and duties, respect for others, fairness and justice, and the development of human capacities. This seriousness raises ethics above etiquette and custom. It is why we think that disagreements over ethics are more important than differences over aesthetic preferences. What ethical values people affirm or reject has impact on others. Ethical norms are of such importance that we use social pressure and education to promote and protect them.

However, ethics as serious business does not entail that there are no limits on its application. Ethics is about a relatively small proportion of actions and norms – those that deal with the good, right, and virtuous. We can imagine circumstances where almost any choice can raise an ethical question. But we should refuse to see an ethical issue in every act, if we want to avoid a fanaticism that would over-regulate our lives.[8]

IMPARTIAL STANCE

Since ethics is an activity, it is distinguished not only by its subject matter. It is also distinguished by how it deals with its three themes.

Ethics adopts an impartial stance. What is a stance? It is an optional approach to the world. For example, I can adopt a cynical stance and believe that selfish motives are behind people's seemingly well-intended actions. I can adopt an egoistic stance and evaluate all actions in terms of what promotes my interests, even if they harm the interests of others. In contrast, the ethical stance is an impartial approach to the discussion of problems. Ethical persons transcend egoism and give fair consideration to the interests of others. They care about how people are treated, and they allow such considerations to restrain their pursuit of goods. That the ethical stance can be ignored is obvious. Every day, people act unethically from uncaring, partial attitudes. Some people, such as sociopaths, are psychologically unable to adopt the ethical stance.

I "show" my impartiality by being willing to universalize my ethical beliefs. What is it to be willing to universalize? It is to agree that what holds for me holds for others, and what holds for others holds for me. If I think that John is obligated to do x in situation y, then I agree that I am obligated to do x if I find myself in y. I am not thinking ethically if I hold that Mary ought to report seeing someone cheating on a test to a supervisor but I am not obligated to tell a supervisor if I see someone cheating. The rules of ethics are universal in the sense that they apply to all persons in similar circumstances. There is no special pleading in ethics. There are exceptions to rules. If I am a surgeon, I am not obligated keep my promise to take my son to a movie if I must return to my hospital to treat severely injured people. However, there are no arbitrary exceptions based on what serves someone's interests. For example, "Do not murder, unless you are Stephen Ward or an Irishman," is not a valid ethical rule because it is not impartial. It is partial toward Stephen Ward and the Irish. An exception based on someone's identity or nationality is arbitrary.

To be impartial is not to lack feelings or goals. It is not a bloodless objectivity. We adopt an impartial stance because we care deeply about being fair and about reaching the correct ethical judgment. We value impartiality as a means to these goals. Ethical caring is not a sentimental feeling. It is a tough-minded commitment to living with others ethically. Ethical caring may include but does not require that I have an emotional bond to the people with whom I deliberate. We can care about correct human relations without loving or even liking the people in question.

The ethical stance is different from other stances for evaluating conduct. At a formal event, I make sure to say the right things and to use my best manners. I adopt the stance of etiquette. My rule-following is neither ethical nor unethical; it is non-ethical. It does not raise ethical concerns. Another stance is that of prudence: reasoning about what is prudent or best for me. I should save more of my salary if I desire long-term financial security. Prudential reasoning need not be egotistic since I may include my family or kin as part of my interests. Also, prudence can take the long view. I accept certain short-term restrictions, such as cooperating with people, because it serves my long-term interests. I can act prudentially without acting unethically. In fact, a certain amount of prudence is required by ethics. For example, it is ethically required that I take care of myself.

The difference between the prudential stance and the ethical stance is that prudential thinking is concerned with achieving certain goods for me or for a particular group. It is not impartial to all interested parties. However, prudence and ethics can coexist, and prudence can motivate ethical behaviour. If I operate a laundry in a neighbourhood where everyone knows each other, it may be both ethically correct and prudent to deal honestly with customers. But the ethical duty to be honest in one's dealings is not based on prudence. It is based on an impartial concern for all concerned. The ethical does not reduce to the prudential because they are different modes of evaluation. The prudential stance is often confused with the ethical stance since both advise us how to live well. Bookstores contain guides on how to be successful or how to achieve mental tranquility. Are these books ethical works? The answer is no. They are works of prudence. Ethics is not about what is in my self-interest. It is not about the self-absorbed pursuit of pleasure, or the quest for contentment. Ethics is about acting rightly in terms of what is good for all, and that can be difficult and disturbing.

LOGICAL GROUND

The seriousness of ethics means that it justifies other types of norms. Law also deals with serious topics. Laws are more important than social mores or etiquette. But legal norms are justified insofar as they support an ethical vision of human life in society. Even modern constitutions, those fundamental legal frameworks, ground their laws and rights in some ethical vision of the good and just society. The fundamental rights and freedoms of constitutions are legal expressions of ethical principles.

Some readers may feel that these four criteria fail to establish a hard line between ethics and other normative domains. They are right. The distinction is a matter of degree, such as ethics being *more* fundamental than law. We should not expect hard and fast boundaries. Etiquette, prudence, law, and ethics all deal with regulating behaviour. All speak of what should or ought to be done, in contrast to what is done. Consequently, we expect overlap in language and among the rules. Stealing is both unethical and illegal. Being boorish and ungracious to a visitor is a matter of etiquette, yet at the extreme it is also unethical since it shows disrespect to another human. Also, human society only gradually distinguished these domains. Originally, to violate the commands of a tribal chief was illegal, socially repugnant, and an ethical breach – all at the same time and with little clear distinction between these types of violation of norms. Law only became a distinct area when societies built legal systems with their own rules, practices, and institutions.

These four features of the ethical stance make ethics a distinct and autonomous way to approach life and the world. Ethics is, in a sense, self-justifying. I either see inherent value in adopting the stance, and the goods, duties, and attitudes that it supports, or I don't. I voluntarily decide to adopt the stance, or not. The validity of ethics does not depend on its ability to prove to skeptics that it is rational and in their interest to adopt the ethical stance. That reduces ethics to prudential reasoning. The answer to "Why be moral?" cannot be "Because it serves your interests." Moreover, ethics may not serve your interests. It may require sacrifice. The answer to "Why be moral?" can only be, "Because these are the values we deeply care about." In recognizing the inherent value of ethical concerns, you know why one should be moral. Ethics is addressed neither to the radical skeptic who doubts the validity of any ethical statement nor to the radically unethical person who cares nothing about ethical restraints. It is addressed to people who are similarly motivated to adopt the ethical stance. The issue is not the validity of the ethical stance. The issue is what principles and actions best express our common and prior commitment to ethics.

Ethics is not philosophically bankrupt if it cannot persuade all people to adopt its stance. If someone can witness pain, suffering, and injustice with indifference; if they care little for goodness or the well-being of others; if, in short, they are unmoved by ethical concerns, there is not much that can be said to persuade them otherwise. And, not much *needs* to be said. Ethical insensitivity and radical skepticism are stances that need as much (or more) justification as the ethical stance. The task of ethics is to deliberate about principles and norms with people who are already disposed to care about its values and concerns. An autonomous ethical stance does not mean that ethical thinking is self-enclosed and dogmatic. As MacIntyre argues, traditions and practices have tensions within and without their sphere that stimulate change and improvement.[9]

In summary, ethics is the natural and necessary human activity of constructing, critiquing, and enforcing norms to guide conduct and interaction in society. It includes the psychological and social processes by which such norms (and related capacities) are inculcated into individuals. Ethics is practical. It starts from the lived experience of ethical doubt and plurality and then seeks integration and theoretical understanding. Ethics is the evolving and dynamic activity by which humans attempt to live an ethically good life. Ethics is a distinct area of society because of its serious and distinctive subject matter and because of its impartial approach.

Theory and Practice

We have described what it is to engage the world ethically. That engagement takes the form of ethical reflection, and that reflection often takes the form of theories – theories about the nature of ethics, of ethical method, of what should be our primary principles. The number of theories and the variations on them are vast and beyond the scope of this book. But it is important to discuss the relationship between theory and practice in ethics, and the types of ethical theories.

Ethics is practical, yet it is also theoretical. We theorize about how we act and why. In the circle of experience and reflection, both poles of ethical thinking play their part and attract us. So, what is the relationship of theory and practice in ethics?

When we think about theory and practice, we should not consider them to be completely separate spheres: a sphere of ideas isolated from the world, and a practical world hostile to ideas. There is almost no theoretical reflection where some amount of practical thinking does not intrude, and no sphere of practical thinking devoid of theory. Our thinking is like a rope of tightly compressed theoretical and practical strands that are difficult to untangle. A good deal of our theoretical thinking, such as our view of what constitutes justice or freedom, is influenced by how such views would work in practice. Conversely, many practical problems, such as digging a train tunnel under a river, have theoretical aspects. Many professions, such as medicine, combine the theoretical and the practical.

The theoretical-practical distinction is a matter of degree. Some thinking is more practical or more theoretical than other forms of thinking. The difference is due to (a) the dominant interest of the thinking in question and (b) the types of reasons that it uses. Practical problems are addressed to us as agents. The dominant interest is what to do. How can we solve a problem, how should we act, or how can we achieve a goal? Theoretical problems are addressed to us as knowers. The dominant interest is what is true, or what to believe and how to explain some phenomenon. For example, we want to know, theoretically, how subatomic forces explain the observable features of ordinary objects, or how certain genes predispose someone to skin cancer. Practical problems are resolved by developing the right practice. Theoretical problems are solved by coming to the right (or true) belief. Theoretical reasons are reasons for believing; they support a proposition. Practical reasons are reasons for acting; they support an action.[10]

Therefore, ethics is practical because its dominant interest is practical and its reasons are practical. It seeks reasons for doing action x, not theoretical reasons for believing y or explaining z. This doesn't mean that ethical reasoning does not use theory. Ethics is not anti-theory, nor is it so practical as to be averse to careful analysis, to the raising of technical points, or to questions of principle. Theorizing in ethics is systematic thinking about what we do when we act according to norms, or give ethical reasons. Theory exposes the assumptions that lurk beneath everyday judgments, the way that most of an iceberg lurks below the waterline. These assumptions quickly surface and come into play as soon as a debate begins. The ultimate purpose of theorizing is to illuminate our ethical experience, examine its tensions, construct new principles, and improve our ethical responses. There is no saying, in advance, how theoretical or arcane our thinking must become to sort out an ethical issue. We should follow our thinking wherever it leads. To insist on a practical "anchor" for ethics is a reminder that this theorizing should be grounded in meaningful, existential questions.

Reflection and theorizing in ethics can be divided into two groups:

Philosophical ethics
(a) The nature of ethical statements and the meaning of ethical concepts.
(b) How we know ethical statements, plus their objectivity.
(c) The purpose(s) of ethics given certain theories of society and human nature.
(d) The history of ethics.

Applied ethics
(e) Criteria of right and wrong; the supreme principle(s) of ethics; universal ethics.
(f) What principles should guide how we act in general and in the professions.
(g) How principles apply to issues.
(h) Methods of ethical reasoning.

Philosophical ethics (or metaethics) studies ethics at a high level of generality and detachment. We step outside of ethics and, like an external observer, analyze it as a social, psychological, and linguistic phenomenon. In practical life, we come to the judgement, "I ought to return the wallet I found in the street." In philosophical ethics, we ask what does "ought" mean in that judgment? One way of putting the distinction between philosophical and applied (or normative) ethics is this:

> Whereas normative ethics is concerned to answer first-order
> *moral* questions about what is good or bad, right or wrong,
> virtuous and vicious, metaethics is concerned to answer second-
> order *non-moral* questions, including (but not restricted to)
> questions about the semantics, metaphysics, and epistemology
> of moral thought and discourse.[11]

Philosophical ethics asks three large questions. (1) What are we saying when we speak ethically? (2) How do we know or justify what we say? (3) What is the purpose of speaking (and acting) ethically? Theories can be categorized according to which question they ask and how they answer it. Among the most prominent theories are moral relativism and moral absolutism, which carry on a debate over whether there are cross-cultural, objective criteria for ethical evaluation. Another general category of metaethical theories is descriptivism, or "moral realism": the view that ethical statements are true and objective depending on whether the statements correctly correspond to external and independent moral properties or facts. In opposition to descriptivism is non-descriptivism, which denies that ethical claims are descriptions of moral facts. Ethical statements are expressions of approval of certain actions or imperatives that certain actions ought to be done or not done. Another metaethical theory is intuitionism, the view that humans know that certain actions are good or right by intuiting the moral properties of the action in question.

Applied ethics is just that – *applied*. It deals with the articulation and application of principles to problems. In applied ethics, we work within ethics. We do not step outside ethics and observe its activity like a sociologist. In applied ethics, we are actors who do ethics, arguing for certain principles and values and their application in controversial cases. Did I do the wrong thing when I refused to give money to famine relief? Should we keep alleged terrorists in an isolated camp, without legal rights? Applied ethics reveals how people understand ethical principles. Values such as respect for life, friendship, and happiness can be so abstract that we need to see how people apply these values to identify where we agree or disagree. After all, both the Quakers and the Mafia agree on the value of friendship.[12]

Applied ethics has two divisions, general and specific: (1) framework ethics – general questions about frameworks of principles; and (2) pragmatic ethics – questions about the application of frameworks to situations.[13] Theories of applied ethics argue for the best framework of principles for life and for specific areas of life. Framework ethics also is interested in specific, substantive issues. Applied ethics uses principles to take positions on assisted suicide, the legitimacy of war, the duty of developed countries to developing nations, and the correctness of government policies.

Applied ethics studies the practice, dilemmas, and tough "judgment calls" of professions to help nurses, public servants, journalists, and others follow proper protocols. For example, how much information should a doctor provide a seriously ill patient about her disease? How should a health organization inform patients that their cancer tests were botched by a pathologist? What is "informed consent" in a business contract? If a financial adviser owns stock in a company, should he promote that company to clients?

The three themes of ethics – the good, the right, and the virtuous – determine the types of applied theories. The most familiar theories of applied ethics can be divided between theories that argue that ethics is essentially about which actions produce the best consequences, which actions respect basic rights and duties, and which actions are chosen by a virtuous person and express his or her virtues. Therefore, framework theories come in three kinds: consequential, non-consequential, and virtue theories. Consequential theories articulate principles that define goodness and identify actions that promote the good; non-consequential, or deontological, theories articulate principles that say what is just and what is our duty. Such principles are intended to restrain the pursuit of our goods and personal interests. Virtue theories describe moral character and specify the virtues that individuals need to be ethical.

Utilitarianism is the most familiar consequentialist theory. In its classical formulation, it holds that the supreme principle of ethics is the greatest happiness of the greatest number. The most famous deontological ethical theory is Kant's theory of the categorical imperative as the ultimate moral principle and duty. The first and most influential virtue theory is Aristotle's analysis of the good for humans as the development of our virtues, as excellences of character.

The division of ethics into philosophical and applied shouldn't be taken too literally. It is a tool to clarify ethics. In abstraction we can separate these forms of ethical thinking. But in reality, they interact. What principles I think should guide conduct is not divorced from my philosophical assumptions about the nature of ethical principles. Some philosophers argue that philosophical ethics is more important than applied ethics because we can only answer the questions of applied ethics – what are good reasons for doing x or y – when we know, philosophically, what counts as good or bad reasoning in general.[14] On the view of practice and theory above, both forms of ethics are equally valid and should influence each other.

NATURALIZED ETHICS

In this section, I stop describing the contours of the ethical sphere in a neutral fashion and advance some substantive ethical positions. I explain my own theoretical approach to ethics: naturalism. It is important to explain my naturalism at this point because it will influence our subsequent reflections on journalism ethics.

My naturalism is primarily a metaethical theory. I stand back from ethics and think about ethical activity as a distinct but natural form of human activity. As a naturalist, I take positions on the main questions of metaethics listed above. These positions have implications for applied ethics. My main concern in this section is to describe the tenets of my naturalism, not to provide a full defence. The reasons for these tenets will become clear as we deal with various topics in the chapters to come.

Idea of Naturalism

Naturalized ethics is the idea that ethics is a natural activity of humans, explained and justified by natural concepts, phenomena, and causes. Ethics is the activity of a social species seeking to survive and thrive in natural and social environments. Humans are moral agents in the midst of life on this planet, wrestling with issues that require decision and deliberation. For naturalism, the motivation for doing ethics arises from natural needs and social aims. The capacities needed for ethical judgment are the natural, psychological capacities of humans. The justification of principles and decisions relies on natural considerations – the consequences of action, the requirements of contract, the satisfaction of desire, and the flourishing of humans. To call ethics "natural" is to hold that ethics should not be regarded as supernatural or extranatural in its motivations, justifications, enabling capacities, or knowledge. A natural theory of ethics does not appeal to supernatural authority, transcendent absolutes, or the intuition of non-natural, moral properties. Naturalized ethics is ethics within the limits of human experience.

There are at least two senses of the phrase "a naturalistic explanation" when we are referring to humans and human behaviour. It can mean (1) an account of some phenomenon of human existence that is continuous with empirical science. To be "continuous with empirical science" means that one appeals only to natural entities, properties, causes, and processes recognized or consistent with the empirical nature of natural science. This approach excludes occult or mysterious properties, non-physical or spiritual forces, and metaphysical entities allegedly existing outside nature. Also, a "naturalistic explanation" can mean (2) an account that explains some aspect of human behaviour in terms of the kind of creature we are, "subject not only to physical and biological laws but also as social and cultural elements."[15] The second sense of naturalistic explanation is a more particular articulation of the first.

My sense of naturalism is the second. Naturalistic ethics utilizes knowledge of who we are as a physical species in the natural world and knowledge of who we are as a species living under (and helping to create) culture, norms, and society. Most major aspects of humans and society are amenable to such an approach, including for example the ethical notions of justice and of rights.[16] My naturalism, therefore, draws ideas from the natural and social sciences and the humanities. For ethics, the most important fact of human existence is that we live under norms that we construct. Humans have this peculiar ability to shape their existence not only according to certain genetic and evolutionary factors but also according to how they think they ought to live. Naturalism seeks a natural explanation of this distinctive ability of humans to reflect upon and alter the conditions of their existence.

Historically, the first naturalists were Ancient Greek philosophers who thought of ethics as the expression and perfection of the nature of "man" – a rational human nature. Rawls speculates that Ancient Greek ethics was naturalistic in spirit because it sought the highest goods for life through logic and dialogue, unaided by Greek civic religion or Homeric epics.[17] Naturalism is as old as Aristotle's definition of the good life as the virtuous development of our natural, rational capacities within a polis. The polis was also regarded as a natural social phenomenon.

This naturalized ethics was replaced for centuries by the supernatural ethics of medieval Christianity, based on divine will and a pessimistic view of human nature as "fallen." Naturalized ethics returned in force by the eighteenth century as part of a renewed faith in the human capacity to improve society and to know nature scientifically. This modern ethical naturalism sought to show how principles and duties derived not from an external source but "from human nature itself (as reason or feeling or both), and from the requirements of our living together."[18]

The crucial issue for early modern naturalists, from Shaftesbury and Hutcheson to Hume, Adams, and Kant, was not the content of ethics; it was assumed that most people agreed on what was right or wrong. The issue was the rational basis of such judgments – indeed, whether the judgments were based on reason or some other source, such as the emotions. The main ethical question was: how do humans come to know the requirements of ethics, and to be moved by those requirements? Both Hume and Kant believed that ethics arose from human nature and that the awareness of how we are to act is rationally explainable to conscientious people. They believed that humans, by nature, had sufficient motives to act properly. Hume's ethics was developed by a scientific analysis of human nature, a complex of faculties and passions. Ethical sentiments such as sympathy and benevolence, and conventions such as justice, arose out of the conditions of human experience and society.

A classic example of naturalistic analysis is Hume's discussion of the origins of justice in *A Treatise of Human Nature*.[19] Hume explains justice as a reasonable convention that is so firmly based on the human condition that it might as well be considered a law of nature.[20] Justice comes about when people seek the advantages of lawful society in a world where there are limited resources and people with limited benevolence. If people were, by nature, supremely benevolent, then the restraints of justice would not be needed. If nature provided people with abundant food and resources, then rivalry would be reduced and the constraints of justice would not be needed. Justice derives from the limited generosity of people combined with the "scanty provision nature has made for [their] wants."[21] Hume's analysis makes no reference to extra-natural causes.

Naturalism was a major approach to ethics well into the nineteenth century. Increasingly, it aligned itself with science. Philosophers assumed that their subject was continuous with the sciences, and facts about human nature were important for the questions of ethics, logic, and knowledge.[22] C.D. Broad wrote: "If naturalism be true, ethics is not an autonomous science; it is a department or an application of one or more of the natural or historical sciences."[23]

However, the twentieth century began with a rejection of naturalism in philosophy, prompted by advances in logic and by a positivistic philosophy of science. A new and powerful formal logic and an ascendant logical positivism distinguished sharply between scientific fact and ethical values, and between empirical inquiry and conceptual analysis. Philosophy was defined as an autonomous non-empirical discipline that uses conceptual analysis to discover formal or "analytical" truths in logic and other fields. Science concerns itself with discovering "synthetic" truths about the world through observation and empirical methods. Frege, for example, argued that "psychologism" in logic – explaining logic by how people naturally and actually think – was a mistake. Logic is an autonomous science with its own methods, truths, and norms. This analytical philosophy is modern rationalism, as conceptual analysis.

The analytical turn led to new forms of non-naturalism in ethics. No longer did philosophers appeal to the transcendent authority of God or Platonic Ideas. Rather, philosophers appealed to reason's ability to discern logical or linguistic truths about ethical concepts. G.E. Moore, in his influential *Principia Ethica* of 1903, claimed that conceptual analysis showed that ethical concepts could not be reduced to "natural" concepts such as pleasure, happiness, or the sentiment of sympathy. Defining ethical properties in terms of natural properties was a logical mistake. It was always an "open question" as to whether natural properties were what we meant by goodness and other ethical terms. "Naturalistic fallacy" was Moore's expression for the belief that "good" *means* some natural property.[24] Moore replaced naturalism with ethical intuitionism. We intuit a non-natural and indefinable property of goodness that belongs to objects, experiences, and activities. Actions are right if they promote the greatest increase of this good in the world. To say I have a duty to do an action is to say that "this action will produce the greatest possible amount of good in the Universe."[25]

It is easy to regard Moore's *Principa Ethica* as a completely new development in ethics. Thomas Hurka, however, has argued that Moore was within a tradition of ethical philosophy that runs from Henry Sidgwick's *Methods of Ethics* in 1874 to W.D. Ross's *Foundations of Ethics* in 1939.[26] Nevertheless, Moore's book stimulated interest in studying metaethics apart from normative ethics. But Moore was careful not to argue that metaethics was superior or should be the only ethical inquiry pursued by philosophers. Similarly, other metaethicists who followed Moore, such as Charles Stevenson, were careful not to suggest that normative ethics was no longer a part of ethics. But others who took the "linguistic turn" in philosophy were not so cautious, such as the positivist A.J. Ayer. Ayer said statements of value in ethics are not significant in a literal sense "but are simply expressions of emotion, which can be neither true nor false." Therefore, it appeared that normative ethics was not a field where knowledge or cognition played an important role.[27] W.D. Hudson introduced his moral philosophy book in 1970 by saying that "[A] moral philosopher ... thinks and speaks about the ways in which moral terms, like "right" and "good" are used by moralists when they are delivering their moral judgments."[28]

Therefore an unintended legacy of G.E. Moore's *Principa Ethica* was to separate metaethics and normative ethics and to place them at odds. Philosophers claimed that either philosophical or applied ethics was the most important part of ethics and the proper concern of philosophers.

The idea of ethics as conceptual analysis, a form of metaethics, protected ethics as a distinct sphere of inquiry, at least temporarily.

But the building of a philosophical wall between philosophy and science, between conceptual analysis and synthetic reasoning, came at great cost to ethics' practical application – the construction of "synthetic" normative positions on issues. Meta-analysis seemed to reveal ethical statements and judgments as empirically meaningless or the arbitrary expression of subjective emotion. Therefore, practical (or normative) ethics was regarded as a somewhat dubious, subjective enterprise that was neither empirical science nor conceptual analysis. In retrospect, the first half of the twentieth century is a strange period for ethics. Philosophers turned away from natural knowledge at a time when the sciences were developing powerful theories about the human mind, human evolution, and human society. Inquiries in psychology, sociology, anthropology, and biology were not seen as a great resource for ethics.

Naturalism, however, did not disappear. John Dewey applied the naturalistic approach in his ethical writings. In the second half of the century, naturalism recovered. Conceptual analysis exhausted itself. Moore's analysis of ethical terms was questioned. Quine, a leader of analytical philosophy, called for a naturalized epistemology, and questioned the "analytic-synthetic" distinction that separated philosophical analysis from natural knowledge. The rise of interdisciplinary theories in cognitive science and linguistics brought philosophy and science closer together. In ethics, Rawls and others ignited a new interest in normative ethics.

Main Tenets

Naturalistic ethics, as a preference for natural explanations of ethics, admits of many varieties. Therefore, I state the tenets of my naturalism in terms of three themes – (1) the nature of ethical statements, (2) ethics as human construction, and (3) ethical activity as natural, and therefore a proper subject for natural inquiry.

AFFIRMING ETHICAL STATEMENTS

In my view, all values, including ethical values, are ontologically dependant on human acts of valuing. Values, including ethical values, do not exist independently of human acts of valuing. There is no external and independently existing order of ethical values and ethical properties in nature, apart from humans. Values are experienced only by humans, in and through purpose-driven activity. Values come into existence through acts of valuing and affirmation. Values, including ethical values, are expressions and projections of human feelings, interests, and reasoning upon ourselves and the world. My view denies that values are objective properties of the world that we discover through intuition or insight into God and the cosmos. Value is a property that an object *has* relative to human appraisal and practices.

A world without human sentience would be a world without value. As William James said, there is "no status for good or evil to exist in, in a purely insentient world. How can one physical fact, considered simply as a physical fact, be 'better' than another?" Goodness, badness, and obligation can only exist if there are creatures with conscious desires and demands. Such conscious beings *make* things good. Otherwise, James says, "things have no moral character at all."[29] We confer value on the objects of our rational choices. We also confer value on persons *as* persons. Our notion of persons as ends-in-themselves is a conferring of value on ourselves as autonomous, rational beings. This is not a scientific discovery. We decide, through reflection, to see ourselves in this manner.[30]

This ontology of value entails that my ethical naturalism is a form of non-descriptivism (or anti-realism). Ethical statements are avowals or affirmations of values that we project onto the world and organize into rational frameworks. Ethical claims are not descriptions of fact but practical proposals about how best to act to live in goodness and right relation. Ethical judgment is an action-guiding choice based on ethical reasoning that is judged reasonable or correct, rather than true or false. Ethical thinking does not seek a true description that corresponds with reality. It seeks reasonable judgments and standards for action. Our ethical statement affirms a type of action, or affirms the principle behind it, as correct or reasonable. We express our ethical evaluation of that state of affairs, for practical purposes.

The purpose of ethical affirmation is not simply to project value onto objects. The primary purpose of avowal is to integrate, coordinate, and influence my conduct and the conduct of others. We affirm certain ethical values to guide our conduct and influence others. For example, when we affirm an ethical principle, we "make it public, or communicate hoping to coordinate our avowals with others." We thereby give direction to our "joint practical lives and choices."[31] Ethics consists primarily of the "practical stances that we need to take up, to express each other, and to discuss and negotiate."[32] Ethical thinking attempts to make the affirmation of values as rational and defensible as possible.

Our tendency to express ethical concepts in factual, representational language can tempt us to think of ethical judgments and affirmations as factual propositions. We say that an action *has* ethical value, in the same way that we say this lamp *has* electrical current running through it. It seems that, in ethics, we are describing the ethical properties of actions in the same way that we describe an object's shape or molecular structure. Moreover, we say that there *really are* universal values, that it is *true* that cruelty is wrong, or that it is a *fact* that one owes a duty to one's children. We say we have come to *see* that discrimination against gays is wrong. We borrow the strong realist predicates of "true," "real," and "fact" to express the strength of our values. We ignore ourselves as authors of the valuing. We ignore the fact that, in ethics, we don't literally *see* anything. Rather, we come to a conclusion, after complex deliberation, or after applying principles to a situation.

Realism pervades ethical language because of history. The idea that ethics and politics were statements about facts, a matter of discovery and knowledge about some state of the world has been the dominant assumption of Western ethical thought. Berlin has shown how the idea that values might be a human invention, only began to gain ground in the late 1700s. Berlin calls this revolutionary conception of values "the largest step in the moral consciousness of mankind since the ending of the Middle Ages, perhaps since the rise of Christianity."[33]

CONSTRUCTION AND CONTRACT

My naturalism holds that ethics, where valid, is the product of human construction and invention that is rational, objective, and non-arbitrary. What this constructivist procedure amounts to with respect to journalism is the subject of the next chapter.

Constructivism holds that how we come to judge an action or principle as reasonable is a matter of practical reasoning following a certain procedure, guided by a set of criteria of evaluation. This makes my anti-realist approach "constructivist" in the tradition of Kant, contract theory, Rawls, and Habermas. On this view, ethics is not based on religion or a common conception of life. We construct our ethics through a process of deliberation. A realist thinks that "a correct moral judgment, or principle, is one that is true of a prior or independent order of moral values." A constructivist thinks "a correct moral judgment is one that conforms to all the relevant criteria of reasonableness and rationality" given by procedures approved by practical reason.[34]

Immanuel Kant's constructivism is evident in his procedures for testing maxims and for applying the various versions of the categorical imperative. Kant's constructivism has been described perspicuously by Rawls in his lectures of the history of moral philosophy. In those lectures, Rawls describes Kant's view of constructivism and moral objectivity: "Moral convictions are objective if reasonable and rational persons who are sufficiently intelligent and conscientious in exercising their powers of practical reason would eventually endorse those convictions, when all concerned know the relevant facts and have sufficiently surveyed the relevant considerations. To say that a moral conviction is objective, then, is to say there are reasons sufficient to convince all reasonable persons that it is valid or correct. To assert a moral judgment is to imply that there are such reasons and that the judgment can be justified to a community of such persons."[35]

According to Kant's constructivism, individuals use their reason to apply the categorical imperative to maxims. In modern ethical theory, this individualist approach to ethical construction becomes a social process. We come to know what we ought to do by considering what we could all agree to. Ethical judgments do not describe ethical facts. They express those norms that we agree should govern our interactions. Contract theory in ethics, or *contractualism*, for example, describes procedures by which all members of a society come to agree on principles and laws. What is "right," "obligatory," or "wrong" in any domain of society is determined by principles that define a reasonable cooperative framework. An action is right or wrong "if the act accords with, or violates principles that are, or would be, the object of a suitable agreement between equals."[36]

Ethics as agreement, as a form of justification, has acquired a social meaning in writers such as John Rawls, Thomas Scanlon, and Jurgen Habermas. Impartial ethical reasoning means we are able to justify to others our norms, our policies, and our reasons for acting.

Justification is an open and fair dialogue among all parties about the impact of a norm on their interests. Each party approaches ethical issues from their distinctive position in the world. According to Scanlon, I have to argue in terms that people with similar moral motivations "could not reasonably reject."[37] Habermas puts forward a discourse morality of equal respect and "solidaristic responsibility for everybody." Habermas argues that in ethics we don't project ourselves by imagination into the place of others, as Adam Smith and others have recommended. Instead, we participate in an actual dialogue with others, where all parties get to give their reasons.[38]

My naturalism is constructivist in this social sense and is close to the views of Rawls and Scanlon. I hold that reasonable and objective ethical judgment is the result of humans following an objective procedure that ensures the judgment is as reasonable as possible.

My naturalism, then, belongs to that tradition of ethical thought that Korsgaard calls "procedural moral realism." In a trivial sense, everyone who isn't a nihilist or who doesn't think ethics is a waste of time is a realist.[39] If all that realism means is that we think there are better or worse ways of answering ethical questions, then most of us are realists. In all forms of procedural realism, there are ways to answer ethical questions, but there is disagreement on how one should go about answering the questions.

I embrace a non-descriptive form of procedural moral realism. I do not think that a correct ethical procedure requires positing the independent existence of moral facts. The correct procedure is to follow a procedure of practical reason that uses objective criteria for evaluating ethical reasoning. There are correct answers because there are correct and reasonable reasoning procedures.

I will explain this view in chapter 2. For now, it is important to see the difference between this non-descriptive procedural realism and realism proper – or "substantive moral realism." A substantive moral realist believes there are correct answers because there are moral facts or truths. Ethical questions are about these moral facts; ethical inquiry is inquiry into these moral facts. The correct procedure is to find ways to align one's beliefs with moral facts, which exist independently of these procedures and which these procedures track. As Korsgaard points out, in substantive realism, the procedures for answering normative questions are ways of "finding out about a certain part of the world, the normative part." Substantive moral realism is distinguished by its views about the subject of ethics. Ethics is conceived of as a "branch of knowledge, knowledge of the normative part of the world."[40]

My social constructivism leads to a belief that ethics performs a certain function. This belief will play a large part in this book. The belief is this: ethics, at its best, functions to define agreed-upon principles for social cooperation. It provides the principles for fair human interaction so that humans can participate in society for mutual benefit. Even if we disagree with his political philosophy, Hobbes was right to see society as a sort of contract among citizens. Humans construct and enforce rules so that society can exist. Rules help society to establish some degree of control, order, and reliability among human interactions. I can act with greater confidence if I know that other people will not steal, lie, murder, and/or arbitrarily break promises. Ethics is natural and necessary to humans as social creatures, and that is why ethics is an important part of society's normative sphere.

Yet, not just any ethical contract will do. Many societies enforce rules that perpetuate an unjust social order. Ethics seeks to articulate and support norms that promote a fair society for the common good. We want ethics to function as a voice for the good and the right and to work for the reduction of harm and evil. The most important function of ethics, then, is to help citizens question existing norms and construct better principles. This is a critical understanding of ethics. In this book, a critical "social cooperation" view provides a basic conception and a starting point.

INVENTION

A naturalistic approach to ethics stresses the non-absolute and changing nature of norms and principles, as the world changes. It takes into account the history of the construction of ethics. These reflections led to the importance of human invention in ethics. Humans invent new standards, ideals, and ethical concepts to address new problems. I go so far as to suggest that we think of ethical rules and principles as *fallible hypotheses*: principles are fallible, experience-based general "hypotheses" that form part of our experiments in living well. They evolve through imagination, dialogue, and social change. For example, principles of justice are hypotheses about how to construct fair systems of justice. The utility principle, the greatest happiness for the greatest number, is not a factual truth about society. It is an hypothesis about how to make social decisions. This process of affirmation and judgment-making is rational. That is, it is under rational restraint. Principles and frameworks are open to rational assessment by a holistic set of norms, which we will examine in the next chapter.

Ethical ideas are analogous to scientific hypotheses in this respect: they are creative conceptions for dealing with complex phenomena. Scientific hypotheses are fallible theoretical proposals on how to explain phenomena. The hypothesis are tested and altered in the course of inquiry and experience. Ethical principles are fallible practical proposals on how best to guide and evaluate conduct. They are tested and altered in the course of inquiry and experience. I do not want to press this analogy too hard. We do not confirm ethical principles in a quantitative, scientific fashion. Nevertheless, ethics is experimental in an analogous sense. It tests its norms by considering their effectiveness in addressing problems.

Why insist on this analogy and why use the language of "hypothesis"? There are several reasons. It is useful to adopt an experimental approach to ethics because it encourages us to challenge lazy assumptions, to ask for evidence, to consider other principles, and to link ethics to natural knowledge. The language of hypothesis and experimentation helps highlight the non-absolute nature of ethical statements, stress their basis in practical reasoning, and underline ethics as a natural, human invention. To think of principles as general hypotheses is to take seriously the history of ethics. The primary purpose of ethics is not to develop a complete and unchanging system of universal truths. The purpose, as Dewey believed, was to develop sufficiently clear, reasonable, and flexible guidelines that allow humans to respond effectively to new and urgent problems. Absolutism and dogmatism are less tempting attitudes when we remind ourselves that ethical systems do not sit idle. They get deconstructed and reconstructed as the conditions of life alter. Pressed by circumstances, citizens, governments, and others redefine their roles, question existing rules or reinterpret principles.

It may appear that ethics can't be so dynamic because ethics must have firm rules. I agree that we hope for firm guidelines, and we usually change specific norms against a background of stable ethical convictions. But we should not consider these rules as unchanging. Nor should we think of ethics as consisting of a static code of principles. Codes are milestones that mark the twists and turns in our continuing ethical journey as a species. Codes are one component of ethics, the end product of our ethical experience to date. Nor does the existence of principles solve all of our problems. To say one understands ethics by citing the rules is like saying one understands Galileo's physics by citing his laws of motion. We can know the rules and still struggle to apply them. If Moses came down a second time from the mountain, and this time arrived with fifty tablets containing five hundred commandments, and even if he supplied us with a detailed manual on how to apply the rules, we would still have ethical debate. We would not escape deliberation and uncertainty. Faced with new and complex situations, we would still have to engage in ethical invention.

Ethical invention is not unique. It is a form of conceptual creativity that occurs in other areas such as science, technology, politics, and art. The inventive process is dynamic, involving imagination and bold hypothesis. Consider the following ethical and humanistic inventions across history: the ancient Stoic notion of a universal humanity; the movement against slavery in the nineteenth century; the idea of a neutral International Red Cross among combatants; Gandhi's idea of nonviolent resistance; the idea of universal human rights; the enlargement of ethics to include issues of gay and lesbian rights, women's rights, and animal rights.

We can learn much about ethical invention by studying invention in other domains, such as politics. In twentieth-century politics, liberal democracy, communism, and fascism proposed ideals for entire societies. Their process of invention was anything but tidy. New ideals were put forward amid the confusion of social revolution, and the course of history altered the original ideal. The long and violent process that produced liberal democracy was not "intellectualist" in the sense that someone articulated a clear and complete concept of liberal democracy and then citizens set about creating liberal institutions to match the idea. Rather, the liberal concepts of tolerance grew out of the confusion of religious wars during the Reformation. Principles of liberal equality evolved out of violent struggles for political representation motivated at times by parochial interests and the unethical pursuit of power. Today, the need for ethical invention remains. For example, the science of genomics gives humans, for the first time, the means of altering the building blocks of human nature. We will need wisdom and imagination to construct an ethics for the sciences of life.

The invention of values is most evident during social upheavals when movements announce new revolutionary creeds. Nietzsche believed that superior individuals were capable of a revaluation of all values.[41] My inventionism does not presume the necessity of radical reform. It depends upon the conditions. Nor do I presume that humans are, or should be, preoccupied with creating entirely new ethical systems from scratch. People also do good work when they propose norms as improvements to existing frameworks.

Natural Ethical Inquiry

Finally, my naturalism holds that natural inquiry into ethics is not only possible but to be encouraged. Two assumptions define my attitude toward natural knowledge and ethics. One, ethics is a thoroughly natural activity of a thoroughly natural organism, the human species. Ethics is part of the human ability to appreciate values and formulate norms for personal reasons and for social coordination. Normative activity is a peculiarity of the human species, as it seeks to survive and thrive in natural and social environments, as natural for humans as is empirical thinking or artistic creation. Two, if ethics is natural activity then natural knowledge shapes ethics. We should expect the evolution of our natural knowledge to shape how we think about ethics. Our understanding of ethics should be informed and constrained by the best available natural and scientific knowledge of humans and society. Recent developments in the scientific study of the mind, human neurology, the human genome, and social systems have made natural knowledge even more pertinent to ethics, and especially to a naturalized ethics. Daniel Dennett has argued that this naturalism should be applied to philosophy in general.

My fundamental perspective is naturalism, the idea that philosophical investigations are not superior to, or prior to, investigations in the natural sciences but in partnership with those truth-seeking enterprises and that the proper job for philosophers here is to clarify and unify the often warring perspectives into a single vision of the universe. That means welcoming the bounty of well-won scientific discoveries and theories as raw materials for philosophical theorizing, so that informed, constructive criticism of both science and philosophy is possible.[42]

To adopt this approach we have to reject standard objections, such as the view that the "is-ought" distinction separates norms and facts, ethics and science. In ethical reasoning, it is true that naturalists (or any ethical thinker) cannot deduce *ought* or *good* from *is*. We can't deduce what humans ought to do from facts about what humans actually do, or from presumed facts about nature or the universe.

Some people think the is-ought distinction is supported by Moore's argument that when we consider concepts such as good that there is always an open question whether good means some natural property such as pleasure or happiness, since we can always wonder whether, in fact, pleasure or happiness is good, or what we mean by good. This seemed to open up a gulf between natural properties and ethical, non-natural concepts such as *good*. But the open question does not prove that *good* is an indefinable non-natural property. The open question is just another way of expressing the widely acknowledged difference between what *is* and what *ought* to be. The persistence of the "open question" can be explained naturally. Humans, because they have developed self-consciousness, can always ask about their existing desires and beliefs. Through human rationality, humans gain the capacity to step back and ask about what they ought to do, desire, or believe. Humans have a distinct and persuasive capacity to question their norms. This fact does not prove that ethical concepts are special non-natural concepts, nor does it erect an unbridgeable dualism between *is* and *ought*.

When it comes to constructing ethical arguments, there are other options than deducing *ought* from *is*. A naturalist can hold that an ethical conclusion is not directly derived from factual premises alone. Ethical conclusions follow from a combination of factual and normative premises. Normative premises must be among the premises. To judge that John's violent action against Mary is wrong, I need the normative premise that such violence in general is wrong. This does not make ethics circular is some fallacious manner. Instead, it indicates the holistic nature of our ethical conceptual scheme. What we judge in one area is influenced by beliefs in other areas. The essential question is not whether we can deduce *ought* from *is*. Clearly we can't. The crucial question is how we defend the ethical beliefs that serve as premises in our arguments.[43] It is impossible for practical reason to draw a well-considered judgment about what ought to be done in a situation unless it uses both normative principles plus all of the relevant facts and circumstances of the case. Often, which facts are relevant is determined by which ethical issues are in question. To support this point would require producing a model of ethical reasoning, which I do in chapter 2.

If we still feel that naturalism and ethics are incompatible, then we should remember that one of the classical discussions of the is-ought distinction, Hume's discussion in book 3 of *A Treatise of Human Nature*,[44] attempts to show that the distinction supports his naturalistic view that ethics is based in the emotional side of human nature. Hume believes that the realization that our ethical judgments are not deductions of reason from facts supports his view that they are the expression of emotions and attitudes toward the object in question. Hume uses the is-ought distinction to support his naturalistic psychology of ethics. He wants to show how the ethical sense of *ought* arises from natural sentiments and worldly conditions. We discover the source of our moral concepts within us, as a fact about our passionate nature, through introspection of our feelings. Hume wants to "show that morality and our practice of it are the expression of our nature, given our place in the world and our dependency on society."[45] Ironically, Hume, a naturalist, was one of the creators of the is-ought distinction, which subsequently was used to cast doubt on naturalism.

The simplistic assumption that the is-ought distinction draws a firm line between norms and facts, ethics and science obscures a more nuanced (and correct) view of the role of facts in ethical reasoning and, conversely, the role of norms in a natural world. Once we set aside such objections to naturalism, we come to see that natural inquiry (and knowledge) can play three important roles in the development of ethical theory: it aids the explanation of ethics as a whole; it aids the evaluation of assumptions; and it aids deliberation about specific issues. The first role places special importance on scientific theories of the evolution of human society and culture. The biological and social sciences provide theories that explain the evolution of ethics as a distinct human phenomenon. Ethics is normative evolution within a larger process of natural and cultural evolution. If the explanation of ethics is natural, then the natural and social sciences provide important information. Ethical behaviour required the slow development of increasingly complex organisms who finally reached the capacity to think, strategize, value, and follow norms in society. Each individual human is "an assemblage of roughly a hundred trillion cells" and "not a single one of the cells that compose you knows who you are, or cares."[46]

Two types of questions are of particular importance. First, what is the biological and genetic inheritance of the human species? How did biological evolution result in human propensities, emotions, rational capacities, and social impulses? For example, what is the biological basis of the capacity to feel sympathy for others, or to act aggressively? Second, how did ethics establish itself in human society? How did humans, as biological creatures, develop societies where agents cooperate and restrain the maximization of their individual goods? Theories in evolutionary psychology, human biology, philosophy of mind, social psychology, game theory, and other fields can help answer these questions and allow us to slowly piece together a picture of the rise of ethics and the origin of concepts of good, right, and duty.

Science can identify the neurological basis of conscience and sentiments such as hatred or benevolence. It can indicate how social cooperation arose. For example, primatologist Frans De Waal has argued that human morality evolved from a long line of animals that care for the weak and build cooperation with reciprocal transactions.[47] While Hobbes and Hume had to speculate on the natural origins of justice and other concepts, today's ethicists can consult detailed scientific theories.

Naturalistic inquiry resists the temptation to treat ethics as something mysterious, religious, or immaterial. Instead ethics is viewed as part of being human in a natural world. We can see how, through a natural process, humans developed into conscious, deliberate, norm-constructors, norm-supporters, and norm-violators with roots, perhaps, in the "customs" of wolves, apes, and other species.[48] We can use this knowledge to identify possibilities of action. Ethicists should welcome well-won scientific discoveries as material for ethical theorizing and informed criticism.

Finally, scientific knowledge can help us evaluate ethical claims. If the sciences can identify conditions that promote ethical behaviour, we can determine whether ethicists make realistic assumptions about human motivations and capacities. Even when we construct ideal ethical theory, such as the principles of justice for a well-ordered society, ideal theory must be at least consistent with common human experience and scientific knowledge of human nature and society. Facts limit theories but they do not determine by themselves which ideal theory is best.

A naturalistic approach encourages ethicists to question age-old assumptions. Consider this conflicting list of generalizations that have propped up political and social philosophies for centuries: humans are motivated only by utility or by pleasure; humans naturally desire their own perfection and virtue; humans are naturally selfish and need authoritarian government; society allows humans to develop into ethical beings; society corrupts humans' natural sentiments; humans agree to ethical restraint as part of an original social contract; ethics is a way for the powerful to keep the masses in line; ethics stunts the growth of the strong individual. Rigorous natural knowledge helps ethics go beyond these speculations to more fruitful hypotheses.

Naturalistic ethics, then, rejects any attempt to protect the distinctness of ethics by erecting walls between ethical and natural inquiry. Natural knowledge is not a threat but a resource for understanding ethical behaviour and assessing the viability of ethical systems. Ideally, we develop an ethical theory that "allows us to act in the full light of knowledge of what morality is and why we are susceptible to its influences, and at the same time to believe that our actions are justified and make sense."[49] The aim is not to reduce ethics to scientific facts, or to expose ethics as a delusional activity. Rather, we use natural knowledge to improve normative reasoning.

JOURNALISM ETHICS

What Is Journalism Ethics?

Now, where is journalism ethics on this large map of ethics? It is a type of applied ethics. Journalism ethics is the analysis and application of ethical principles of relevance to a particular domain of society – the practice of news media. Journalism ethics studies the principles that should guide conduct among journalists and should regulate their interactions with other citizens. The framework of journalism ethics includes principles, rules, practices, and conceptions about the purpose of news media. Journalism ethics addresses ethical issues at two levels. It considers "micro" problems of what individual journalists should do in particular situations and "macro" problems of what news media should do, given their role in society. Like ethics in general, journalism ethics has three areas of concern: principles appropriate to journalism, their critical application to problems, and virtuous character so journalists are disposed to follow the principles.

Why do journalists have an ethics? That is, why do we presume that they have certain duties and must honour certain principles? Why do they not simply have the freedom to publish what they want within the legal limits of libel and hate speech? Journalists have ethical norms and duties because of their social role. Our society protects their freedom so that journalists can inform citizens in a responsible fashion. Every group that has significant influence on the public, including journalists, accrues certain duties. Power and impact entail social responsibilities, whether specific individuals accept them or not. Journalists also have an ethics because they can do both substantial public harm and substantial public good.

On the negative side, journalists can destroy reputations, deal in malicious rumours, demonize minorities, plagiarize and fabricate stories, manipulate images, intrude on private lives, and add to the trauma of vulnerable people. They can manipulate elections, spark racial tensions, accept kickbacks for doing (or not doing) stories. They can sensationalize and misrepresent issues. In times of tension, they can support the removal of civil rights, support unjust wars, and act as a megaphone for demagogues.

There is also the positive side – contributing to the public good. Ethics is not just about restraints on journalism or what you should not do. It is also about what you should do. Ethics encourages journalists to seek truth without fear or favour, to act independently, and to do the sort of reporting that our society needs.

No one, and certainly no profession, that has power can avoid ethics. Freedom does not give journalists a sort of ethical immunity. Press freedom is not a "get out of jail" card with respect to ethics. Freedom to publish is valuable as a means to ethical journalism. Otherwise, such freedom can be harmful and its ethical value questioned.

How does journalism ethics differ from ethics in general, and how do we distinguish an ethical norm in journalism from a non-ethical norm? Journalism ethics shares with ethics in general such principles as truth-telling and promise-keeping. But journalism ethics focuses on the problems and norms specific to the domain of journalism. For example, journalism ethics pays special attention to journalists' relationships with sources, the conflict between reporting the truth and causing harm to story subjects, and what objectivity means in a news report. Journalists may apply ethical principles differently. Investigative reporters argue that there are situations where journalists may deceive someone or tell a lie to get a story, such as the abuse of elderly people in a nursing home. The journalistic tolerance for deception is greater than we find in many other professions. Take another example: society does not usually demand that people go to jail to keep their promises. Yet many journalists believe they have a duty to protect the identity of a source who has been promised anonymity, even if it means time in jail.

The question of how to distinguish ethics from other normative spheres (that we discussed above) arises also for journalism ethics. When it comes to journalism, how do we distinguish ethical questions legal or prudential questions? For example, in a newsroom, consider a debate over whether to publish a sharp and sensational story on a well-known public figure. Should I publish it? As it stands, "Should I publish?" is an ambiguous question. It could mean, "Will the publication further the career of the journalist who wrote it, or attract the attention of readers?" Or, it could mean: "Are we legally permitted to publish this story, which defames the person's reputation?" Or, it could mean: "Would it be ethically right to publish it, even if it is legal?" Ethical deliberation must distinguish these senses. A story that sensationalizes the personal life of a public figure may be legal – it may be legally safe to publish – but it may be unethical in being inaccurate and unfair. Nevertheless, there is no necessary incompatibility between ethical values and other types of values. A story may be well-written, legal, and career-enhancing, yet also ethical. A question about journalism is an ethical question – as opposed to a question of prudence, custom, or law – if it evaluates conduct in light of the fundamental public purposes and social responsibilities of journalism.

What one regards as a question of journalism ethics depends, ultimately, on one's conception of the primary functions of journalism and the principles that promote those aims. Consequently, there is room for disagreement on the level of practice, in applying norms, and on the level of theory and principle.

A major task of journalism ethics is to determine how existing norms apply to the main ethical issues of the day. Some current problem areas are:

- *Limits of a free press in a pluralistic society*. Should online journalists receive the same protection as newspaper reporters? Should journalists be allowed to offend religious and ethnic groups, including those groups on the margins of society?
- *Accuracy and verification*. How much verification and context is required to publish a story? How much editing and editorial gatekeeping is necessary?

- *Independence and allegiances.* How can journalists be independent despite their close relations with their employers, editors, advertisers, and sources? When is a journalist too close to a source, or in a conflict of interest?
- *Deception and fabrication.* Should journalists misrepresent themselves or use recording technology, such as hidden cameras, to get a story? Should literary journalists invent dialogue or create composite characters?
- *Graphic images and image manipulation.* When should journalists publish graphic or gruesome images? When do published images constitute sensationalism or exploitation? When and how should images be altered?
- *Sources and confidentiality.* Should journalists promise confidentiality to sources? How far does that protection extend? Should journalists go "off the record"?
- *Special situations.* How should journalists report hostage-takings, major breaking news, suicide attempts, and other events where coverage could exacerbate a problem? When should journalists violate a person's privacy?
- *Ethics across media types.* Do the norms of mainstream print and broadcast journalism apply to journalism on the Internet? To citizen journalists?

Five Stages

The history of journalism ethics can be divided into five stages. The first stage is the invention of an ethical discourse for journalism as it emerged in Western Europe during the sixteenth and seventeenth centuries. Gutenberg's printing press gave birth to printer-editors who created a periodic news press of newssheets and newsbooks. Despite their primitive newsgathering, and the partisan nature of their times, editors assured readers that they printed the impartial truth based on matters of fact.

The second stage was the creation of a "public ethic" as the creed for the growing newspaper press of the Enlightenment. Two things were central: the idea of a public, and the legitimacy of its collective opinion. Journalists in the eighteenth century claimed to be tribunes for the public, protecting their liberty against government. Leading journalists claimed the press was a Fourth Estate that represented the public better than Parliament did. The press was indispensable to governing because it formed rational public opinion.

The third stage was the evolution of this public ethic into the liberal theory of the press, during the nineteenth century. Liberal theory began with the premise that a free press was necessary for the protection of the liberties of the public. The hope of liberalism was that a free press would be a sober educator of the masses, a promoter of liberal society. Liberal theory coincided with the advent of a mass commercial press devoted to news, not opinion, in the second half of the 1800s. This was a time of extraordinary growth in papers as they moved from dependence upon political parties to dependence upon circulation and advertising.

Meanwhile, at the height of the liberal press, we see, paradoxically, the rise of a modern ethics with an emphasis on rules and restraints. We see new journalism associations and new codes of ethics, the first ethics textbooks and growing media criticism. Modern standards start to take shape – independence from political parties, the separation of news and opinion, and the value of impartial news. What sort of ethics was this? It was an ethics in service not to an elite liberal society but to an egalitarian liberal democracy. Journalism served, first and foremost, a self-governing citizenry of all classes.

Now, why did journalists, who had just achieved a tolerable freedom, create associations and codes of ethics? Why did they agree to rules of reporting that restrained their freedom? Many factors were at play. I will stress one. The birth of ethics was a response to a withering belief in the liberal hope that a free press would be a serious public informer. As the press gained its freedom in the late 1800s, people witnessed something different. They worried about the growing power of newspapers controlled by press barons with strong commercial ties. There was a growing criticism of the sensational and "yellow" free press. It was no longer obvious that a free press was the people's tribune or that the free press made the public's interest its chief concern.

Journalism ethics was born in an attempt to respond to deficiencies in the idea of a free press and a marketplace of ideas. In part, the solution was ethics – the development of standards to evaluate how the press should use its freedom for the public good. These concerns set the stage for the fourth era of journalism ethics: the elaboration of ethical standards and duties for the free press across the twentieth century. From the early 1900s to the middle of the twentieth century, objectivity was a dominant ethical ideal for mainstream newspapers in the United States, Canada, and beyond, although it was less popular in Europe. By the 1920s, major journalism associations in the

United States had adopted formal codes that called for objectivity in reporting, independence from government and business, and a strict distinction between news and opinion. The result was an elaborate set of newsroom rules to ensure that journalists reported "just the facts."[50] For example, in the early 1900s, the press was said to have a duty to be objective in news; reporters should be balanced and get both sides of a story.

By the 1940s, journalists, scholars, and others in the United States had constructed the social responsibility theory of the press.[51] The theory held that the press had an ethical duty to provide accurate, comprehensive news and a forum for diverse voices, even if the voices differed from the newspaper's own views. While liberal theory recognized the idea of press responsibility, social responsibility theory argued that the press had neglected these responsibilities. In the United States, the Hutchins Commission into the Freedom of the Press in the late 1940s gave the theory a clear and popular formulation. In its report, *A Free and Responsible Press*, the commission stressed that the main functions of the press was to provide "a truthful, comprehensive, and intelligent account" of the news and events and "a forum for the exchange of comment and criticism." The press should provide a "representative picture of the constituent groups in society," assist in the "presentation and clarification of the goals and values of society," and "provide full access to the day's intelligence."[52] If journalistic self-regulation failed, social responsibility proponents warned that government regulators might intervene. Today, the ideas of social responsibility theory have "won global recognition over the last 50 years," such as in European public broadcasting.[53] Moreover, the theory continues to provide a vocabulary for new ethical approaches, such as feminist and communitarian theories, while providing standards for the evaluation of media performance.

In the 1960s, activists argued that journalism should help bring about a more equitable society by fairly representing and empowering the many groups seeking recognition. At the same time, scholars in the rapidly growing area of media studies asked journalists to look at themselves more critically. Journalists should be aware of how they framed issues and stereotyped groups; and how the media is itself a power to be monitored. In addition, communitarians called on the press to strengthen communal values, rather than encourage individualism. Feminists sought a journalism that did not demean women and fostered caring relations among citizens. Civic journalists argued that journalism's primary purpose was to re-ignite public engagement with politics.

So, the result of these developments was that journalism ethics in the twentieth century added new values and new duties to the original stress on liberty. Nothing like this was envisaged by the original, partisan journalists who fought for a free press, such as John Wilkes in England or Tom Paine in the United States. Nothing like this was part of the original liberal theory of the press. Ethics arose as an attempt to make the free press a democratic press that would be more reliable, more objective, and less tied to partisan groups. The assumption was that being free was a necessary but not a sufficient condition for good journalism.

Where do we stand today, with respect to ethics and democracy, a century after the invention of modern journalism ethics? This question will be addressed more fully in chapter 4. But, for now, we can say that journalism is in a period of increasing doubt about this traditional democratic model. We have entered a fifth stage of journalism ethics – an attempt to rethink ethics, to articulate the purposes and standards of a mixed, interactive media of global impact. Amid a media revolution, traditional views are embattled and we lack consensus on basic concepts. One source of doubt is the questioning of standards such as objectivity and professionalism. But there is a deeper challenge. In a world dominated by the freewheeling internet and citizen journalists, does democratic journalism really need a restraining, cautious ethics? Maybe what democracy needs today is not restraining standards but more freedom – more voices across the internet, diffusing the power of mainstream media and democratizing media. I detect in some of these arguments a new liberalism for cyberspace: democracy will be at hand if we make the new media free for everyone.

A Code of Journalism Ethics

The preceding sections indicate what journalism is and how it has developed. To gain a more concrete understanding, it may be helpful to examine a typical set of journalism principles and how they are structured into a code of ethics. For the sake of familiarity, let's pick an example from Western journalism. Take, for example, the code for the Society of Professional Journalists (SPJ) of the United

States. This code is one of the oldest national codes, and it has been influential in the writing of other codes around the world. The SPJ code expresses most of the major ethical principles of Western journalism today.

The code presumes a social contract between journalists and the public, whereby a free press has duties to promote democracy. The liberal idea of a social contract[54] is used to justify the claim that professional journalists are allowed to report freely in return for responsible coverage of essential public issues.[55] The social contract assumes that the purpose of journalism is the promotion of democracy. Although there exist other views about the ends of journalism, the democratic model of journalism is dominant in Western countries. The ethical purpose of journalism is explained by journalism's social role as an informer of citizens. Journalism has some higher democratic purpose. On this view, a question about journalism is an ethical question if it evaluates media practices in light of journalism's responsibilities to a democratic public.

This liberal social contract gave rise to two types of principles in the SPJ's code of ethics: proactive and restraining.[56] These principles are, in turn, defined by more specific rules, standards, and practices. In the SPJ code, the two primary proactive principles are "seek truth and report it" and "act independently." "Seek truth" includes such rules as accuracy and the proper verification of claims. "Act independently" is defined in terms of avoiding undue influence from all groups and avoiding conflicts of interest. Proactive principles assert that journalists do not simply have freedom to publish, but they also have a duty to publish the most accurate and comprehensive truth on matters of public interest, and to report independently without fear or favour.

Restraining principles call on journalists to use this freedom to publish in a responsible manner. Restraining principles include the duty to minimize harm to vulnerable subjects of stories, such as children or traumatized persons, and the duty to be accountable to the public for editorial decisions.

This professional model favours a holistic, contextual approach to the application of principles. For every situation, journalists are expected to weigh principles, standards, facts, expected consequences, rights, and the effect on reputations.[57] When norms conflict, such as when reporting the truth conflicts with the desire to minimize harm, such as to *not* report a sensitive fact, journalists will have to decide which principles have priority.

Journalism Ethics Naturalized

The application of naturalism to journalism means that certain ways of looking at journalism ethics are favoured and other ways are rejected. Naturalism for journalism ethics means that we regard the activity of journalism as part of the distinctive and natural human activity of responding rationally and consistently to issues and problems in a domain of society. The accent is on *doing* journalism ethics in terms of stressing the dynamic nature of applying principles to difficult new conditions. The principles of journalism are not regarded as absolute laws, and we are mindful that they vary across societies. Journalism rules and norms are proposals, or hypothesis, about how best to conduct responsible journalism in the public interest. Those norms will change and require reinvention as journalism, democracy, and the world change.

Naturalism also favours certain types of justifications for journalism principles. Naturalized journalism ethics grounds journalism ethics in natural and social considerations such as the empirical consequences of reporting in certain ways and in social philosophies such as democracy and the secular idea of social contracts. It rejects any attempt to ground journalism ethics on a supernatural basis, such as the presumed commands of God or any religious "holy" book. It may be that certain values of Christianity or Islam agree with certain journalism values such as freedom, respect, and democracy. This would be a happy convergence. Religious values may provide additional support to journalism values. But journalistic principles are not grounded in such religious views; rather they must find logically independent grounds in naturalistic ethics and naturalistic approaches to society and politics. We will discuss this point in greater length in chapter 3, when we discuss the ultimate ends of journalism.

CONCLUSION

The first half of the chapter explained the basic idea of ethics, why ethics is distinct, the role of theorizing, and my naturalistic approach to ethics as hypothesis and invention for the common good. The aim of ethics is to live well individually and socially by responding reflectively according to basic values and frameworks. Responding reflectively faces the problem of integrating values given the human condition, natural conditions, and current problems. Ethics was not

identified with a static code of absolute principles defended dogmatically. Instead it was defined as a distinct and dynamic human
activity with wide scope – the critical analysis and application of
our basic norms and values as a guide to conduct. Ethics is different
from other activities by virtue of its subject matter and impartial
approach. Ethical theorizing was divided into two types, philosophical and applied.

A naturalistic approach to ethics was defined as a commitment to
natural explanations of human normative activity, a non-realist view
of ethical statements, and the idea that ethics is a rational construction that changes over time, not a discovery of absolute principles.
Ethics is rooted in praxis, and should be forward-looking and pragmatic in aim, fallible in its epistemology, and dialogic and experimental in method. The challenge is not to make ethics safe from
skepticism, subjectivism, and relativism. The challenge is to ensure
that humans have ways to rationally, intelligently, and fairly decide
the ethical rules under which they live.

The second half of the chapter defined journalism ethics as a type
of applied ethics, one area of the ethical sphere. It examined the
nature of journalism ethics, and examined its history. It explained
one typical code of ethics, the spj code with its Western democratic
model. It explained the code as based on a liberal social contract
idea and consisting of a tension between proactive and restraining
principles. The chapter advocated a naturalistic approach to journalism ethics, which favoured natural justifications of journalism
principles as opposed to non-natural forms of justification. In the
next chapter, we learn how this general understanding of ethics leads
to a three-level model of ethical reasoning about journalism.

Reflective Engagement

In the previous chapter we took as our starting point the features of the ethical sphere and the features of journalism ethics. I identified ethics as a natural normative part of human experience defined by the attempt to live in goodness and right relations with others by responding reasonably and consistently to problems and new conditions. Engagement with ethical questions in journalism or elsewhere begins with doubt prompted by complex situations and a tension between values. Ethics seeks to integrate our basic values and guide conduct. The ethical response is distinctive because it adopts a caring yet impartial stance toward fundamental issues, and this response is best understood by a naturalistic approach to ethics as a whole.

In this chapter, I examine how this reflective engagement should be conducted through reasoning. My answer is that we should use a three-level holistic theory of ethical reasoning, accompanied by a practical model of how to apply the theory to journalism ethics. I use the phrase "reflective engagement" because ethics is the application of practical reason to the ethical problems of the world. Ethical problems require sustained and thoughtful engagement.[1] Engagement is reflective if it is independent, critical thought that is not biased by a narrow activism or an unthinking partiality. By reflection I do not mean a withdrawal to the quiet of one's study to contemplate life's meaning. Reflection is not the activity of someone who has resigned from the world. It is the activity of engaged inquirers who distance themselves from their beliefs, for a limited period of time, so as to critique them. The act of distancing is not the sign of an aloof or uncaring attitude. On the contrary, distancing is the first step in deciding how one should act. We take a critical stance toward our beliefs for the sake of constructing more informed beliefs. We construct more informed beliefs to prepare us for action. Reflective engagement means bringing our full rational capacity, including our emotions and other sensitivities, to bear on difficult issues that require careful thought and complex policies.

I begin this chapter by describing how practical reasoning becomes ethical reasoning. I describe my three-level theory of ethical reasoning. I identify the main elements of ethical reasoning and how these elements are related dynamically and holistically. In the second part of the chapter, I show how to use this holistic approach to think about three types of ethical subject matter: (a) deciding on correct action in concrete situations; (b) the use and justification of ethical frameworks to evaluate situations; and (c) the ultimate aims of ethical thinking and action. As we move across these three topics, we move from reasoning about concrete cases to general frameworks of principle to philosophical reflection on the ultimate aims of ethics. This sets the stage for my model of reasoning about ethical issues in journalism. I conclude the chapter by examining the deeper philosophical conceptions that ground this theory and model: holism, the fusion of philosophical and applied thinking, and ethical objectivity.

PRACTICAL THINKING

Practical Reasoning

Ethical thinking is one expression of the human ability to think practically: determining what to do, how to reach a goal, or how to solve a problem. It need not be systematic or guided by explicit method. It may not amount to anything we care to call theorizing or reasoning. Practical thinking is influenced by many factors other than reasoning, such as our emotions, biases, and values.

In this chapter we are interested in practical reasoning about ethics as a regimentation of our everyday practical thinking. Practical reasoning is the process of giving ourselves explicit reasons for acting intentionally in certain ways under certain conditions.[2] The most explicit form of practical reasoning is deliberation. Practical reasoning is the capacity to respond cognitively to a problem in a certain way. I construct a set of reasons that, when made explicit and formal, resembles a logical argument leading from premises to conclusion. By resorting to practical reasoning I respond differently than if I had responded by using my gut instinct, intuitions, emotions, or random choice.

Consider these two examples of practical reasoning:

Example 1: resolving differences. Suppose that while I am visiting the house of a married couple I hear them argue over their plans for the weekend.[3] Both have made separate plans for the weekend, without telling each other, and now there is no one to take care of their two children for the weekend. The woman complains that her husband doesn't spend enough time with the children; the husband says he has a crucial business meeting on the weekend that he cannot avoid. I want to prevent a serious quarrel between my friends. It occurs to me that I can assist them by offering to take their children for the weekend. My weekend is clear, I have the space for the children, and my wife loves visitors, especially children, and so on. I conclude that the solution is to offer to take care of their children for the weekend.

Example 2: starting an inquiry. Suppose I become director of the Vancouver branch of a major corporation. Within a month, I hear rumours that the previous director misused budget monies to sponsor unjustified travel and to purchase personal items. The financial officer is conducting a review of the previous year's budget for our head office in Toronto. He identifies several questionable expenditures by my predecessor, which he brings to my attention. As a new director, I am not sure how to approach the problem. Do the rumours and the questionable expenditures justify an inquiry by me or not? Furthermore, the previous director was well-liked and received several company awards for outstanding service. Might I damage a reputation needlessly by my actions? I decide that I want to know more and that it is my duty as director not to ignore the case. I need to know the facts, consult company policy, and consider what options exist if wrong-doing is established. Therefore, I ask the financial officer to gather all the facts and report back within a week. If the report contains damaging allegations, I will contact the former director and give him a chance to answer questions. Only then will I decide whether the facts warrant a full investigation and possible action.

The two cases are attempts to respond rationally to problems. They involve putting together a set of reasons that lead to a conclusion that supports some action. The premises of my argument include:

(1) *Motivational premise(s)*. In both cases, I, the agent, have certain desires or motivations. I care enough about the problems to be moved to respond, and the problems are sufficiently complex to require practical reasoning. In one case, I want to ensure harmony between friends; in another, I want to address allegations of financial wrong-doing.

(2) *Background premise(s)*. In both cases, I, the agent, rely on a wealth of background factual premises about each situation, implicitly or explicitly.

(3) *Means-ends premise(s)*. In both cases, I, the agent, use means-ends reasoning about how specific actions or decisions could help me reach my goals.

(4) *Normative premise(s)*. In both cases, I, the agent, use premises about what ought to be done, what is appropriate, and what norms are in question. For example, in starting an inquiry into a former director I think about the norms and best practices of my company and what they demand of me. Normative premises include means-ends statements that are hypothetical imperatives, e.g., I *should* do certain things if I want to achieve certain ends. Practical reasoning includes an evaluation of my ends.

These examples support the point made in chapter 1 that, in ethical reasoning, the agent does not reason directly from *is* to *ought*.[4] One reasons from a mix of factual, motivational, and normative premises that converge upon a normative conclusion, "I should do *x*." The reasoning provides both causal (motivational) and rational support to do *x*. When all goes well, practical reasoning results in Aristotle's "deliberate desire," where the reasoning is correct and the desire right.[5] Of course, many factors can bias reasoning and prevent the agent from carrying out the action. I may encounter "weakness of will" (acting against one's better judgment). Nevertheless, practical reasoning is a factor in determining action.

Audi depicts practical reasoning as an inferential process having three main premises: a motivational premise, "I want *x*"; a cognitive, instrumental premise, "My doing *A* would contribute to realizing *x*"; and a conclusion or practical judgment, "I should do *x*."[6] Audi's claim is that all practical reasoning embodies this abstract form even though, in actual reasoning, the number and types of premises vary enormously, from a syllogism to more elaborate trains of ethical reasoning. I agree with Audi's approach, but I add to the structure two types of premises – background and normative premises.

In summary, practical reasoning is problem-based, explanatory, intelligible, causal, inferential, and normative. It is explanatory since appeals to practical reasoning explain actions and make them intelligible to the agents themselves and others.[7] Practical reasoning is causal because it motivates the agent to carry out the conclusion of his reasoning, and it is inferential and normative by inferring that certain actions should be done. Practical reasoning guides my response and strengthens my motivation.

ETHICAL REASONING

However, there is nothing inherently ethical about practical reasoning. It can be used as an instrument for ethical or unethical purposes. Therefore, we need to explain how practical reasoning becomes ethical reasoning. This explanation is a theory about *normative* ethics – about how we argue for various normative positions and judgments. A full explanation answers several key questions. What is meant by ethical reasoning, and what is its role in ethics? What are the elements of ethical reasoning? What types of premises and what forms of reasoning are prominent? How should these elements be related and combined to produce well-considered judgments?

Practical reasoning becomes normative ethical reasoning when it addresses the serious problems of the ethical sphere. *How* one reasons is important. Four things are paramount. First, the agent must adopt the critical and impartial attitude described in chapter 1. Second, the agent must wish to arrive at the correct ethical conclusion, not just a prudent or legally correct conclusion. Third, the agent must introduce ethical premises into the reasoning. These are premises about ethical values and norms that supplement non-ethical normative premises. The ethical premises join existing background and means-ends premises. Fourth, the agent draws an ethical judgment from the premises. Like practical reasoning, ethical reasoning is problem-based, explanatory, intelligible, causal, inferential, and normative. In ethical reasoning, a convergence of normative and empirical premises results in an ethical conclusion. Some actions are so obviously bad, e.g., malicious lying for personal gain, that they do not require much thinking. But other problems require careful reasoning.

Consider the previous example of starting an inquiry. The reasoning could be practical but not especially ethical. The director could see the problem as one of prudence. How should he act so that he isn't accused of ignoring a problem? He may consider company norms not out of a desire to act ethically but to avoid being blamed later. The reasoning, however, starts to become ethical when the director sincerely wants to know what the ethically correct action is. How should he act so as to balance his ethical duty to serve his company and employees with his ethical duty to respect the rights of the former director? The director reasons ethically if he asks not whether the actions of the former director were inappropriate but whether they were unethical. Did they violate a trust? Did it involve lying and deception? He adopts an impartial attitude and surveys all relevant facts and norms. In such cases, several forms of practical reasoning can occur. The director may reason about what to do from a prudential, legal, or ethical point of view. The reasoning is ethical when it takes on the characteristics noted above.

This is how practical reasoning becomes ethical. But we still have not answered the most difficult question. We can think ethically in many ways, and we can construct many different views about the correct way to combine the elements of ethics into an argument. So, what is the best theory of ethical reasoning? That is, what theory best captures how these elements should be related when we reason ethically?

A "Horizontal" View

A traditional way of thinking about ethical reasoning is to see it as a "vertical" or top-down process. In this view, our ethical beliefs form a system ranging from the highest or most abstract principles to lower, more specific judgments about what we should do in concrete situations. This traditional view identifies three types of premises, according to their level of generality: (1) ethical judgments – claims that a certain act is good or right; (2) mid-theoretical premises – general normative principles that we consult to decide how to act; (3) supremely general principles about what is ethically good, right, or virtuous that act as ultimate criteria for what is right or wrong.

The ultimate principles include Kant's categorical imperative, Mill's utility principle, and Rawls's principles of justice. Mid-theoretic premises are rules, standards, or norms whose application is not as encompassing as the ultimate principles, such as "It is a duty to come to the aid of someone in trouble, if such assistance does not put one's own life or well-being in jeopardy." Codes of ethics of professions contain principles at this mid-theoretic level, such as the principle of objectivity in news reporting. This level also includes maxims for specific occasions, such as the rule in journalism that investigative stories using anonymous sources must be based on at least two independent sources that are known to the reporter and the editor. Finally, ethical judgments state the goodness or rightness of particular actions or types of actions, such as "This act (act of racism) is wrong" or "This type of act (racism in general) is wrong."

The point of this analysis is not only to sort out the types of premises that occur in ethical reasoning but also to help us see how they are to be organized. The traditional view argues that good ethical reasoning moves from the top to the bottom, from the theoretical to the concrete.

To its credit, the traditional view does organize the amorphous terrain of ethics into a coherent structure. It helps us avoid the grossest types of errors, such as confusing ethical questions with non-ethical questions. However, I think the scheme has its limits. The scheme imposes a hierarchical scheme on ethical thinking that is untrue to its dynamic nature. Too often, the scheme leaves students (and others) thinking incorrectly that we can draw a hard line between philosophical and applied ethics and that the two modes of thinking don't influence each other. The scheme may induce some people to think that the "higher" philosophical theories are prior in method and in importance than the "lower" reaches of applied ethics. In the previous chapter, we saw how at least one modern ethicist argued that we *first* have to figure out what we are saying when we make an ethical claim, before we can have any solid normative views about what is right or good. Other metaethicists are more modest about their area of research. Charles Stevenson, for example, claimed that by engaging in metaethics he was only "sharpening the (conceptual) tools" for normative questions, which constitute "by far the most important branch of ethics."[8] The vertical view also puts too much distance between the detached attitude adopted by philosophical ethics and the attached stance of the actor adopted by anyone who engages in applied ethics. It fails to explain the close relationship between these two forms of ethical inquiry. Moreover, the traditional approach encourages the same misunderstandings within normative ethics, or applied ethical reasoning. The approach suggests that all or most ethical reasoning starts with general principles from which one then deduces mid-theoretic principles and judgments.

I believe there is another way to conceptualize ethics that distinguishes philosophical and applied ethics yet avoids these misunderstandings. We need a categorization of ethics that is closer to the dynamic and holistic thinking that characterizes reflective engagement. I propose that we replace a vertical analysis by a horizontal scheme that shows how all elements of ethical thinking influence each other. I prefer to conceptualize ethical thinking in a way that does not encourage a hierarchy of philosophy versus practice, does not identify one area as superior, and does not set up a dualism of actor versus detached thinker.

REASONING ACROSS THE ETHICAL SPHERE

Scheme and Model

What would a horizontal scheme look like? In this section, I provide an overview of the scheme, leaving the details for later.

The key, as always, is to start with practice as the primary concern of ethics and let the demands of practice shape theorizing. This means that we take seriously the previous chapter's claim that ethics is something we do and that theory's purpose is to help us understand the ethical issues in our lives. Even the abstract reaches of philosophical ethics may be relevant as part of a unified effort to understand and improve our practice.

The second step is to look at the occasions that prompt us to reason ethically. We construct a theory of reasoning according to the main types of occasions, from judging a specific action to reforming an ethical ideal. Such a theory needs two closely related parts: (1) a scheme and (2) a model that applies the scheme.

What is a scheme of ethical reasoning? A scheme is a systematic categorization of the types of reasoning that we find across the ethical sphere. The scheme, because of its general nature, is not a complete theory of reasoning. It needs practical models that show how individuals are to use the scheme in specific domains and situations. A model shows, through a specific series of steps, how different types of reasoning apply to the problems of different domains and professions, such as journalism, medicine, or scientific research. We will examine a model for journalism shortly.

An ethical scheme or model is not an empirical theory. It does not purport to describe how people actually reason. There is a good deal of work on the psychological and sociological processes involved in practical reasoning. I am not trying to add to that literature. I am putting forward a normative theory about how we ought to reason. It is a theory of good reasoning. I offer a normative scheme and an accompanying model that says how people, and journalists in particular, should reason ethically. My scheme and model do not give reasoners a precise formula for generating answers to ethical questions. The scheme and model are part of the art of reflective engagement.

In what follows, I present my scheme for ethical reasoning. Then I describe a model for applying the scheme to journalism.

THE SCHEME

Three occasions prompt ethical reasoning: questions about cases, questions about frameworks, and questions about ultimate aims. Each occasion requires a distinct form or "level" of reasoning. Therefore, we need a scheme of three interconnected levels. The following diagram outlines the scheme.

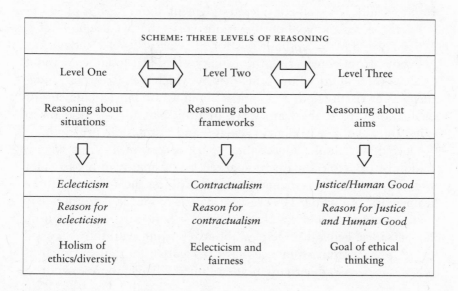

SCHEME: THREE LEVELS OF REASONING		
Level One ⟺	Level Two ⟺	Level Three
Reasoning about situations	Reasoning about frameworks	Reasoning about aims
⇩	⇩	⇩
Eclecticism	*Contractualism*	*Justice/Human Good*
Reason for eclecticism	*Reason for contractualism*	*Reason for Justice and Human Good*
Holism of ethics/diversity	Eclecticism and fairness	Goal of ethical thinking

The diagram shows how reasoning about cases, frameworks, and aims are related. The three forms of reasoning correspond with three levels of generality. As our reasoning moves from cases to frameworks to ultimate aims, we move from discussing practical ethics to applied ethics to philosophical ethics. We use the method of reflective equilibrium to check the overall coherence of our ethical reasoning.

On level 1, the occasion is a concrete problem of pragmatic ethics concerning the right thing to do; level 1 is reasoning about cases. We reason to an ethical judgment about what to do in situation s or situations of type s. Typically, these occasions are difficult because values conflict, the facts are complex, and several courses of action are possible. For example, should a journalist report on a secret military mission if such a report might endanger the safety of soldiers from one's own country? How should journalists balance their feelings of patriotism and their desire to avoid causing harm with their duty to report the truth freely and independently? Level 1 reasoning is also prompted by debates over ethical issues, such as the decriminalization of marijuana, pornography, and the death penalty.

Level 1 proceeds by asking how a framework of principles and values, such as we find in codes of ethics, applies to a particular situation or issue. For example, we ask about the ethics of altering media images by using new technology. Or, we want to know how our religious framework applies to the question of gay rights. The result, ideally, is a well-considered judgment about topic x or y.

Level 2 is reasoning about the frameworks that we use on level 1. We analyze the conceptual tools for arriving at level 1 judgments. We move from considering the validity of ethical judgments about cases to the validity of the principles by which we justify such judgments. The result is not a judgment about a case but a judgment (or evaluation) about the framework of principles for the domain in question. Level 2 reasoning articulates and justifies the principles.

Once again, doubt and conflict spark reflection. Level 2 examination of principles might be sparked by trouble with a particular principle, a clash of principles, or doubts about the adequacy of the framework as a whole. For example, a code of journalism ethics may be too general to address practices in a specific area of journalism. For instance, general principles about reporting truthfully may fail to address deceptive practices in investigative journalism, such as when it is permissible to use hidden cameras. This failure to address a practical issue may lead to a decision to formulate a subcode for investigative journalism.[9] In all of these cases, level 2 reasoning asks: "What framework is appropriate for this domain or this profession?" The focus is on the validity of some (or all) of the principles of the relevant framework.

Levels 1 and 2 ask questions and use forms of normative reasoning that belong to applied ethics. Level 1 raises questions that belong to pragmatic (applied) ethics. Level 2 raises questions that belong to framework (applied) ethics.

Level 3 asks questions at the metaethics level. We reason about metaethical questions, such as the nature of ethics, naturally arise in the course of ethical thinking. Level 3 theories also analyze the basic ethical concepts, articulating what we mean by the good, the right, and the virtuous. Level 3 includes normative reasoning about the ultimate aims of ethics in general, or the ethical aims of the domain in question. One of the most important questions that prompts level 3 thinking is: what are the aims of normative reasoning on levels 1 and 2? Our answer to this question helps to justify our framework of principles on level 2 and our considered judgments on level 1.

A feature of my scheme is that each level should employ a distinctive form of ethical reasoning. For evaluating cases on level 1, I advocate an eclectic application of principles, or a framework of principles. For evaluating frameworks of principles on level 2, I advocate the ethical approach of contractualism. A contractual approach evaluates principles as fair terms of cooperation among interested parties. To evaluate our reasoning on levels 1 and 2, I argue that we need to employ a holistic, naturalistic level 3 approach to ethics, as sketched in the previous chapter. This approach combines naturalism as a view of ethical judgment, the method of reflective equilibrium for evaluating the coherence of our ethical beliefs, and the idea that the ultimate aims of ethics is the promotion of the human good within the right. Naturalism views norms as inventions of practical reason, not as descriptions of the world. Reflective equilibrium seeks coherence within each level and across the three levels. In the diagram, I place arrows between levels to indicate the idea of equilibrium among levels. The aim of the good *within* the right is explained in chapter 3.

In the rest of this chapter, I explain in more detail the three levels of reasoning, develop a model to complement the scheme, and explain the features of my theory.

Level 1: Eclecticism about Cases

Ethical reasoning about cases is best conducted by adopting an eclectic approach.[10] My meaning of eclecticism follows the standard dictionary definition. I am eclectic in thinking if I combine ideas from various sources to achieve a certain purpose. For example, my theory of human nature is eclectic if I combine ideas from Plato, Kant, and Jean-Paul Sartre. Eclecticism can be used well or poorly. In philosophy, we should not mix ideas willy-nilly. Unrigorous eclecticism is a hodgepodge of ideas. A systematic eclecticism carefully combines concepts to produce a coherent system of thought that improves on previous theories.

In ethics, eclecticism is a pluralistic form of thinking. It recognizes a plurality of values and concerns. It insists that ethical reasoning reflect that plurality. Eclecticism is opposed to ethical monism, which denies or downplays the significance of plurality. Monism holds that there is one supreme principle or one supreme criterion of right or wrong. Ethical judgments about situations are determined by reference to a supreme, or master principle, such as maximizing the happiness of the greatest number of people. In contrast, eclecticism is a pluralistic approach to ethical reasoning that consists in a context-based weighing of several (or many) principles that have *prima facie* ethical weight, none of which is supreme. No principle always trumps any other principle.

Eclecticism is not the common observation that ethical situations have many features. The monist can always reply, "Sure, but only one feature counts, or counts the most." Eclecticism holds that a plurality of ethical features – and the tension between them – is an essential and ineliminable part of ethical reasoning. For eclecticism, the most important part of ethical reasoning is neither the reduction of values to one master value nor the deduction of right action from a supreme principle. Nor does eclecticism think that the logical relationship of principles and judgments about cases is a hierarchical relationship between the judgment and one supreme principle. To the contrary, the most important part of ethical reasoning is holistic reasoning that balances principles in different contexts.

Eclecticism holds that there is no way to judge the plurality of valid considerations in ethical cases by reference to a single ethical criterion. Considerations about ends and duties, fair process and ultimate aims, the good and the right – all are equal and fundamental aspects of ethical life. All are fundamental components of ethical thinking. Even where we formulate principles to guide our thought, plurality reappears as a plurality of conflicting principles.

Consider the task of an editor deciding whether to publish graphic war images. The responsible journalist, faced with the decision whether or not to publish these images, attempts to honour different types of duty – to inform completely, to minimize harm to the families of soldiers, and so forth. The decision to publish gruesome images of dead combat soldiers may be deemed right, because it portrays war realistically, or wrong, because it exploits death to sell the news. *Not* to publish the images may be commended as responsible restraint or condemned as censorship that sanitizes the conflict. Within and without journalism, we confront a diversity of goods and duties that are best analyzed through an eclectic form of reasoning.

Philosophically, my eclecticism agrees with the pluralism of deontologist W.D. Ross, who believed that there is no one supreme principle or duty of ethics, such as utility.[11] Instead, there are *prima facie* duties of promise-keeping and gratitude that are weighed in given situations. Even when it is shown that one duty trumps another, the trumped duty continues to have ethical weight. The doctor who realizes his duty to injured patients trumps his promise to take his son to the movies still understands that his promise to his son retains some ethical force – enough to encourage him to set another date for the movie. The journalist's decision to not report the kidnapping of an aid worker in a war zone because it would endanger the person's life puts prevention of harm above freedom to publish. Yet freedom to publish retains ethical weight. Reasoning must weigh principles and other considerations according to the circumstances of each problem. One cannot specify in advance which principles to consider and what their relative weight will be. It depends on the situation, the agents, and the facts of the case.

Eclecticism makes level 1 reasoning context-sensitive. This is as it should be. It also makes level 1 reasoning less tidy. The advice is to identify the relevant principles in a given situation and adjust them to the facts. But how does one do so? This is a controversial area of ethical theory. Aristotle thought that one needed virtue and *phronesis*, or practical wisdom.[12] Whatever theory one adopts, the fact is that ethical reasoning follows past experience and deliberation. There is no formula for "proving" ethical judgments from absolute rules. To be sure, it would be simpler if one could do ethics by declaring: "Never, ever, break promises. Period." Or: "Always, and everywhere, maximize utility." Unfortunately, the ethical sphere is too complex for absolute pronouncements. The reality of ethics is complex and defies simplification. Yet, on the other hand, our rationality prefers economical forms of thinking. The best approach is to remain true to the complex phenomena of ethics. We should shape our reasoning to the complexities of the ethical sphere, not shape the ethical sphere to the wishes of reason.

APPLYING FRAMEWORKS

Much of level 1 thinking, especially in the professions, consists of eclectically applying a framework of potentially conflicting principles. To see why the framework form of eclecticism is an attractive approach to case-reasoning, consider this example from journalism: suppose you are a reporter covering a federal election in Canada for *The Vancouver Sun* newspaper. Someone tells you at a social event that John Jones, the Liberal candidate and former member of Parliament for the riding of Vancouver Centre, is alleged to have sexually harassed women on his office staff. That "someone" is Jason, a senior election worker for the Conservative candidate for the riding. Jason mentions that a woman in the Jones's office, Martha, has told fellow staffers about his actions. You contact Martha. She confirms that she was sexually harassed and hints that there may be other victims, but refuses to go into detail. Martha says she is considering laying a complaint with either the police or the Human Rights Commission. She asks for confidentiality: "Please don't use my name."

What should a responsible journalist do? Anyone who carefully analyzes the example should come to see the value and necessity of eclectic reasoning. One needs to bring together separate and independent considerations. From a consequential perspective, there is the impact of such a story on the election campaign. From a duty perspective, the journalist should act as watchdog on abuse of power. From a rights perspective, Jones has the right not to be falsely accused. The principle of minimizing harm urges us to protect the confidentiality of alleged victims of sexual harassment. From a utilitarian view, the politician's happiness might be secondary to the greater good of publishing the allegations. These are not the only rights, duties, or considerations possible. There is, for example, the journalist's right to publish. It is not plausible to maintain that such decisions can or should be made by consulting only one principle, such as utility. Within and without journalism, we confront a diversity of goods and duties that cannot be evaluated according to a single moral criterion.

A common way to reason about complex cases is to consult a framework of principles, or code of ethics, and then weigh the major principles. Most Western codes of journalism ethics begin with eloquent preambles that stress the value of a free press while recognizing that freedom implies duties. The codes provide a list of principles of two types – what I call "proactive" and "restraining" principles. Principles of free and independent news-gathering urge the journalist to be proactive and courageous in collecting news and investigating stories in the private interest. Such reporting supports the role of journalists to act in the public interest and as watchdog against abuse of power. However, such activity is restrained by principles of verifying information, minimizing harm, respecting rights, and being accountable to the public. The influential code of the Society of Professional Journalists in the United States (at www.spj.org) summarizes the framework of principles for journalism by placing all specific standards and norms under four principles: seek truth and report it, act independently, minimize harm, and be accountable. The list of principles and standards is eclectic in the sense that it reflects the manifold ethical considerations that arise in journalism, and also in the sense that the principles reflect different ethical traditions. The principles of seeking truth and of acting independently reflect a liberal idea of the press, while those of minimizing harm and of accountability reflect the deontological and compassionate side of ethics. The code assumes that the principles and rules will conflict in many cases; therefore, journalists must reason eclectically. They must balance principles and decide which principle has priority in any given case.

In their well-used textbook, *Doing Ethics in Journalism*, authors Jay Black, Bob Steele, and Ralph Barney explain that the four principles of the Society of Professional Journalists are "intended to work in tandem, and not alone," and ethical dilemmas entail "a balancing act between or among two or more of the principles." Also, there is a ranking of principles: "All things being equal, journalism's first objective is to seek out and report the truth."[13]

In the case of the allegation of sexual harassment by a politician, the evaluative task is clarified by applying this code of ethics. The ethical decision amounts to whether the principle of freedom to publish independently, and to act as watchdog against abuse of power is, in this case at this time, trumped by the duty to substantially verify serious claims and the right of the politician not to have a career destroyed by allegations. Whatever decision is taken, in the end, the journalist must be accountable to the public. She should be able to justify the decision to publish or not to publish.

How frameworks apply to level 1 cases can be understood by considering a real-life example. In 2008, Melissa Fung, a reporter with the Canadian Broadcasting Corporation (CBC), was kidnapped by militants while reporting outside Kabul, Afghanistan. The CBC feared that media coverage of her kidnapping could damage efforts to obtain her release. Media coverage might encourage escalating demands for ransom or for the release of terrorists from prison. Also, media coverage could prolong Fung's time in captivity and, worst of all, threaten her life. The CBC decided not to report the kidnapping and asked the same of other major news organizations. Assume that the CBC's concern about the consequences of coverage is plausible. How would one use the principles of journalism to evaluate the CBC's request to refrain from reporting?

A non-eclectic, monistic approach would stress the overriding force of one principle, such as freedom to publish. For example, we might argue that the freedom to publish is a supreme principle of journalism. It always trumps the duty to consider the consequences of publishing. In fact, just such a view was advanced by journalists and media commentators in Canada after Fung was released by her captives and the news blackout was revealed.

A more plausible method of evaluation is the eclectic approach to journalism principles. We start by recognizing that any journalism case worth discussing will require the balancing of conflicting values; slogans and intuitions won't cut it. Instead, we stand back and take all the major principles of journalism ethics into account and seek to balance them with respect to the facts of this case. For example, journalists could argue that in Fung's case the news blackout is ethically valid because the restraining minimize-harm principle trumps the proactive principle of reporting freely and independently. Of course, the justification of this judgment would require a complex argument. The justification accepts the burden of balancing various principles and facts. It recognizes that simply emphasizing one principle won't be persuasive. Instead, one must construct a more careful argument that weighs many considerations.

The value of a framework, such as the SPJ framework, is not that it provides instant and unequivocal answers. The value is that the framework embodies an eclecticism that encourages a nuanced reasoning that balances values, rights, and duties, given the facts of the case. In the Melissa Fung case, responsible journalists must construct an argument that incorporates both a love of freedom and a concern for others.

Level 2: Evaluating Frameworks

In the previous section, I used the examples of reporting on alleged sexual harassment and not reporting on a kidnapping to show how eclecticism is an attractive approach to level 1 reasoning. Eclecticism often operates through the use of frameworks of potentially conflicting principles. Despite the tension between component principles, a framework provides a basis for deciding if x or y is the ethically preferred option in situation s. Further, frameworks tell us which facts and principles are relevant.

Yet, how do we know *which* frameworks are ethically valid? The question identifies a second, more general, level of ethical reasoning – reasoning about the frameworks themselves. This reasoning about frameworks is prompted by such questions as: how do we ethically evaluate and justify frameworks? how do we identify the "best available" framework? what restraints guide the formulation and espousal of frameworks and their principles? To answer these questions, we engage in ethical thinking at level 2 of the scheme. The object of our attention is not a concrete situation or issue but something more abstract: the legitimacy of mid-theoretic and supremely general normative principles.

I propose that level 2 reasoning about frameworks should use a three-step process of evaluation. The first step is to ask whether the framework satisfies general rational criteria for evaluating normative frameworks. The second step is to ask whether the framework satisfies criteria derived from a contractualist approach to ethics. The third step is to evaluate the framework with respect to the methods of reflective equilibrium. Together, the three levels of evaluation provide a substantial degree of rational restraint on existing or proposed frameworks. Epistemologically, it is false that "anything goes" in ethics. People can espouse what they please, but that does not make their espousals plausible or reasonable. Their claims must be

able to withstand the scrutiny of other espousers and their demands
for evidence, principles, and argument. This testing of principles is
close to MacIntyre's idea of evaluative standards within practices.[14]
These schemes of evaluation are "devised and only fully intelligible"
as parts of human activities and practices. Evaluative schemas are
"practices of rational justification" embedded within larger practices aiming at truth or correct conduct.[15]

The rational criteria are:

Normatively complete. A framework should contain principles
that deal with the general features of all or most ethical situations
in a domain. These general features include the consequences of
actions, moral obligations, and the duties of various public officials.
Pragmatically fruitful and realistic. A framework should provide
the conceptual resources for insightful and useful analysis of both
recurring and novel problems. The principles are realistic if they fit
the practice in question. For example, a principle that asked journalists not to publish anything unless it was completely proven
to be true, without a shred of doubt, is too high a standard for a
deadline-driven practice. A more realistic principle would stress
the need for as much verification as possible, collaboration among
multiple sources, and a process for correcting errors.
Expressively adequate. The framework should express the main
values of the activity in question and place them in some priority. Eclecticism does not rule out priority rankings within frameworks. Some principles will have more *prima facie* ethical weight
than others in many circumstances. Eclecticism only rules out that
one principle is always (or almost always) prior. Eclecticism holds
that priority rankings can be questioned and adjusted for types of
problems. For example, one could question the general tendency
in journalism ethics to give priority to truth-telling and independence with respect to minimizing harm and the promotion of social
cohesion (and other civic ideals). One could argue that a journalism ethics that prioritizes social responsibility and cohesion is
more appropriate for certain cultures.
Expressively meaningful. In expressing the main values of an activity,
frameworks "make sense" of the activity as a whole. Frameworks
indicate what the point of the activity is, what its ultimate aims
and functions are. Principles should be consistent with the role of

the profession. For example, a principle that requires journalists never to publish offensive images would violate the journalists' duty to inform the public about important events.

Coheres with existing judgments. The framework of principles should attempt to support our well-considered moral convictions and judgments. For example, a framework that sanctioned untruthful communication and deceptive actions by journalists in most situations would be unacceptable.

Coheres with ultimate principles. A framework should be consistent with ethical principles outside the domain in question, such as a conception of the ethical life and just social arrangements. Journalistic principles of truth-telling and independence, for example, cohere with general commitments not only to truth and individual liberty, but also to egalitarian democracy.

FAIR CONTRACT

If a framework passes evaluation by the above criteria, it has gone a long way to being judged ethically valid. But the framework must satisfy a second kind of test: does it express a fair and ethical contract between interested parties in the domain in question? The aforementioned criteria presume that frameworks are social contracts. They are not the constructs of individuals who formulate an idiosyncratic or private set of rules. But frameworks must be more than contracts, they must be ethical contracts, with fair principles that can be accepted by all interested parties. We ask whether the framework is a fair and reasonable instrument for guiding action in the domain in question.

Therefore, I add one more criteria:

Procedurally fair. The principles should be justifiable from a contractual perspective. An evaluative approach must check for fair process under some conception, whether it is Habermas's ideal conditions for ethical discourse or Rawls's contracting under a "veil of ignorance."

My naturalism encourages a contractual approach to principles. On a contractual view, frameworks are not religious frameworks, or the expression of a pre-existing moral order in the universe. Instead, they are human inventions to regulate conduct. Contracts are only ethical if they are the result of a fair deliberative process, as explained in chapter 1. Frameworks, where ethical, contain agreed-upon terms for fair social cooperation within a profession, or across society. For my contractualism, what is "right," "obligatory," or "wrong" in any domain of society is determined by principles that define a reasonable cooperative framework. An action is right or wrong "if the act accords with, or violates principles that are, or would be, the object of a suitable agreement between equals."[16] Contractualism, as a form of constructivism, implies that the ethical validity of frameworks is determined by the process that leads to fair principles through uncoerced rational consent among all parties. Stated hypothetically, the principles could not be reasonably rejected by free and impartial parties, given the goals of the activity in question.

Only contracts that originate in a fair process can mediate between conflicting interests or impartially settle professional issues. For instance, a framework of principles that supports apartheid violates our social and political ethics. A framework for physicians that excludes women, or a code of journalism ethics that overlooked the impact of reporting on the vulnerable, is a framework that should be rejected. Such a framework is a non-starter, ethically speaking.

The criterion of fair contract is a plausible restraint on journalism frameworks since journalism ethics is rooted in a contract with the public. Journalism ethics is, to a large extent, what the public can legitimately expect from its press. A contractual approach asks what journalists implicitly or explicitly promise the public. An action by a journalist or news organization is either right or wrong if its performance under the circumstances would be disallowed by any system of legitimate rules for the regulation of journalistic behaviour, given the social role of journalism. As in all social contracts, fair process and consent is important. Journalistic principles are legitimate if they could be recognized by all parties involved in the social process of journalism through a fair process of deliberation. Principles should reflect the concerns of the practitioners and those who may be affected by their actions. For example, principles concerning privacy should reflect not only the journalist's desire to expose wrongdoing, but also recognize the harm such stories do to the alleged wrongdoers. The development of new practices and standards should include meaningful input from members of the public to understand their expectations of journalists.

Level 3: Ultimate Aims

We have discussed level 1 and 2 reasoning. But what about level 3? In the next chapter, I explore level 3 thinking in some detail. In so doing we will outline the ultimate anchor for our ethical beliefs and forms of reasoning. We will articulate what Taylor calls our "inescapable" ethical framework.[17] But at this point, to round out this outline of the scheme, I need to say a few things about the special importance of ultimate aims as a form of level 3 thinking.

Appeal to ultimate aims is a major way to judge our frameworks on level 2 and, by extension, the application of those frameworks on level 1. We ask: does our reasoning promote our ultimate ethical goals? What are those goals? Philosophers have advanced many candidates for the ultimate goals of ethical reasoning, and of life itself. The candidates include the perfection of human nature, human welfare and flourishing, the development of great individuals, freedom, happiness, a just society, and various forms of utopian society from a Christian "heaven on earth" to a communist society.

The role of aims is evident in the history of journalism. Judgments about what journalists should do has been heavily influenced by views about journalism's ultimate aims. Moreover, if people differ on journalism's purpose, they will likely differ on the value of certain types of journalism. This should not be surprising, given the close link between means and ends in our thinking, especially when we are dealing with a practical profession like journalism. For example, if journalism's primary role is thought to be supporting the existing social order, government policies, and public authorities, as is often the case in many non-democratic countries, then little emphasis is placed on a critical press that embarrasses authority, questions policies, and generates debate. However, if journalism's role is thought to be that of helping citizens govern themselves and hold authorities to account, there will be strong emphasis on an independent press that facilitates debate, that challenges, that embarrasses. What are the main views about the ends of journalism across the four hundred years of modern journalism? They can be summarized thus: to report and disseminate information; to interpret events and trends; to act as watchdog; to advocate for reform or revolution; to be an activist for certain causes; to educated the public and guide public opinion; to serve the public, the party, or the state. These ends form a continuum from factual reporting and interpretive writing to social activism. Ideas about the aims and methods of journalism have been combined in many ways to create different ethical (and political) theories of the press. Of relevance to us is the liberal democratic tradition that defines journalism as serving a self-governing citizenry, first and foremost. The press's primary allegiance is to this public, not to its leader, not to their government, not to the state or any of its institutions.

Views about the ends of journalism justify and, in fact, give birth to certain journalistic norms and principles. The idea that journalism serves liberal democracy justified and gave birth to the principles of journalistic independence, the watchdog role of the press, and the right to criticize public officials. The idea that journalism ought to impartially provide facts gave birth to the doctrine of news objectivity.

The importance of social and political aims in the history of journalism indicates that the philosophical basis for journalism ethics is beyond journalism. The ultimate goals are not *within* journalism. The activity of journalism, as a form of human expression, has inherent value. But the primary value of journalism is instrumental, as a means to the sort of society we wish to maintain or create. To enter into a discussion of the ends of journalism inevitable takes us beyond the professional aims of journalists. With level 3 thinking, we link journalism ethics to basic social and political philosophies. That is why one of the criteria for evaluating frameworks is "coheres with ultimate aims" where the aims are presumed to be values affirmed outside journalism.

Reflective Equilibrium

Finally, a framework has to meet a third general test. Does the framework exhibit an internal coherence among its principles, and does the framework cohere with our ethical judgments on level 1 and our ultimate aims (and metaethical positions) on level 3? This search for coherence is the method of reflective equilibrium.

To see how reflective equilibrium works, consider again level 1 reasoning. What are we attempting to achieve when we balance principles from different levels to discuss a situation or issue? We seek a process that helps us respond intelligently and ethically to serious problems. We want to improve our chances of arriving at the correct interpretation of a principle or a reasonable practical judgment. But what the correct principle or conclusion *is* depends on how well it fits our ethical web of belief. I understand "fit" in terms of reflective equilibrium. A holistic form of ethical reasoning, because of its stress on mutually supportive and influencing elements, gravitates toward reflective equilibrium as both the goal of reasoning about specific problems and the goal of ethical theory.

John Rawls introduced the idea of reflective equilibrium in *A Theory of Justice* and again, with modification, in *Political Liberalism* to explain the construction and evaluation of a theory of justice.[18] In *A Theory of Justice*, the general test of reflective equilibrium is applied to the principles that emerge from the deliberation of individuals under a "veil of ignorance."[19] In constructing a theory of justice, we seek reasonable principles that "match our considered judgments duly pruned and adjusted" and "at all levels of generality."[20] We ask whether the principles "match our considered convictions of justice or extend them in an acceptable way." Under reflective equilibrium, "no one level, say of abstract principle or that of particular judgments in particular cases, is viewed as foundational. They all may have an initial credibility."[21]

Reflective equilibrium expresses our desire for integration of beliefs. If we can adjust our principles and intuitions at all levels of generality into a coherent system or a theory, then we have reached reflective equilibrium. The process, when successful, reaches equilibrium because our principles and judgments coincide. It is reflective because we know to what principles our judgments conform and the premises of their derivation. Our state of mind can be described by this phrase: "At the moment everything is in order." Yet the equilibrium can be upset by further reflection, which leads to further revision.

As Nussbaum says, Rawls's ideas of justification are "holistic" and "internal."[22] Reflective equilibrium presumes that we are "starting in the middle" of an imperfect conceptual scheme with inevitable tensions between levels and with problems in the application of principles. The scheme provides "provisional fixed points" for the start of reflection.[23] These are judgments, concepts, and principles that we feel are basic and sound *at this point of time*. However, such convictions are fallible, and we would be prepared to change them if confronted with a strong counter-argument. New cases may shake our confidence in a principle, or in our theory as a whole. The challenge is to re-establish reflective equilibrium. We cannot say in advance what the result will be.

I believe the method of reflective equilibrium extends beyond the construction of a theory of justice to the construction of ethical theory and to the way we reason ethically. Through reflective equilibrium, we have a general method for reforming our ethical conceptual scheme and for justifying judgements.

Applied to my tri-level scheme, reflective equilibrium seeks to adjust ideas on all three levels until they cohere – that is, provide a consistent and systematic theory of ethical reasoning. Construction in ethics does not start with a Cartesian method of radical doubt whereby the constructor starts from scratch, placing all existing ideas aside as doubtful until principles known with certainty can be found. Nor does one construct by ignoring existing principles and intuitions. In ethics, our construction usually seeks partial or gradual justification and reform. We improve upon a particular principle or area of ethics, while holding the rest of our ethical conceptual scheme intact.

Reflective equilibrium is applied on each level of my three-part scheme. On level 1, we seek the best possible fit between our judgments and principles. On level 2, we seek a fit between (a) the framework and our judgments about cases on level 1 and (b) the framework and our ultimate aims on level 3. On level 3, we seek to develop a metaethical theory of ethics and a theory of ultimate aims that are not only intrinsically attractive but fuse with and make sense of our reasoning on levels 1 and 2.

Elgin sees the process of reflective equilibrium as a way of being rational amid uncertainty and complexity:

> A system of considered judgments in reflective equilibrium is neither absolute nor arbitrary: not absolute, for it is fallible, revisable, revocable; not arbitrary, for it is tethered to antecedent commitments. Such a system neither is nor purports to be a distortion-free reflection of a mind-independent reality. Nor is it merely an expression of our beliefs. It is rather a tool for the advancement of our understanding.[24]

We have reviewed three general methods for testing frameworks. The existence of this constellation of evaluative criteria defeats the charge that ethics (and constructivism) is arbitrary or subjective. To the contrary, ethical thinking that observes these evaluative criteria bears all the hallmarks of rationality. We think and act within identifiable conditions and according to certain norms to reach certain practical, ethical goals.

A Practical Model

Let's assume that we embrace the three-level scheme of ethical reasoning. Let's assume further that we have validated some frameworks. Imagine that we are journalists and find that the ethical framework of the Society of Professional Journalists – its code of ethics – satisfies the scheme's evaluative criteria. How would we then go about using this scheme and this framework to reason about situations in journalism?

What we need is a model. A model is a series of steps for the ethical analysis and evaluation of any journalism situation on level 1. A model leads us to a well-considered judgment about what to do. A model translates the scheme and framework into a specific set of questions and reasoning techniques. The model operates at level 1, helping frameworks to be applied to cases. I now propose one such model for journalism ethics. My model is not unique; other models are possible. My claim is merely that this model promotes critical analysis of journalism issues on level 1.

The analysis consists of four stages to be carried out by individual journalists or groups of journalists in newsrooms: awareness, analysis, evaluation, and judgment.

STAGE 1: AWARENESS OF PROBLEM

The application of the model begins with the recognition of an ethical problem. This is not as obvious a step as it appears to be. Often, journalists fail to recognize that their actions raise ethical issues. They may confuse ethical issues with legal issues. The model presumes that journalists can recognize lurking ethical problems in practice. Recall, for example, the ethical conflict felt by the reporter who was informed about allegations of sexual harassment by a politician on the campaign trail. When they recognize a problem, journalists should share their uncertainty and begin an ethical discussion.

STAGE 2: ANALYSIS

The ethical discussion begins with analysis. Journalists analyze situations by identifying the ethical issues and the facts most relevant to the ethical issues. The skills of this analysis are many, as we will see below.

STAGE 3: EVALUATION OF OPTIONS

Using the analysis, journalists identify what appears to be a range of ethically permissible actions. They evaluate those options by reference to a framework that specifies the principles and aims of journalism. Journalists choose the actions that best adhere to the framework, after carefully balancing choices and weighing principles. In this stage, the focus is not on analysis but on justification of possible actions.

STAGE 4: CONSIDERED JUDGMENT AND REVIEW

Evaluation leads to a considered judgment about which action is best. After the action has been carried out, the journalist reviews the wisdom of the decision based on the outcomes. The outcomes may be so negative that they prompt a revision of some part of the framework.

For this chapter, the most important stages are analysis and evaluation: stages 2 and 3. Let's break down these two stages into their main components.

Analysis consists in distinguishing the key ethical issues from legal, commercial, prudential, and etiquette considerations. It involves distinguishing what should be done from the idea that "this is the way we usually do things around here." As explained in chapter 1, ethical issues are questions about the ultimate public aims of journalism and what actions and principles promote or violate these aims. The analysis should be guided by questions about consequences, the honouring or violating of someone's rights, the impact of a story on various groups, and the integrity of journalists and their profession. At the same time, the analysis should determine what facts are most important to the case. Are there any important facts unknown or uncertain? It may be helpful to check codes of ethics to review relevant principles.

Stage 3, the evaluation, begins with the identification of a range of possible actions (or types of reporting) in a situation and the subsequent identification of a subset of actions that are *prima facie* ethically permissible. In many cases, the ethical choice is not between dozens of possible actions since many of these actions will be clearly unethical and require no sustained reasoning, such as recklessly publishing a libellous story. The decision comes down to a choice among two or three possible actions, each of which has some ethical weight.

To return to the sexual harassment example, one option may counsel publishing sexual harassment allegations against a politician because that is what a free press does, or that it is information that the public ought to know. Another option counsels not reporting the allegation because that would cause real harm to the subject of the story. Another option may steer a middle course. It agrees that the story should be published but argues about when and how. Is it preferable to wait until more facts are verified or to publish the article without revealing the name of the complainant?

Having identified the apparent ethical options, the journalists should evaluate each option by using level 1 reasoning – assessing each option in light of the major principles and values of journalism ethics such as reporting truthfully and independently, while attempting to minimize harm and be accountable to the public. This holistic weighing of principles and values leads to the conclusion that one action is best, ethically considered. "Best" means that the proposed action comes closest to fulfilling the ethical principles and aims of journalism, duly weighed and balanced with respect to this situation. Let's apply the model to another situation.

CHILDREN OF ADDICTED PARENTS: SENSITIVE PHOTO

Imagine that John is one of your newspaper's best photographers. He has just returned from an area of town frequented by drug dealers and heroin addicts.[25] John has a compelling photo to accompany a story on the effects of drugs on children. The photo shows two children, Maria, age five, and her three-year-old brother, Jorge, whose parents are addicts. The parents think their children don't see what they do, but the photo tells a different story. It shows the children playing junkie in a gritty public alley outside their home. They pretend to stick needles in their arms. Maria and Jorge's parents gave your photographer permission to take pictures of the children for publication. Since then, however, the children's grandmother has heard about the photo and called your newsroom to ask that you not run the photo. There are mixed opinions in the newsroom. Should the photo be published?

Applying the four steps of the model, step 1 is easy. It is clear that ethical issues are involved. A responsible editor would feel at least some doubt or uncertainty about publishing such a dramatic picture of children. Step 2, analysis, reveals that the ethical issues include journalism's duty to independently report the unvarnished truth versus the duty to not exploit or harm the subjects of stories. The situation is made more difficult by the fact that crucial facts are unknown. Under what circumstances did the parents agree to this photo? Why did they agree? Were they in a condition to provide informed consent? Is consent needed in this case?

The evaluation phase, step 3, begins by identifying the options, which appear to be: publish the photo as is; don't publish the photo; or publish the photo under certain conditions, such as not naming the children or family, or their address; or obscuring the faces of the children. The evaluation of these options requires the balancing of two major principles: the principle of journalistic truth-telling in the public interest – drawing public attention to a serious social problem (parental addiction) – versus minimizing the harm of publishing the faces of the children. Proponents of publishing the photo may argue that, in this case, reporting the unvarnished truth is consistent with journalism's duty to draw attention to serious social problems. Perhaps the story could prompt officials and child protection agencies to do more to protect children in such situations. The opposing response could argue that the photo exploits the children for the sake of a dramatic story to sell newspapers. Publication would violate the privacy rights of the children and would stigmatize them indefinitely. Moreover, it could be argued that it is not journalism's role to fix social problems.

Step 4, considered judgment and review, requires a decision about which possible action is most plausible, ethically. The decision won't be easy. It is difficult to predict with any certainty the long-term consequences of publishing the picture. Will publication actually prompt remedial action by officials or significantly increase public awareness of the problem of parental drug abuse? Will the published photo really stigmatize the children? However, despite the uncertainty, the model does show what the ethical options are, the uncertainties involved, and how one might construct a full ethical argument for or against publication. This model doesn't provide the answer, but it ensures, through a step-by-step process, that the ethical framework is applied, relevant questions are asked, and rival values are identified. The model shows how one should practice the general skill of ethical reasoning through eclectic weighing and balancing. It shows us how to reason on level 1 in journalism.

FEATURES OF THE THEORY

I have described a tripartite scheme of ethical reasoning and an accompanying model. I have briefly described how reasoning proceeds on each of the three levels, and I have provided criteria for evaluating frameworks of principles. I conclude the chapter by explaining in more depth the central philosophical features of the theory. I will discuss holism, the relationship of applied and philosophical ethics, and the objectivity of ethical reasoning. Some of these ideas have been mentioned in this and the previous chapter. In this section, I provide a fuller discussion.

Holism

In chapter 1, I noted that value pluralism was a stimulus to ethical thinking. In this chapter, I advanced eclecticism as the best form of ethical reasoning given the plurality of value.

The main reason for eclecticism is that it embodies a form of holistic reasoning. My assumption is that holistic reasoning is the best approach to practical reasoning in ethics for two reasons: (a) the holistic nature of the things we value, and (b) the holistic nature of our minds and their conceptual schemes. Holism rejects monism because monism misconstrues the nature of value and of the mind.

The fact that, in ethical reasoning, we feel compelled to recognize many principles with prima facie ethical weight is not a coincidence. It has to do with the way our minds organize and evaluate information. Our minds are holistic processing devices, whether the topic be ethics, the syntax of grammar, or the best scientific hypothesis. The psychological basis of holism is the fact that humans understand their world, and come to practical conclusions through webs of belief, or holistic conceptual schemes. Different beliefs in that web, from the practical to the theoretical, influence each other when we think and judge. These holistic forms of thinking defy attempts by philosophers to replace holistic reasoning with linear forms of reasoning using deduction or induction. In ethics, eclectic reasoning is best because our web of belief ensures that the reasons for doing anything are context-bound, plural, and connected.

"Holism" contrasts with "atomism" as an approach to understanding objects, processes, and systems. The debate over holism or atomism involves the age-old philosophical problem of the relationship between part and whole. Atomism holds that the individual parts of a system – the atoms – are most important for understanding the whole. The whole is understood through the actions of the atoms, or individuals. Holism holds that the whole is more than the sum of its parts. The relationships among the elements are equally or more important than the elements themselves. While atomism focuses on the parts, holism focuses on the interactions of the parts. Their interaction defines the behaviour of the system and the very nature of the elements. Holism emphasizes the web of relationships in which the parts participate. Methodologically, atomism seeks to understand phenomena by analyzing them into their component units. Holism seeks to understand how the atoms are synthesized into complex wholes.

It might seem that an abstract dispute about the part and the whole would have little theoretical or practical effect, but it does. Over many centuries, contending approaches to the understanding of language, society, and other phenomena have been divided over the merits of atomism and holism. Atomism in psychology led to the British empiricists of the eighteenth century, Hume and Locke, and their attempt to analyze knowledge as an association of simple impressions or ideas. Not so long ago, behaviourists dreamed of explaining complex human behaviour, such as language, as a combination of atoms of behaviour cued to stimuli through operant conditioning. Atomism in social psychology has been associated with "methodological individualism" – the idea that social facts can be reduced to facts about individuals. In ethics, some contract theories reduce ethics to the rational calculations of self-interested individuals.

To get a sense of holism, we can note a few examples outside ethics. The importance of a web of relationships is evident with language. When individual symbols are organized in certain ways, they become a language, a holistic system of great expressive power. In linguistics, Ferdinand de Saussure argued that any individual symbol in a language is defined by its internal, "synchronic" relationships with other symbols. Less abstractly, we can consider Aristotle's contention that one cannot conceive of the good for individuals apart from studying the good of individuals in society. In psychology, gestalt theories showed how our perception of individual objects is influenced by the perceptual context or "gestalt" in which the object occurs. In the philosophy of science, Quine argued for a holism of empirical meaning and theory evaluation. A scientific theory as a whole – not its individual sentences – has empirical meaning. The theory as a whole obtains empirical meaning by implying or predicting empirical observations. Also, scientific theories are evaluated holistically by weighing a variety of related norms, from empirical prediction to theoretical economy.

Turning to ethical reasoning, atomism is often expressed by two related views: a monism of ethical value and a top-down approach to reasoning. A monistic, top-down approach was mentioned briefly above.[26] I now want to examine this approach more carefully so as to contrast it with my holism.

Monism is the view that there is one form of value, or there is one value that is supreme. The idea of one supreme value leads to the idea of top-down ethical reasoning. Monistic, top-down analysis strives to show how our many ethical norms and judgments form a single, logical system that extends from the most general to the most particular. The idea is this: if there is one supreme value, then all other value judgments must de deducible from this one value. The "derivation" is conceptualized as the deduction of particular ethical judgments at the bottom of our ethical conceptual scheme from a supreme principle at the top of the scheme. In this way we organize our reasoning, around one element such as happiness. Typically, top-down theorists contend that the top principles are better known, have greater authority, and are more important to ethics than lower elements such as mid-level rules and particular judgments. The top principles are universal precepts that hold independently of context.

Most monistic, top-down theories do not argue that one can deduce all ethical judgements directly from a supreme principle. Rather, the supreme principle applies to judgments through the mediation of less general, or mid-theoretical, principles. For example, one might argue that a particular act of promise-keeping is justified because it promotes reliable human relationships and, in turn, reliable human relationships are valued because they promote a supreme value –

well-ordered communities. The principle of reliable human relationships is a mid-theoretical principle that mediates between the
judgment and the supreme principle of well-ordered communities.
Similarly, rule-utilitarians can argue that a particular act, say of following the rule not to cheat others in financial transactions, is justified by the fact that the greatest good for the greatest number is
secured when people follow the rule. The rule of not cheating mediates between the judgment and the supreme principle of utility.

Overall, monistic top-down theories regard ethical justification as
something that flows downward through our ethical system. Ethical
reasoning derives a practical conclusion from principles of ascending
generality up to and including a supreme principle. The justification
of judgments may not always require tracing the argument back to
a supremely general principle. Yet the top-down analysis presumes
that such a possibility exists, if the dispute requires it.

An example of a top-down theory is the version of philosophical
intuitionism favoured by the English ethicist Henry Sidgwick. On
this view, philosophical intuitions bring ethical rules and mid-theoretical principles under one or two fundamental principles that are
true and evident. For Sidgwick, the supreme principle of philosophical intuitionism was utilitarianism, or "Universalistic Hedonism."[27]
Classical utilitarianism, as we find in the writings of Bentham and
Mill, is also a monistic, top-down theory in the teleological tradition. Mill begins his *Utilitarianism* bemoaning the lack of progress
in ethics over what is "the criterion of right and wrong" or the *sum-
mum bonum*, "the foundation of morality." Mill's use of the definite
article "the" in this opening passage of chapter 1 indicates that he
takes a master principle approach to ethical reasoning.[28]

Mill reasons that if all actions are for the sake of some end, then in
ethics we need "a clear and precise conception of what we are pursuing." Mill notes that both utilitarianism and moral intuitionism
believe in the "necessity of general laws" and that "morality must
be deduced from principles." But the trouble, Mill continues, is that
schools of ethics fail to place their principles and intuitions under
"some one fundamental principle or law, at the root of all morality."
If there are several basic principles, "there should be a determinate
order of precedence among them." Mill argues that the utility principle is the best candidate for a supreme principle, an ultimate criterion or right and wrong that can act as a "common umpire" between
conflicting principles.[29] Bentham, in some writings, indicates that the

utility principle is not just the maximization of the total good but also the distribution of good among individuals – the "greatest equal happiness."[30] Regardless of how this issue is settled, these forms of utilitarianism are top-down theories.

Of special concern to the top-down approach is how one justifies supremely general principles. Mill believed that the supreme principle of utility, like all questions about ultimate ends, is "not amendable to direct proof" since whatever is proved to be good is a good that is shown to be a means to another good that is "good without proof." But assent to the supreme principle is not arbitrary. It can come "within the cognisance of the rational faculty," which includes appeals to intuition but also to various considerations that lead us to assent to the doctrine. For example, we may produce a conception of utility that encompasses recognized particular goods, accords with our lived experience, does not conflict or rule out ethical principles such as duty, justice, or virtue, and is useful in sorting out ethical problems. Another source of proof is that a principle, such as the promotion of happiness, is actually desired by humans, and hence recognized as a plausible candidate for the greatest good. For Mill, this rational argument and assent is, in ethics, "equivalent to proof."[31]

HOLISTIC STRUCTURES

Holism challenges the monistic, top-down approach in two ways. First, monism is rejected, Holism doubts that the pluralistic of basic values can be reduced to one principle. Second, it rejects the top-down approach as the best model for the nuanced and complex activity of reflective engagement. It offers holistic reasoning as an alternative.

Let's take a closer look at the structure of this holistic reasoning. Two ideas are primary. First, various types of premises are related holistically. The premises form a system of mutually supporting elements within a conceptual scheme. Premises are nodes in a web of belief where the lines of influence, evidence, and evaluation run in all directions. Second, the aim of ethical reasoning is to reach a reflective equilibrium among elements.

A holistic approach differs from a top-down approach in several ways. No level in the system (no type of premise) has automatic priority over other elements. No element at the top, middle, or bottom of the system has a privileged logical or epistemological status.

There is no "master" element. Holistic analysis does not attempt to organize ethics into a system where elements are linearly ordered from the top to the bottom or from the bottom to the top. Holism does not regard ethics as a house whose upper structure rests on absolute foundations. Rather, ethics is an arch of mutually supporting blocks (beliefs) that together maintain the arch's structural integrity (conceptual system).[32]

Top-down approaches portray the logical and epistemic relations among ethical beliefs (or premises) as unidirectional and asymmetrical. The lines of justification, by deduction, induction, or intuition, run one way: upward or downward. One element lends authority to another element but not vice versa. A holistic view sees the lines of justification moving in both directions. The holist regards the relations as multidirectional and symmetrical. The holist asks: why should one element of an ethical system be the ultimate source of justification? Maybe the ultimate source of justification is the coherence of the whole conceptual system. Why should the lines of support run in one direction rather than back and forth? Holists posit a plurality of relations among elements. In addition to deduction and induction, there are other relationships such as the balancing of principles.

According to holism, premises at any levels of our ethical conceptual scheme can strengthen or weaken our commitment to premises at any other level. This dynamic affects ethical reasoning. For example, it means that, if our intuitions conflict with principles, the latter do not always override the former. We may have great confidence in the correctness of a particular ethical judgment. We may be firmly convinced that John should make amends to Mary because of what he did in circumstance c – say he maliciously and falsely accused her of cheating on her husband at a social occasion attended by her peers. We cannot conceive of a principle or theory that would change our minds. Take another example: if a general principle of justice conflicts with a firm judgment or leads to unacceptable judgments, such as sanctioning racism or the unequal treatment of minority groups, the principle itself comes under question. Conversely, if we adopt a new principle, such as the view that animals have rights, then such a principle will require changes to our existing judgments about how to treat animals, whether humans should be vegetarians, and so on.

Reflection on difficult cases may lead to changes in upper-level ethical and legal principles. Consider the case where we ethically evaluate a new government treaty with a group of British Columbia

aboriginals in an attempt to repair historical wrongs and to establish a framework for cooperation in the future. Suppose the treaty
provides financial compensation and recognizes aboriginal communal rights, such as the right to have its own salmon-fishing season,
despite the objections of environmentalists and non-aboriginal fish-
ermen. As we examine the case, we realize that the treaty's principles
and provisions conflict with existing notions of justice and equality.
Using existing notions only, we might conclude that the treaty is discriminatory toward non-aboriginals in granting special fishing rights
and we may note that "communal" rights are nowhere supported by
existing legal principles. However, the matter does not have to end
there. We can argue that a correct (or improved) principle of equality should allow for special adjustments based on history, systemic
discrimination, and tradition. In this manner, our reflections, initially
focused on a specific case, may lead to changes in our theories of
social justice and of the distribution of resources.

In the professions, the dynamic nature of holistic reasoning is evident. Changes in basic concepts reverberate across the web of belief
and practice. For example, if doctors adopted the principle that they
should *never* withhold any information from patients, that would
require basic changes in the practice of medicine and in its code
of ethics. In times of war, journalists may become confused as to
how to act both as a patriotic citizen and as a critical, truth-telling
journalist. Should journalists question a military campaign, even if
some citizens think this is unpatriotic and may aid the enemy? One
response to this debate over patriotism is an attempt to redefine the
journalistic principle of serving the public so as to allow journalists
more freedom to act as critical public informers. Or, journalists may
be troubled by public demands to restrict their coverage of a hor-
rendous serial-murder trial so as not to cause offence to the public
and the families of murdered people. But this demand only raises
questions about the correct interpretation of the journalistic principle to avoid harm in reporting. This principle, if understood as "do
no harm," is too strong because it would make most of journalism
impossible. Almost any type of article, from a scathing book review
to an investigation into political port-barrelling, does some harm
to someone. Perhaps the correct principle is to minimize harm. But
how does the principle work? Thinking holistically, there is no saying in advance what changes will be required across our belief system to re-establish reflective equilibrium.

According to my holism, ethical thinkers start in the middle of things. They approach situations with an existing set of standards and beliefs, a conceptual scheme. Philosophers have provided metaphors to convey this idea of holistic thinking and evaluation within evolving conceptual schemes. Otto Neurath compared the inquirer to a sailor who repairs his boat while he sails along. Quine added that scientific inquirers are sailors whose boat they "must rebuild plank by plank while staying afloat in it."[33] Epistemically, this means that inquirers can't start from scratch by rejecting all standards and beliefs. Rather they employ a limited skepticism that questions specific beliefs from within their evolving conceptual scheme. They stand on planks to repair other planks. The goal is to improve and reform our conceptual schemes by paying attention to internal tensions and revealing cases, and by comparing perspectives.

Fusion of Philosophical and Normative Ethics

In my horizontal view of ethical reasoning, I stress how elements interact. There is one further form of interaction that plays a central role in my theory – the interaction or fusion of philosophical and normative ethics.

My fusion view is close to the position put forward by philosopher Stephen Darwall, who argues against the separation of metaethics and normative ethics discussed in chapter 1. He claims that it is impossible and undesirable to completely "seal off" philosophical issues from intelligent normative discussion. Although metaethics and normative ethics address different issues, "systematic ethical philosophy thrives when these areas are brought into dynamic relation and pursued in an integrated way we might call 'philosophical ethics.'" Metaethics and normative ethics should be pursued independently, as "complimentary aspects of a comprehensive philosophical ethics." The aim is to integrate both forms of thinking into a coherent ethical theory – an aim that was held by systematic ethical thinkers in previous centuries.[34]

One reason that we can't seal the borders between applied and philosophical ethics is that the subject matter of ethics is itself a matter of philosophical dispute. What one takes to be part of ethics depends in part on one's philosophical view of the nature of ethics. As we've seen, ethicists think that ethics is primarily about the realm of the good, or of the right, or of virtue. Or, take for instance, how we should understand virtue theory as a normative theory. What is the subject matter of virtue theories? Is virtue theory only about virtues that are ethical? Or does virtue theory include virtues that go beyond the ethical sphere? To decide this is to engage in metaethics as to how we distinguish various normative spheres, and how we should understand the scope of ethics. Moreover, how we reason normatively is influenced by our metaethical views about the nature of ethical judgment. If we are expressionists, our approach to normative ethics will be different from those who are descriptivists. The same applies to whether we are absolutists or relativists. Therefore, normative ethics has trouble talking about its subject matter and methods without making fundamental metaethical assumptions.

Overall, there are several occasions that prompt us to align or "fuse" our normative and philosophical views. The complexities of normative questions prompt us to think deeper about the aims of ethics and the nature of ethical statements. We anchor our beliefs in philosophical positions, and in return we adjust our philosophical positions given our normative experiences. We also seek a fusion when we check our three levels of reasoning for overall coherence. We align our metaethical views with the rest of our ethical conceptual scheme, and in return we seek to align the rest of our conceptual scheme with our metaethical views. The desire to fuse normative and metaethical ethics is part of our holistic reasoning about ethics and the attempt to reach reflective equilibrium.

Is Ethics Objective?

What does my discussion of ethics and ethical reasoning in these first two chapters imply about the issue of ethical objectivity? Do I think ethical statements are objective or subjective, absolute or relative? Are there answers in ethics? Is there something to be right or wrong about? My answer to all of these questions is "yes." But it is important to understand how and why I answer in the affirmative.

Ethical reasoning, conducted according to the methods described above, is objective in the sense of not being subjective or arbitrary. To be subjective, an ethical position comes to its conclusions based on subjective biases and factors that are not under rational restraint and evaluation. Ethics, as invention, is objective and non-arbitrary since there are rational evaluative criteria – criteria that rational agents who share the ethical impulse could not reasonable reject.

There are answers in ethics, insofar as judgments are supported by this method and rational criteria. Yet, ethics is relative in a moderate sense since our evaluations occur within historically contingent conceptual schemes; one cannot show there is only one correct scheme for all times and places.

What could we mean by the question, "Are ethical judgments or ethical standards objective?" It is a version of the more general question, "Is x objective?" where x is a person, attitude, method of belief. There are two senses of this general question worth worrying about. These two senses have dominated discussions of objectivity across the history of Western culture.[35]

One sense is ontological objectivity. To be ontologically objective, a belief must correctly describe or correspond to the way the world is. It must refer to some actually existing object or state of affairs; and it must truly describe certain properties of an object or state of affairs, such as size or mass. My belief that there is a flock of pink flamingos in my bedroom is not objective because it is due to my imagination or my dreaming. My belief that there is a yellow tree in my backyard is not objective because the tree is actually dark brown. So, to ask if ethics is objective in the ontological sense amounts to the question: "Do ethical judgments or statements correctly refer to (or describe) ethical objects, properties, or facts external to my mind?" In chapter 1, in a non-descriptive, naturalistic approach to ethical statements, I argued that this ontological approach to ethical statements is wrong. Ethical assertions are not true or false in a literal or primary sense. There are avowals of ethical value and proposals put forward by practical reason as guides to action.

A second sense of objectivity is more relevant. It is what I call "epistemic objectivity" or "methodological objectivity." We may struggle to know what is true, or what corresponds to reality. Yet we can understand objectivity in a different manner. It is the *way* we approach issues and draw conclusions. On this view, my beliefs on any subject, including ethics, are objective to the extent that they are formed by good reasoning and rigorous methods that detect bias and reduce error. They are beliefs that withstand sustained public scrutiny and are tested for evidence and logic. Objectivity in this methodological sense does not guarantee truth or correct practical judgment, but it improves our chances of getting closer to the truth or the most reasonable judgment. In science, the hypothesis that a group of genes in the brain is causally related to Parkinson's disease is tested for plausibility and objectivity according to certain objective methods and standards of evidence. In journalism, my story is epistemically objective if its claims are based on the best possible journalistic methods for gathering data, collaborating facts, checking sources, and so on. Similarly, ethics is objective to the extent that its statements are the product of the best available objective procedure and forms of inquiry.

Epistemic objectivity is a good place to start when we are thinking about objectivity in ethics. We saw in chapter 1 how Rawls described Kant's view of ethical objectivity: moral beliefs are objective if reasonable and rational persons who are sufficiently intelligent and conscientious in exercising their powers of practical reason would eventually endorse those convictions, when all concerned know the relevant facts and have sufficiently surveyed the relevant considerations.[36] How we come to judge an action or principle as reasonable is a matter of practical reasoning following a certain procedure. This is the essence of my epistemic objectivity and "procedural realism" in ethics.

My notion of objectivity in ethics is an elaboration on this constructivism, with an emphasis on the social nature of the evaluation process. An objective judgment is the result of humans, united by a desire to do what is ethical, following an objective procedure that ensures the judgment is as reasonable as possible. To say that a moral conviction is objective, then, is to say there are reasons sufficient to convince all reasonable persons that it is valid or correct. To assert a moral judgment is to imply that there are such reasons and that the judgment can be justified to a community of such persons. As a constructivist, I think "a correct moral judgment is one that conforms to all the relevant criteria of reasonableness and rationality" given by procedures approved by practical reason.[37] This procedure is an open, social process of subjecting claims to public scrutiny. The normative-guidance system for ethics is not solipsistic. It is an intersubjective system that features dialogue and deliberation.

The procedure depends not only on the ethical stance and dialogue, but also on reasoning according to certain objective standards. Hence, an ethical statement is reasonable if it is a construction of ethical reasoning that uses criteria to weigh facts, norms, principles, and consequences. The result is not an absolute truth as sometimes imagined for theoretical statements. It is not a correspondence of ethical statement with fact or external reality. Instead, it is the most reasonable and well-considered ethical judgment given the best available evaluative criteria.

In this chapter, I have indicated how one would apply this epistemic objectivity to ethical reasoning by using a three-part scheme and model. In addition, I have provided several types of criteria for rational evaluation and objective restraint, such as criteria for evaluating frameworks, the restraints of contractualism, and the method of reflective equilibrium. Reviewing these criteria is one of the best ways to cast doubt on the charge that ethics is simply subjective or arbitrary. We show, in a concrete manner, that there exist plausible and reasonable norms to test and restrain claims. Even if ethics is a human construction, or an invention, it can claim to be a rational enterprise and, more so, an objective enterprise to the degree that we can point to rational and objective forms of evaluation on judgment, reasoning, and theorizing.

This constructionist, criteria-based notion of ethical objectivity is what Putnam has called "ethics without ontology" or ethics without objects.[38] Putnam writes:

> What I am saying is that it is time we stopped equating *objectivity* with *description*. There are many sorts of statements – bona fide statements, ones amenable to such terms as "correct," "incorrect," "true," "false," "warranted," and "unwarranted" – that are not descriptions, but that are under rational control, governed by standards appropriate to their particular functions and contexts.[39]

In *The Invention of Journalism Ethics*, I used the ideas of holism and epistemic objectivity to put forward a new view of objectivity for journalism that I call "pragmatic objectivity."[40] According to pragmatic objectivity, objectivity in journalism consists of a general attitude and the application of a set of evaluative criteria. The objective journalist must be willing to adopt the objective stance. The objective stance is a set of virtuous attitudes that includes a disposition not to prejudge stories, to fairly represent other views, and to follow where the facts lead. Taking up this stance, the objective journalist conducts a holistic evaluation of stories according to a set of standards, from factual evidence to the coherence of claims with existence knowledge. In addition, these general criteria support more specific rules for the gathering and verification of claims within stories.

Pragmatic objectivity replaces the doctrine of traditional objectivity in news reporting – the notion of objectivity that arose in journalism in the early 1900s. Traditional objectivity narrowly construed objectivity as reporting "just the facts" and the elimination of all interpretation, opinion, and theorizing by the reporter. Traditional objectivity was, and is, a form of ontological objectivity. It aims to describe events and objects just as they exist, independent of conceptual schemes and interpretations. To accomplish this description, the reporter is to act as a passive recorder of facts.

Pragmatic objectivity regards ontological objectivity as inappropriate for journalism, and it views traditional objectivity in journalism as a spent force. Pragmatic objectivity begins by viewing journalism not as a passive recording of events but as an active inquiry into, and interpretation of, events. All reports and stores in journalism are interpretations of varying degrees of perspective, editorial choices, and theorizing. For the pragmatic enterprise of journalism, objectivity is not the elimination of interpretation but the testing of interpretations by a set of standards. The goal is epistemic objectivity – applying methods to make sure stories are as well-evidenced and coherent as possible. Pragmatic objectivity is not only an epistemological ideal, but also an essential part of ethical and responsible journalism. It is a complex ideal and method that takes in a number of crucial ethical norms such as truth-seeking, accuracy, and fairness.

Objectivity and Relativity

For a constructivist, the question, "Is ethics objective or subjective?" is not the same as "Is ethics relative or absolute?" The question of objectivity is whether we can provide evidence and reasons for our claims and judgments. Ethics is objective in the sense that judgments and decisions are not arbitrary, based on nothing more than a subjective feeling or desire, or act of will. To respond to the charge of subjectivity, the objectivist needs to show that it is possible to submit ethical judgment to rational evaluation and restraint. The objectivist needs to show how ethics can be based on a set of criteria and procedures that other people could not easily or reasonably reject.

Securing the objectivity of ethical judgments, via a conceptual scheme, does not adequately address the debate between relativism and absolutism. This debate introduces additional, higher-order questions about the status of the conceptual schemes themselves. So far, I have argued that judgments of objectivity are objective, relative to a set of criteria. We can go on to ask: is this conceptual scheme objective in a higher sense? Which higher sense? In the sense that it is absolute. To ask, "Is this standard or set of standards absolute," is to ask: is it the one uniquely correct system for evaluating and forming judgments? Or is ethics – its criteria and principles – relative? That is, are ethical judgments relative to the conceptual scheme one adopts? Are there are several plausible and rival conceptual schemes?

The debate between relativism and absolutism can be understood as a debate about the limits of objective thinking. The question is whether a relative form of objectivity is the best that we can achieve in ethics. Can we only claim that ethical statements are objective within a given domain where statements have the support of an accompanying conceptual scheme? We can call this modest view of objectivity "objective relativism" or "contextual objectivity." The phrase "objective relativism" sounds odd because we are accustomed to thinking of objectivity as requiring absolutism, and therefore as opposed to relativism. In contrast, absolutism prompts us to seek objectivity at a higher plane of thought – absolute objectivity. Absolutism in ethics seeks a set of ethical criteria that are objective in an absolute manner. The set is known to be true or reasonable per se. It is not relative to a particular conceptual scheme, among many potentially rival schemes. There is only *one* conceptual scheme, and it absolutely grounds our judgments of right or wrong.

To be "absolute," then, a theory or belief must be true or objective independently of perspectives and current conditions, in the same way that there might be absolute position in space, independently of the perspective of any observer. If torturing babies for fun is said to be wrong, absolutely, what is meant is that its "wrongness" is not dependent on what people think or believe. It just *is* wrong, period. Absolutely. In the same way, if criteria of right or wrong, such as the principle to reduce pain, are said to be absolute, what is meant is that the authority of the criteria is not based on what people think or believe. Absolutism, in this sense, moves toward an ontological sense of objectivity, or describing absolute moral facts, and thus "substance realism."

In addition, absoluteness is often associated with universality, uniqueness, and certainty.[41] It is thought that an ethical principle can only be absolute if it is universal – holds for all rational beings, say. Also, absolutism is associated with the idea that ethical judgments or principles are uniquely true or reasonable. There is no other rival principle that is equally authoritative, and absolute principles are supreme in resolving conflicts between other principles. Absolutists tend to think of ethics as one set of principles that hold for all humans, or all cultures.

Ethical relativism can now be defined more specifically, in contrast to absolutism. Ethical relativism believes that there is no one ultimate ethical principle or set of principles by which all ethical judgments are to be evaluated for objectivity and rational support. Ethical claims are held to be true or reasonable relative to a background theory or culture, and we lack the means to show that one of the schemes is absolutely true or reasonable, or superior. Judgments about right or wrong are not to be understood absolutely, but rather by reference to "particular standards that are made relevant by the context of the action in question, or by the context of the judgment itself."[42] Ethics relativism comes in different "strengths," from radical to moderate. Radical relativists hold that any ethical system is as true or as justified as any other. Moderate relativists deny that there is any single true morality but also hold that some moralities are truer or more justified than others.

Relativism, properly understood, is not *just* an empirical claim about the existence of different systems of ethical evaluation and practice across cultures or across time. The plurality of different ethical beliefs is obvious. Seventeenth-century England believed slavery was correct; twentieth-century England does not. Today, our culture would criticize female circumcision in tribal countries. But the fact of ethical differences is not sufficient to establish the relativist's case. Why? Because non-relativists can agree that there is a plurality of ethical systems. Philosophers have known for centuries that ethical values differed but many did not conclude that relativism was true. The absolutist may claim that differences in belief are consistent with a belief in truth and absolute standards. For instance, the fact that you and I disagree whether the world is round or flat does not mean there is no correct answer or that the dispute is just a matter of opinion or relativity of belief. The fact that many people have different beliefs about the cause of climate change doesn't mean there isn't a correct belief. Why shouldn't the same fact about opposing beliefs hold in ethics? The fact that there are many different beliefs, by itself, proves nothing. The absolutists can argue that correct thinking can identify absolute standards and truths below the surface of opinion.

Another reason that ethical plurality is insufficient to establish relativism is that the absolutists may argue that the differences are only "apparent" or local, and not substantial. It is possible that differences in belief and practice are only variations on objective, universal principles. It is possible that researchers find that all cultures agree on general ethical values such as a respect for life, truth, and non-violence, but the cultures differ on how they understand those values and put them into practice.

That relativism is not just an empirical claim is clear by looking at the problem in another way. What if, as a matter of fact, humans did *not* have substantial differences on ethical principles? Imagine a time in the past when there was agreement on basic ethical beliefs among all humans. Or, imagine that tomorrow for some remarkable reason all humans will agree upon the same ethical principles. Would these facts refute relativism? I don't think so. The relativist might reply that a consensus doesn't prove absolutism to be true if only because the consensus could break down at any time.

Relativism is a metaethical position about normative principles. It contains strong philosophical assumptions. Relativism must hold that, whether in fact people agree or do not agree on standards, we cannot *in principle* justify the claim that a standard, set of standards, or an ethical system is ultimate and unique. The problem is largely epistemological. There is no rational way to show that one principle or system is rationally superior or has better evidence or is more objective. We cannot show, rationally, how such standards achieve a higher order of objectivity. Relativism contains the premise that when we compare candidates for absolute standards we reach the limits of rational, objective evaluation. We must rest content with relativism. At the least, it is always possible to imagine different ethical principles that are as justified, or as methodologically objective, as the universally dominant ethic. There is no further step we can take to justify one set of ultimate standards as absolutely correct. At this level of evaluation, we run out of reasons, just as we run out of rungs on a ladder as we climb to the top.

My constructivism and naturalism, with its emphasis on the evolution of norms and the invention of ethics, is naturally inclined toward relativism. I think of objectivity as objectivity within conceptual schemes, an objectivity within a moderate relativism. I cannot imagine what a set of ethical criteria of evaluation might be like apart from a perspective or conceptual scheme. However, I am a moderate relativist because I believe that not all evaluative schemes are equal. In ethics, it is not "anything goes." Some schemes are better than others. Also, I am not an absolutist because I do not think that all ethical differences can be shown to be variations in major common principles. Substantial and non-reducible differences exist is ethics. I believe that my view of objectivity should be persuasive to many people, and it appeals to general notions of rationality and human conditions, but I do not claim that is an absolute scheme. My theory is general in scope but not absolute in authority.

I accept the relativistic view that absolutism exceeds the limits of rational evaluation in ethics. It is always possible, in theory, to imagine two or more ethical evaluations schemes, or two or more conceptions of objectivity, that are nearly equal in plausibility and for which we lack further resources to determine which is uniquely correct. I believe that it is perfectly possible to speak of judgments being correct or reasonable within certain conceptual schemes or ethical systems. We can develop non-arbitrary, reasonable criteria for evaluating ethical reasoning yet still hold out the possibility that other, different, and reasonable systems are possible.

So far, my relativism works at the abstract level of metaethics about what we should say about ethics to be consistent and rational. I have agreed that relativism is always a distinct theoretical possibility. Yet, I also believe that, when we come "down to earth" and actually observe how humans construct their ethical systems, there is a good deal of common values – enough commonality to encourage cross-cultural dialogue. The commonality exists because humans construct ethical systems for similar purposes from (generally) similar circumstances. The basic needs of humans in society, the common desires and goals of humans, and the fact that humans share a biology and inhabit the same planet leads to the espousal of common ethical values across borders and cultures.

Every society has common problems such as the need to obtain security; to ensure reliable human interactions and contracts; to care for the young, elderly, and seriously ill. As a result, most societies value the principles of truth-telling, promise-keeping, reduction of harm, non-violence, and the satisfaction of essential needs. Societies also need to specify the duties and roles of a variety of social roles and institutions. How societies construct ethical norms to reach these goals will vary. To this degree, the absolutist's idea of the variation of basic ethical norms is true. How societies interpret and realize the values of freedom, dignity, promise-keeping, and other general principles will vary according to conditions and history. As Scanlon says, variations in what is right or wrong arise "from variations in what people have reason to reject in different societies."[43] Therefore, a moderate relativism of a constructivist sort can recognize the existence of basic principles in ethics that not only anchor our own conceptual scheme but also the schemes of other peoples. From a contractual, constructivist perspective, it is to be expected that different ethical systems exhibit both commonality and difference, given the fact that humans share common and yet different forms of life. Commonalities and differences are to be expected since the construction of ethics in any society uses natural and social facts about humans *and* the particular and distinct cultural facts of that society.

I also hold that moderate relativism is an attitude that has the best practical consequences for a liberal, democratic society. Moderate relativism avoids the negative consequences of adopting absolutism or extreme relativism. Absolutism and extreme relativism are incorrect emotional and practical responses to the variability of ethical belief and the existence of ethical disagreement. Absolutism attempts to compensate for plurality and variability by declaring certain values to be absolutely true or right for all because they are based on non-relative sources such as God, nature, or metaphysical insight. Absolutism seeks to get below the shifting sea of human belief to find some unassailable rock upon which to stand. It suggests, incorrectly, that ethics is only possible if there is absolute truth and absolute objectivity. On the other side, extreme relativism concludes that the fact of variability proves that there are no absolutes; therefore, there is no rational or objectivity in ethics *at all*. Assuming that objectivity and reasonableness must be absolute, extreme relativism concludes that there are no objective and reasonable restraints in ethical debate, and no objective way to resolve disagreements. Both absolutism and extreme relativism start from the premise: either there are absolutes or there is nothing; there is no middle ground.

My "objective relativism" seeks the middle ground, arguing for the possibilities of reasoning about ethics in a non-arbitrary manner. The possibilities for non-arbitrary ethical discourse and disagreement are much greater than acknowledged by extreme relativism (or extreme subjectivism). One of the negative practical consequences of extreme relativism is to discourage cross-cultural dialogue. According to extreme relativism, if ethics is hermetically sealed within specific cultures, cross-system dialogue is futile. This attitude, at times, can turn into the dangerous idea that, where there are serious ethical disagreements, the only resort is to ignore each other or to respond with force. It is true that, at a very high level of metaethics, we run out of rungs on our ladder when we try to compare systems. This does not excuse the avoidance of seeking greater understanding and perhaps agreement on some ethical values and issues. The mantra of "everything is relative" should not short-circuit the practically important effort to put our energies into intercultural dialogue on ethics.

Ethical absolutists often accuse relativists, even moderate relativists, of having dangerous effects on human attitudes and behaviour. Relativism is associated with nihilism, extreme skepticism, and a refusal to stand up to unethical practices in other cultures. Absolutes fear that relativism will leave us with no way to say what is actual right or wrong, or unable to justify our claim that Hitler or some other tyrant was objectively wrong. It is all a matter of opinion. In reply, extreme relativists accuse absolutists of being ethical fascists who want to enforce one dogmatic set of values. It is thought that extreme relativism contributes to a more tolerant world by refusing to judge the ethical practices of other cultures, that judging other cultures smacks of cultural arrogance or intolerance. Relativism, it is argued, is more in line with liberal democratic thought.

It is important to avoid such overheated rhetoric. The best approach is to adopt a moderate relativism that stands between absolutism and extreme relativism. The true menace for ethics and for democratic societies is a society that swings between absolutism and extreme relativism.[44] The danger of absolutism is well documented historically by the cruelty and intolerance of absolute religion and absolute forms of government. The idea that reasonable people could hold different comprehensive views on ethics, politics, and religion, and that such a plurality should be tolerated, arose in the seventeenth century as a practical necessity, not as a high-minded ideal, only after the exhaustion of armies in bloody religious wars across Europe.

Meanwhile, the social danger of extreme relativism is passivism and an inability or reluctance to judge. If no cultural and ethical traditions are better than any other, then why not passively acquiesce to whatever tradition one was born into? Why bother to reform? On what basis can I judge another view or practice to be incorrect? We need to recognize that liberalism and liberal tolerance is not based on, and does not require, extreme relativism. Liberalism is committed to a substantial set of values that it considers the best for human society. Liberalism is not the attitude that "anything goes." It is based on a specific, historically contingent political scheme that includes tolerating views insofar as they do not reject a commitment to basic rights and liberties. Liberalism presumes that some forms of life and some principles are better than others, and there is reason to believe so.

Extreme relativism has no necessary connection to liberalism. It can be used to support unattractive political philosophies. It can be used to justify extreme political egoism – if no view is any better than mine, why not pursue my own interests? Extreme relativism can be used to justify traditionalism and even authoritarianism – the view that ethics is following established traditions and values. Therefore, if ethical views are relative and no view is better than any other view, why bother to critically assess and improve ethics? What does "improve" mean if ethics is extremely relative?

My constructivism, and its moderate relativism, avoids the dilemma between absolutism and extreme relativism by seeking a middle ground of reasonable but not arbitrary forms of reasoning, and a reasoned affirmation of ethical values according to the best available norms. Ethical reasoning and ethical systems are fallible and always open to revision. I recognize the need for stable ethical frameworks, but I also leave open the possibility of reform. Not all values are to be doubted; not all values are to be accepted. One works critically from within the best tradition available, and one remains open to other traditions. My liberal constructivism gives up the ontological search for absolute truths below the conflicting, changing ethical opinion of humans and replaces it with a common human dialogue about fair and reasonable terms of social cooperation in a liberal democracy. The search for absolutes is not only illusionary – there are no such foundations – but absolutism is unnecessary and potentially more harmful to ethical progress and tolerance than moderate relativism.

Finally, what about the presumed threat of meaninglessness when we regard ethics as a human construction? This is absolutism's attempt to persuade through fear and exaggeration. Such fears are rhetorically effective only among some people. Absolutists may decry the rise of science and its materialism in the early modern era, and the "disenchantment" of the world whereby value became a human-relative property. Absolutists can complain that the modern view has lent a "meaninglessness" to life and encouraged nihilism in ethics. Or, one can see such developments, as I do, as liberation from the heavy weight of tradition and absolutism. Ultimately, whether we praise or decry the collapse of an ancient paradigm of value is beside the point; we need to deal with the world as it is today. We need to mature ethically as a species. This means accepting that there may be no metaphysical meaning to life on earth, or at least none that is knowable in absolute terms. I fear the inflexible, uncompromising imperatives of absolutists much more than the tolerant, open-mindedness of the relativists. I do not fear that moderate relativism entails unstable and dangerous citizens. Citizens don't turn into barbarians simply because they come to understand, philosophically, that their values are not absolute. Historically, the greatest mass murderers have been absolutists, from the popes who supported the medieval crusades and the Spanish Inquisition to Hitler's fanatical and "absolute" plans for humankind.

The spectre of nihilism does not move me to accept absolutism. Humans are meaning-creating organisms who cannot live long with a vacuum in values. Extreme skepticism or nihilism about all ethical beliefs, or all beliefs in general, may be a (barely) possible theoretical attitude; but, as practical guides to life or action, they are not viable options in the long run. Even if values are human creations and are therefore in that sense "subjective," the project of ethics continues. Humans are forced by the nature of social life to come to some defensible ethical principles and ethical agreements that respond to the conditions of life. To live together, humans must attempt to construct common values, whether or not the values are eternal or temporary, subjective or objective. Humans have *always* constructed ethics and always will, whether or not we want to call our constructions "absolute."

Absolutism is not the only ethical life raft in a dangerous world. Humans should have the courage to embrace the uncertainties of a non-absolute ethics as the best option for a reasonable, tolerant ethics able to adapt to new circumstances. The challenge to ethics is not to discover some code of absolute principles.

These considerations lead me to regard absolutism as an unpersuasive metaethical view of the nature of ethics and ethical reasoning. In addition, it has unattractive practical implications for liberal society and for a contractual approach to ethics. As William James wrote, the challenge of ethics in a pluralistic and rapidly changing world is this: "Invent some manner of realizing your own ideals which will also satisfy the alien demands – that and that only is the path of peace."[45] James stated what it meant to take seriously the act of invention in ethics:

> There is no such thing possible as an ethical philosophy dogmatically made up in advance. We all help to determine the content of ethical philosophy so far as we contribute to the race's moral life. In other words, there can be no final truth in ethics, any more than in physics, until the last man has had his experience and said his say."[46]

CONCLUSION

In chapter 1, I explained my naturalistic conception of ethics as the construction of a normative guidance system for practical problems, a construction that honoured reasonable but fallible restraints. In this chapter, I described a holistic approach to reflective engagement that explained what such a system might look like. I presented a three-level theory of ethical reasoning, and an accompanying model for journalism. I concluded the chapter by explaining the main philosophical features of my theory – holism, the fusion of applied and philosophical ethics and objective relativism. Taken as a whole, this theory is my reply to the question: "How shall we reflectively engage issues ethically in general and in journalism?"

In the next chapter, I turn to describing the ultimate aims of ethical reflection in terms of the "good in the right." This is the level 3 task of providing a philosophical goal for level 1 and 2 reasoning about cases and frameworks. I provide a theory of ethical flourishing that combines a Rawlsian view of the just society and a notion of the human good. I argue that our ethical frameworks must advance a general goal: to move toward just social arrangements that promote the human good through the development and perfection of basic capacities. I believe that this theory of aims is a powerful perspective from which to understand the purpose of ethics and the purpose of journalism ethics.

3

Ethical Flourishing

Human excellence grows like a vine tree, fed by the green dew, raised up, among wise men and just, to the liquid sky.

Pindar[1]

The reasonable generates itself and answers itself in kind.

John Rawls[2]

This chapter completes the presentation of my approach to ethics. In chapter 1, I described the nature of ethics. In chapter 2, I explained my three-level theory of ethical reasoning. In this chapter, I provide a theory of the ultimate aims of ethics in terms of ethical flourishing. These theories form the foundation not only for my approach to journalism ethics but also for the construction of a global journalism ethics in the second half of this book.

I argue that ethical flourishing is the ultimate aim for ethics in general and, therefore, for journalism ethics in particular. The ideal of ethical flourishing is a combination of the two sub-ideals – flourishing and just society. To explain ethical flourishing, I put forward two theories: a theory of the good as flourishing on four levels; and a Rawlsian theory of right for a liberal democratic society or well-ordered society. I then describe how the theories combine to form the concept of ethical flourishing. Ethical flourishing is a congruence of the good and the right.

THEORIES OF THE GOOD

Why Aims?

Aims are part of our everyday explanations of actions and policies. In ethics, teleological theory makes the ends of action the primary consideration. In journalism, notions about the aims of journalism have influenced beliefs and justified practices.

Theories of the good, like all ethical theories, arise from uncertainty about our aims – what goods are worth pursuing and which goods have priority. Should I take the good of maximizing pleasure as my aim? But what if it conflicts with my desire to live a life of service to others? We construct a theory of aims because common sense provides insufficient guidance for our pursuit of the good.

An ultimate aim is the goal for ethical life. It is an ideal that expresses what all of our ethical reasoning and striving is attempting to achieve. It is a target at which the ethical impulse should aim. An ultimate aim is a "final" good in the traditional philosophical sense of what is valued for its own sake and in terms of which we value other things. I use the word "aim" because it is broad enough to include both the pursuit of goods and the pursuit of justice. The concept of an aim does not prejudge whether goods or the duties of justice are the primary concern of ethics, and it does not presume the correctness of a specific ethical theory such as utilitarianism.

The question of ethical aims is important for journalism ethics. Many codes of journalism ethics assert that their principles are justified because they support certain aims such as democracy and justice. In chapter 2, I summarized the main aims found in the history of modern journalism. Many of these aims, such as acting as an effective watchdog on power, are justified because they promote the larger aims of society, such as accountable democratic government. The philosophical basis of journalism ethics is a *deep* view of the ethical and political aims of life and society. Therefore, this chapter's discussion of ultimate aims is an essential step toward a philosophy of journalism ethics.

Theories of the Good

Ultimate aims are ultimate goods. Therefore, a theory of ultimate aims is a theory of the good, or a large part of a theory of the good. What are the features of a theory of the good? How do we evaluate them? What are the main types of theories of the good?

By considering the function of a theory of the good, we identify five features:

(1) *Integration of values.* A theory of the good provides a unifying goal for ethical striving. It offers an ideal to inspire humans and to

measure their ethical development. A theory is a hypothesis about how best to organize our lives ethically.

(2) *Explanatory function.* A theory tells us what "good" means, which goods are most valuable, and how the good is related to the right. It explains the reasons behind our judgments of what is good. A theory shows how it relates to other theories and how it can incorporate insights from the history of ethical theory.

(3) *Holistic "fit."* Ultimate aims should help us to think about cases, justify frameworks of principles, and achieve a reflective equilibrium among the three levels of reasoning.

(4) *Goods of common experience.* The theory clarifies and corrects existing beliefs, but it should not be exoteric or strongly counter-intuitive. It should not promote goods that are not recognized as goods by most humans. It should not recognize goods that are so difficult to obtain (or know) that they are beyond the experience of most human beings.

(5) *Informed by natural knowledge.* A theory should be informed by psychological and social facts about humans, their biology and psychology, and their conditions of growth.

Theory Options

My conception is an "expansionist" developmental theory of human flourishing. To understand this description, we need to know something about the types of theories.[3]

Theories about the good can be philosophical conceptions or practical metrics that measure the amount of good produced by various policies. My theory is a general conception of the good. It is not a metric for quantifying, with some precision, the contribution to human welfare of specific policies in specific situations. The social sciences, especially economics and psychology, have developed metrics to measure the quality of life enjoyed by various societies. The United Nations Development Program measures economic, educational, and medical levels in societies to assess human well-being across the world. Metrics usually imply some philosophical conception of the good or welfare, such as defining the good as the satisfaction of desire.

Philosophical theories investigate the various concepts and conceptions of the human good. Rawls's distinction between concepts and conceptions is useful here.[4] For Rawls, the concept of justice states a general problem, e.g., how people living in a society are to share fairly the benefits of cooperation. A conception of justice puts forward a particular solution to the problem in the form of a theory (or set of principles) that explains how the benefits should be distributed. Rawls's conception of justice is "justice as fairness." Justice as fairness aims at a society where things are as good as possible for the least advantaged insofar as this is consistent with basic freedoms. Classical utilitarianism's answer is to maximize utility. The concept-conception distinction applies to other ethical concepts. The concept of good refers to the problem of what we should aim at in our lives. Conceptions of the good offer solutions.

Once we understand our conception as philosophical, the next step is to decide what sort of theory to construct. The first decision is whether we want our theory to be what I call "expansionist" or "non-expansionist" in its understanding of the good. Do we prefer a non-expansive, minimalist theory of the good that understands the good in terms of a few subjective factors such as pleasure or the satisfaction of desire? Or do we prefer a theory that includes other factors, such as objective facts about human development and human capacities.

There are two kinds of non-expansionist theories: hedonic and desire theories. Hedonic theories are subjective because they understand the good in terms of pleasurable or agreeable mental states and experiences.[5] The good life is a life of agreeable experiences where what is agreeable is determined by the individual in question. Hedonic theories are non-expansionist because they limit their theorizing to the quality of subjective experiences. Hedonistic theories differ by emphasizing different mental states such as pleasure, happiness, or tranquility. Hedonic theories offer an attractive economy of thought. We decide ethical issues by measuring an empirical fact common to all humans, e.g., the amount of pleasure.

A second form of non-expansionist theory is desire theory. The good is the satisfaction of desires or preferences. The simplest form of desire theory is "actual desire" theory. The good is the satisfaction of the desires that an individual happens to have. Desires and preferences, while they include subjective states of mind, can be defined more objectively in terms of dispositions to act in certain ways under certain conditions. Economists are drawn to desires and preferences because they can be measured in situations of choice, such as consumer behaviour.[6]

A metric associated with non-expansionist theories is welfarism. Welfarism assesses human welfare by measuring hedonic states, desires, or preferences. Human welfare is defined in terms of (a) desirable (or agreeable) experiences and states of consciousness; or as (b) desire-fulfillment or preference satisfaction, where a preference is satisfied when a relevant state of the world exists or obtains. On this approach, welfarism can be a component of utilitarian theories.[7] One method of the welfare metric is to measure objective objects and properties associated with well-being. For example, economists have measured "opulence" criteria, such as income or wealth, GNP, or bundles of essential commodities as prime indicators of well-being and prosperity. The policy that helps to generate the greatest subjective well-being, as agreeable conscious states or desire-satisfaction, is best.[8] An entire branch of psychology seeks to measure how subjective states of welfare, such as positive experiences and judgments of well-being, correlate with objective factors such as education, wealth, and culture.[9]

Other non-expansionist theorists amend actual desire theory. They worry that, if the good is defined as what one actually desires, the good includes unreasonable, uninformed, pathological, or perverted desires. The good is whatever impulse moves us. As a result, theorists have defined the good as informed or rational desires – desires that are based on knowledge and can withstand the scrutiny of reason. Richard Brandt identified the good with "rational desires," defined as desires that "survive maximal criticism by facts and logic."[10] Other thinkers, such as Rawls, have argued that what is good is judged against a rational plan of life.

The status of informed desire theory in ethical theory is ambiguous. It can be viewed as a non-expansionist theory of desire or as an expansionist theory that appeals to rationality and includes objective information about the world.

EXPANSIONIST THEORIES

Expansionist theories use a greater number of information sources and types of reasons in judging the good than non-expansionist theories. Expansionist theories make "substantive claims about what goods, conditions, and opportunities make life better."[11] Ethical theory can be expanded along six dimensions:

(1) *Experiential.* Theories can expand the good beyond the current experiences or mental states of individuals by including their past and future experiences as well as the experiences of others in similar circumstances.

(2) *Rationality.* Theories can expand by stressing the role of rationality and reason-giving in determining the good. Scanlon argues that, in almost all non-trivial cases, we are expansionists. Our judgments of what is desirable are based on reasons that go beyond simple appeals to subjective pleasure or desire.[12]

(3) *Intersubjective deliberation.* Theories can expand beyond the rationality of one person to include intersubjective deliberation among agents as determinative of the good.

(4) *Third-person perspective.* Theories expand by adding to ethical reasoning a third-person perspective. A non-expansionist theory regards the good as a subjective affair of what I as a subject think is good. An expansionist approach stands back and considers what is good for people in general. It observes how humans live, what things tend to make life go well for many people, and what capacities are needed for living well.

(5) *Objective or natural knowledge.* This opens the door to scientific facts and theories, and knowledge of human nature and society.

(6) *Social goods and ideals.* Theories can expand beyond the good of individuals by including the good of humans in society.

There are many kinds of expansionist theories.[13] One form is the freedom and opportunity approach: the good is defined as the opportunity to freely and actively pursue our desires and goods. What is essential is not just the existence of desires and preferences but *how* we pursue those desires and preferences. Berlin thought that the most valuable form of life was a life characterized by a negative freedom where the right to choose and not to be interfered with is both instrumental and intrinsically valuable – what makes humans have dignity. For Berlin, in today's overly bureaucratic world, it was more important to make people free than to make them happy or teach them to fit in with existing patterns of thought and life.[14] The good life is not defined hedonically as the passive experience of pleasures or the satisfaction of desires. The good life is a matter of how we seek our desires and how we live the good life.

Libertarians also emphasize the good of negative freedom – the active agent who can pursue goods with a minimum of government interference. Nozick, for example, argues that we not only want to feel and experience things, we want to do certain things with excellence. We want to be free and autonomous agents.[15] Nozick brings out the importance of choosing by posing a thought experiment in which someone spends their entire life attached to a machine that stimulates experiences of choosing. Nozick thinks that most people would not count this as a good life. The good for humans is more than the experience of positive mental states.

Other forms of liberalism are more expansionist. They go beyond the good as a freedom of choice and a lack of interference to talk about the good as what such freedom should aim at – the aims of human freedom. Berlin called this "positive freedom" – the opportunity to develop my self according to some idea of self-actualization. True freedom is the freedom to become my "true" self according to some philosophical or religious view of human nature and the world. Some liberals do not embrace positive freedom as some pre-established end of self-actualization, but they do believe that negative freedom is an insufficient notion of the human good. In addition to a lack of interference, individuals need assistance from society to ensure that they have the resources and skills to exercise that freedom. For example, the social liberalism of T.H. Green and L.T. Hobhouse at the turn of the twentieth century argued that liberalism's ethical ground was the goodness of self-development and the opportunity for development. Some liberals straddled the space between negative and positive freedom, presenting a vision of what a free person would be like but not positing one pre-established end for self-actualization. John Dewey, for example, put forward a liberal theory of human growth that imagined humans as critical, informed inquirers using pragmatic methods and "social intelligence" to solve problems and reform education and democracy.

Another form of expansionism is development theory. The good is human development, according to some conception. Developmental theory includes freedom, and it may even make freedom a central element of the good life. But theories also tend to stress the importance of developing many other human capacities. Development theory is clearly expansionist. Instead of looking to subjective mental states, development theory looks to objective patterns in human development and growth.

Amartya Sen has advanced a form of development theory that he calls the "capacities approach." The good is freedom to develop one's basic capacities as a rational human being. Human welfare is to be measured by capacities and not states of consciousness since the states are too subjective, varying widely among individuals and cultures. The capability of a person is an active concept. Well-being is not the having of experiences but rather the ability of a person to "do valuable acts or reach valuable states of being." Living is "a combination of various 'doings and beings' with quality of life to be assessed in terms of the capability to achieve valuable functionings." Some functionings are simple and valued by all, such as being adequately nourished or in good health. Others are widely shared but complex, such as self-respect. The capability approach does not claim that personal utilities, such as pleasure or getting what one desires, are not part of the good. However, such factors are not "the measure of all values." The capability approach differs from utility-based approaches in regarding "the state of being happy as one among several objects of value."[16]

For other developmentalists, such as Nussbaum, these capacities provide an approach to a theory of justice. They are a "source of political principles for a liberal pluralistic society." They are fundamental entitlements that deserve constitutional protection.[17]

Theories of human flourishing and perfection also can be considered forms of development theory in a broad sense, since they stress the importance of human development. In Aristotle's ethics, the aim of human development is the excellence and flourishing of the distinct rational capacities of men. In the ethical tradition of perfectionism, the perfection of individuals is the ultimate end of life.[18] Perfectionism considers what human life would be like if certain capacities, freedoms, opportunities, and other goods were either developed to a high degree or to the highest degree possible under the circumstances. Sir William Hamilton defined "perfection" as "the full and harmonious development of all our faculties, corporeal and mental, intellectual and moral."[19] Some forms of perfectionism emphasize the development of a subclass of capacities, such as rationality.[20] Some perfectionist theories pick out one form of life, such as the religious ascetic or the philosopher-king, as the end of perfection. Other theories are pluralistic. They believe that perfection can be realized in many forms of life.[21]

Advantages of Expansionism

I prefer an expansionist approach because of the limitations of non-expansionist theories and because expansionism suits my naturalism.

Hedonic and desire theories provide empirical insight into what people value and how they make choices. But they fail as ethical theories about what people *ought* to choose and value. Hedonic theories
struggle with the psychological fact there appears to be no one type
of mental state that is common to all the things we find pleasurable
or agreeable. How then do we measure the good? Moreover, we
often think the good is what is non-pleasurable. We prefer to learn
the bitter truth about ourselves, or to endure uncomfortable mental
states, rather than live in deception or ignorance. Also, many things
are good for reasons other than that we find them pleasurable.

To define the good in terms of desires and preferences improves
matters, since they are more objective phenomena. However, as
noted, the concept of actual desire is too wide and non-discrimina-
tory to support an ethical theory of the good. As mentioned, I may
find satisfaction in unreasonable, pathological, or cruel desires. Also,
we may be mistaken about what things we should desire and what
things are in our interests.

Hedonic and desire theories face one other problem. Mental states
and desires, such as being happy or feeling contented, can be poor
guides as to what a person values and to what we should count as
the good for humans. We need to be careful about "adapative preferences" where people's desires and expectations – and sometimes
even their judgment about how happy they are – is distorted by their
situation in life. For instance, a poor person, a dominated female, or
a slave may adapt or downgrade their desires and expectations to
the point of being of being satisfied with their lot in life. We should
not use these people and their desires as a guide to a theory of the
good. The fact that some people, like Dickens's Tiny Tim, say they
are happy shows the limitations of taking mental states like happiness as a criterion of human well-being.[22]

Informed desire theory improves upon actual desire theory, but
the theory is still incomplete. Informed desire theory, like a liberalism of negative freedom, doesn't provide specifics about what
our rational desires are, or should be. It analyses "good for S"
as what S desires upon informed reflection. But this doesn't say
what those desires are, or should be. It doesn't say how we might
reconcile conflicts among desires. Informed desire theory is procedural, not substantive. It defines the good as whatever results
from informed reflection. However, as I will argue, a complete
ethical theory needs a substantive conception of the human good

that says what the ends of action should be and what sort of desires we should value.[23]

The more expansionist one becomes, the more one is inclined to argue that the good is *not* whatever a subject thinks is good or bad for them. Personal judgments based on what one desires must become "considered judgments" by considering a broader range of factors. These judgments need to be knowledgeable about the properties of the objects desired. The person judging needs to reflect on his or her desires.

From a naturalist perspective, an expansionist approach is to be preferred because ethics is not something reducible to what is internal and individualistic – what promotes the satisfaction of my individual desires or pleasures. Ethics is an external, intersubjective process. A rational, biological species living in society is confronted by real-world problems. It seeks to agree on values and norms deemed fair by reasonable people. The expansionist approach is to be preferred because it requires that I do more than consult my feelings and desires. It requires that I start an ethical dialogue between me and others, between me, the world, and our knowledge of that world. It encourages holistic, eclectic thinking. Expansionist thinking appreciates the complexity of reasoning about the good and it prevents the domination of one factor, such as pleasure maximization. In short, non-expansionist theories lack sufficient resources for ethical deliberation about the good. An expansionist theory will have the best chance of correctly determining the good because it considers a rich constellation of factors and it encourages inquiry into the full conditions of human existence.

These considerations favour an expansionist approach. But what form of expansionist *theory* is best? I contend that development theory is the most attractive form. An emphasis of freedom and opportunity is correct, but at what should freedom aim? Development theory offers an answer that avoids dictating one narrow and pre-established end to life. In the next section, I argue that the aims of development are specified by a rich conception of human flourishing on four levels.

GOOD AS FLOURISHING

Idea of Flourishing

My theory of the good understands flourishing as the fullest expression of human development under favourable conditions.[24]

"Flourishing" is a term that describes and evaluates. To say something is flourishing is to point to certain objective features of the object while also approving of those features.

The concept of flourishing originates not in ethics but in biology – in attempts to understand the phenomena of life as development, maturation, and flowering. Flourishing is a biological concept referring to growth. "To flower" and "to flourish" are cognates. For organisms, to flourish is to be healthy. Organisms flourish when they are (a) unimpeded in organic development and normal physical functioning and supported by favourable environment conditions, so that they (b) realize the fullest development and expression of their capacities according to their nature.[25] To say that a tree is flourishing implies that the tree has the capacity to grow, flower, and reproduce itself. "It is not sick, weak, mutilated, injured, or stunted. Anything that impedes that development or the exercise of those mature faculties – disease, the sapping of vigour and strength, injuries – is bad for them."[26] The tree is said to flourish relative to its ability to develop and express a set of capacities and functionings for objects of that species.

Theories of human flourishing interpret human development as analogous to organic growth. The ideal is a full flowering and unimpeded development of the powers and capacities of humans within society under the most favourable environmental conditions. We can, however, also speak of various degrees of flourishing, whereby humans approach the ideal but do not achieve it. Human flourishing includes physical and organic development. But it expands the idea of flourishing to include the development and expression of psychological, social, and cultural capacities. Human flourishing includes the ability to communicate symbolically and to invent new forms of technology. It includes the capacity to create artistically and think philosophically. It is the development, maturation, and expression of the capacities of the species.

To occur, flourishing requires the convergence of many types of goods. Some are means to flourishing and others are components (or expressions) of flourishing. Good soil is a means to a flower's flourishing, while producing an abundance of flowers is a component of the plant's flourishing. Being able to express myself artistically is a component and expression of my flourishing, while having sufficient food is a means to (or necessary condition of) my artistic flourishing.[27]

A theory of flourishing attempts to determine the good by looking to species-wide features. Judgments about flourishing depend on knowledge about what constitutes flourishing for the species in question. The flourishing of a tree depends on what constitutes the flourishing of trees, given the nature of trees and the kinds of environment suitable for things of that kind. The flourishing of humans depends what constitutes flourishing of its species, given the nature of humans and the kinds of physical and cultural environments suitable for that species.

The good, then, is what is conducive to, or part of, flourishing. G is good for S if G is conducive to S's flourishing, or is part of S's flourishing. "G is good for S" means G has properties that are suitable or appropriate for the development and flourishing of S, given its properties and conditions. "Good for" indicates that there is a compatibility between the properties of G and S. Kraut puts the point this way: to say "G is good for S" is best understood as indicating that G has a "certain kind of suitability to S: their properties are so matched to each other that G serves S well ... It indicates that G is well suited to S and that G serves S well."[28] Applied to humans, this scheme means that G is good for John or Mary if G has properties that are suitable or appropriate for the development and flourishing of John or Mary, as members of the human species. A theory of flourishing adopts expansionism's third-person perspective. We ask what is good for human beings, just as we ask what is good for horses. Discussions of the human good occur against background knowledge about the development of the sensory, affective, cognitive, and social capacities of humans, and the suitability of certain things in the environment.

What a theory of flourishing prescribes for individuals may conflict with the desires of those individuals and their judgment of what is good. The phrase "G is good for John" does not mean that G is good simply because it is desired by John, although that may be the case. To determine what is good for John we have to become expansionists and go beyond John's desires to knowledge of his conditions and facts about development.

Flourishing theory should be a flexible account. It should not see human development as a narrow, deterministic process that *must* result in some particular form of life or society. The expression of human capacities, such as the capacity for language or social organization, can take many forms, depending on the natural and cultural environment. Flourishing persons in different parts of the world, say in Canada and China, inhabit quite different environments. We expect such persons to express their flourishing in different forms of art, culture, and social life.

A theory of flourishing determines what is conducive to flourishing by referring to human self-knowledge and knowledge of how humans interact with their environment. Flourishing implies some understanding of who we are as a species – our capacities and propensities, and their individual and social development. Flourishing must take into account the environment in which those capacities are exercised, nurtured, or stunted.

Flourishing as Ethical Concept

It may be objected that development theory, derived from biology, the social sciences, and the humanities, amounts to facts about humans. How does knowledge about the empirical causes and conditions of development amount to an ethics about what humans ought to value? Moreover, not every natural desire or ability is worth developing. We do not want the capacity to be cruel or selfish to be part of flourishing or ethics.[29] Any human capacity can be used for unethical purposes. Therefore, in ethics, we adjust the concept of flourishing to include only those capacities, and only those expressions of capacities, that fit our sense of the ethically good life.

The central concept for ethics is *ethical flourishing,* a form of flourishing. An inquiry into ethical flourishing is an inquiry into how to develop our capacities morally and what external conditions promote such moral development. A theory of ethical flourishing has two major parts. One part is knowledge about the development of major capacities and talents, and the attainment of certain skills and excellences, as indicated by empirical theories of human development. These capacities include the development of our ability to express ourselves, to link means to ends, and to participate in fulfilling social relationships. The second part is a theory of how to use those capacities virtuously and how to achieve ethical aims, such as moving toward a just society. Through ethical flourishing, we enjoy ethical goods such as trust, friendship, and reciprocity. Humans "flower" ethically, as well as physically. In addition to the concept of a flourishing person, physically and socially, we have the concept of an ethically flourishing person.

Ethical development is a deep part our nature, a natural extension of natural human capacities. In ethical flourishing, we realize our full potential as a species.

Flourishing, then, becomes an ethical concept when we espouse ethical flourishing as the ultimate aim of ethical life and use it as a source of values and principles. We argue that some conception of flourishing is what humans *ought* to pursue. The good is *now* defined as what is conducive to ethical flourishing, a combination of natural and ethical goods. To say that G is ethically good for S is to say that G is conducive to S's ethical flourishing or is part of S's ethical flourishing.

In the next section, I define ethical flourishing in terms of the development of capacities on four levels of human development. The ideas underpinning my four levels – the good as flourishing – have a long history. Aristotle developed an expansionist ethics of *eudaimonia* or well-being. *Eudaimonia* is the flourishing of the distinctive capacities of the rational soul as exhibited in the virtues.[30] Humans naturally seek such flourishing just as all living things seek their ideal form. Eudaimonia is a composite good, a convergence of virtues and excellences. Flourishing is "developing and actively exercising different kinds of virtue (arete) through a lifetime shaped by nature, habit, and education" and supported by favourable conditions over a lifetime.[31] Further, every good is located in a hierarchy that constitutes the human good.[32] The lowest rung consists of goods necessary for existence, such as food and shelter. Above this rung are intrinsically desirable goods such as honour, and on the next rung are ethical goods such as the virtues of justice and temperance. The hierarchy is capped by the highest form of life – philosophical contemplation.[33]

Across the medieval and early modern era, philosophies of flourishing became doctrines of perfection within religious or metaphysical views.[34] Humans judged their development with respect to a perfect moral order, or God. Aquinas said being and goodness are the same. The perfect being of God is perfect goodness. Realizing our *telos* fulfills the purpose of God. Spinoza said ethics and knowledge bring us closer to the perfection of God. Ethics is "the transition of a man from a less to a greater perfection."[35]

In modern philosophy, human flourishing was secularized in terms of natural development, abandoning references to God. Kant believed we have a duty to increase our natural perfection. A person "owes it to himself (as a rational being) not to leave idle and, as it were, rusting away the natural predispositions and capacities that his reason can someday use."[36] Hegel and Marx viewed human development as a historical evolution of the species in terms of reason or the material forces of society, respectively.

Liberals developed the idea of flourishing into liberal self-actualization. Humboldt said the highest good was the "self-activity and self-development of human individuals."[37] The idea of flourishing was implicit in appeals to liberty and self-development, for what is the purpose of liberty if not to flourish? Mill used the metaphor of organic growth: "Among the works of man, which human life is rightly employed in perfecting and beautifying, the first in importance surely is man himself ... Human nature is not a machine to be built after a model, and set to do exactly the work prescribed for it, but a tree, which requires to grow and develop itself on all sides, according to the tendency of the inward forces which make it a living thing."[38]

At the turn of the twentieth century, T.H. Green and L.T. Hobhouse argued that liberalism's ethical ground was the goodness of self-development. Green, who called his idealist morality, "The Theory of the Good as Human Perfection," wrote: "The ideal of true freedom is the maximum of power for all members of human society alike to make the best of themselves."[39] Hobhouse, in his *Liberalism* of 1914, said: "The foundation of liberty is the idea of growth ... Liberalism is the belief that society can safely be founded on this self-directing power of personality, that it is only on this foundation that a true community can be built."[40]

For Dewey, to flourish was to grow, in liberal ways. He thought philosophy was the study of how to develop and unleash the potential of humans to overcome problems, identify new opportunities, and achieve richer experiences, or "consumatory experience." In the late 1900s, Bernard Williams thought the idea of flourishing could be used to evaluate the values of different societies. We looked to see whether their values made the social world a "good place for human beings to live."[41] We look at the flourishing of the people who live in it. Williams thought, as I do, that a theory of human nature and flourishing, drawing on the natural and social sciences, can help our ethical reflections.[42]

Levels of Ethical Flourishing

This section analyzes ethical flourishing into the development of four levels of human capacities and their goods. Ethical flourishing is realized to the degree that humans are able to enjoy goods on all four levels. The goods, taken together, make a dignified, creative, and full life possible. Practically, ethical flourishing depends on the degree to which humans can construct societies that promote the fullest expression of these capacities.

The four levels of goods arise from my exploration of empirical studies on development and the aforementioned research on well-being.[43] They also arise from reflection on the meaning of flourishing and from the attempt to develop a theory of the good that achieves reflective equilibrium among intuitions and ideas.[44] The aim is to place goods "within a convincing and attractive picture of human life as it should be lived when all goes well."[45]

My approach is similar to Nussbaum's. She combines a Kantian emphasis on dignity and a capabilities approach to produce her own list of basic capacities. These capacities define her developmental approach to justice. This approach, she says, is "informed by an intuitive idea of a life that is worthy of the dignity of the human being." Her approach relies on "some deep moral intuitions and considered judgments about human dignity" that are "never immune from criticism in the light of other elements of the theory (of the human good)."[46] Some goods on the four levels could be arrived at by other routes. David Held uses a political approach to identify eight universal principles for a global ethics to protect and nurture each person's equal significance "in the moral realm of all humanity." Some of his goods are similar to mine.[47]

THE FOUR LEVELS

When I review the goods of life, I find that they can be placed into four groups – individual, social, political, and ethical. By individual goods, I mean the goods that come from the development of each individual's capacities. By social goods, I mean those goods that come from individuals participating in society and community. By political goods, I mean the goods that accrue to us as citizens. By ethical goods, I mean the goods that come from living among persons of ethical character.

Level 1, the level of individual goods, contains physical goods and the goods of rational and moral capacity. The physical goods give a person physical dignity. All persons need food, shelter, and security to live a normal, healthy life. The *rational and moral goods* allow physical capacity to flower into distinct human traits. A person develops capacities to observe and think critically and to carry out a rational plan of life. Such a person is able to form emotional attachments and to use their imagination to produce (or enjoy) creative and intellectual works. Also, the person is able to be a moral agent who can empathize with others and act from a sense of justice.

Level 2, the level of social goods, arises when we use our rational and moral capacities to participate in society. Human reality is social not just because humans need society to develop language and culture; humans are inherently social creatures. Humans come to value participating in common projects as a good-in-itself. Among the social goods are the freedom to enter into and benefit from economic association, the goods of love and friendship; the need for mutual recognition and respect. In this manner we achieve a social dignity.

In addition to the social goods, there are the political goods of level 3. These are the goods that humans enjoy when they live in a society that has a reasonably just political structure. These goods include the basic liberties, such as freedom of speech and freedom to pursue one's goods, together with the opportunities and resources to exercise these freedoms. Citizens are able to participate in political life, to hold office, and to influence decisions. The primary means to these public goods are constitutional protections, the rule of law, barriers against undue coercion, and the means for peaceful resolution of disputes. A citizen who enjoys these goods has a political dignity through self-government.

There is also a fourth level of goods: ethical goods. To enjoy a full measure of the human good it is not enough to live in a society of rational people; that is, people motivated to pursue their own interests. A society consisting of only rational agents would be a terrifyingly private society. We also need to live among people of ethical character. Such persons are rational agents who are disposed to be what Rawls calls morally "reasonable."[48] Reasonable citizens are motivated to consider the interests of others and the greater public good. Of course, many people are not motivated to adopt the ethical stance. Nevertheless, under certain conditions, humans can appreciate interacting ethically as a good-in-itself. The goal is an ethical flourishing among citizens.

Therefore, to sum up, I provide an outline of the goods on four levels. I divide each level into the major capacities, the primary means of development and the ethical goals associated with each level. For achieving ethical flourishing, all four levels are important and are mutually supportive. What these goods really mean in a practical sense will be explained in the rest of the book.

LEVEL 1: INDIVIDUAL DEVELOPMENT
These goods concern the development of individual capacities and powers, considered in abstraction from social structures necessary for their existence.

Goods of Physical Capacity
(1) Able to live a normal lifespan that is not so deprived or enslaved as to be not worth living. (2) Able to develop one's body and to grow physically and in health. (3) Able to pursue one's own pleasurable activities while avoiding non-beneficial pain and subjection to the pleasure or wishes of others.

Primary means: the physical and other necessities for good health, protection from treatable diseases, adequate nourishment, and shelter; security of body and property: freedom from domestic violence, threats, assaults, theft.

Ethical goal: physical dignity.

Goods of Rational and Moral Capacity
(1) Able to sense, imagine, and think as a critical and free individual. (2) Use of imagination, emotions, and expressive powers: able to form emotional attachments and experience the range of emotions of humanity; able to use imagination and expressive powers to produce or enjoy creative and intellectual works. (3) Powers of theoretical reason: able to think conceptually and critically, to understand and participate in philosophy, science, and culture; able to think critically about major conceptions of life. (4) Able to be a rational agent: able to conceive of a rational plan of life and to pursue one's own interests. (5) Able to be a moral agent: able to empathize with others and to form a sense of justice; able to deliberate about one's good and the good of others; able to form one's ethical identity and to integrate values.

Primary means: education (including literacy), basic mathematics, and scientific knowledge.

Ethical goal: rational and moral dignity through self-actualization.

LEVEL 2: COMMON GOODS
These goods are due to social interaction and community. New capacities and new goods arise out human sociability.

Goods of Economic Association

Able to participate in and benefit from social interaction that allows a division of talents and an exchange of goods not available in isolation.

Primary means: free, non-monopolized markets and economic systems where citizens have the capacity and opportunity to participate in economic associations.

Ethical goal: economic dignity.

Goods of Kinship, Association, and Friendship

(1) Able to enjoy and benefit from family, friendship, and discourse. (2) Able to join others in fulfilling associations through common projects. (3) Able to understand, enjoy, and participate in a diversity of cultures. (4) Able to employ the capacities of level 1 (individual goods) within society.

Primary means: supportive social and political structures, means for peaceful resolution of disputes, sufficient equality of resources, tolerance of diversity.

Ethical goal: social dignity; life in a society that allows self-respect, equality, and dignity; a flourishing social sphere.

LEVEL 3: POLITICAL GOODS

These are the goods of a just political structure, a subspecies of common goods. They may be called "public goods."

Goods of Political and Legal Freedom, and Participation

(1) Able to enjoy basic liberties such as freedom of speech, freedom of association, freedom from discrimination, and other constitutional protections such as civil liberties based on the rule of law. (2) Able to enjoy the "political goods" of participating in political life, political office, and major decisions of society. (3) Able to enjoy the full value of these liberties (or positive freedom): able to exercise these freedoms for self-development and therefore able to enjoy goods on levels 1, 2, and 3.

Primary means: constitutional protections against state torture and undue influence by authorities; the rule of law; political distribution of sufficient resources and goods of social cooperation to allow full value of freedoms; sufficient political tolerance and opportunities to allow meaningful political participation; education in the political goods and their achievement.

Ethical goal: Political dignity.

LEVEL 4: ETHICAL GOODS

These are the goods of a shared ethical life in society. Our flourishing is ethical and just. We exhibit the characteristics of ethical persons and societies. They require developing capacities in ethical directions.

Goods of Moral Reasonableness

(1) Capacity to act according to the virtues and one's sense of justice. (2) Capacity to combine rationality and reasonableness in life and in society.

Primary means: ethical education.

Ethical goal: reasonable citizens.

Goods of Justice

(1) Capacity to understand and apply appropriate principles of justice to organize society and distribute advantages. (2) Capacity to adopt an impartial ethical perspective on issues; to deliberate according to public reason.

Primary means: ethical education, just institutions, sufficient numbers of citizens who have such abilities and motivations.

Ethical goal: shared ethical life among citizens in society.

Features of the Theory

1. The theory is teleological. It specifies the basic goods and ends of living for all humans. The scheme's goods are universal yet flexible. They allow for a wide range of expression of capacities and goods in different cultures. For example, cultures will vary on how they realize "rational and moral capacity," or how they design political systems to allow for public goods.

2. The theory is a naturalistic, expansionist account of good. It includes much more than mental states or desires. It includes objective features of the human species and its environment. It includes what is good for humans as self-conscious, reason-responsive, and value-evaluating persons.

3. The scheme is holistic. The levels are mutually supportive. The satisfaction of one type of good allows another to exist, and vice versa. Physical goods are so necessary to a good life that they support all other goods. Yet this doesn't mean that upper-level goods are secondary. The provision of social and political goods is crucial to the provision of physical goods. In many countries, unstable

political structures interfere with attempts to provide physical goods to citizens. As well, individuals fail to properly develop their rational and moral capacities unless they are nurtured by the social and political goods.

4. The levels are conceptual tools for evaluating to what degree our lives are flourishing. To evaluate how close anyone is to the ideal, we look at how well they have secured the goods across all four levels. In light of these goods, we discuss what political structures, ethical frameworks, and social polices are best.

The scheme is not a practical manual. It does not presume to tell development workers what strategies to employ in underdeveloped countries. We need to distinguish between "What constitutes the ideal of ethical flourishing?" and "What should we do to help people in country x emerge from chaos and dire need?" To deal with extreme poverty in developing countries, agencies rightly focus on a small number of basic needs. However, my theory is not without some practical implications. The four levels provide criteria by which to judge development. Also, the theory suggests a two-stage approach to development in poor countries. The first stage aims at a decent and minimally flourishing life, where physical goods are primary. The second stage aims at an ethically flourishing life, not just a decent life, by developing all four levels.

Open-Ended Nature

Does the appeal to knowledge of the human species and of human nature indicate that, beneath my theory, there exists an implicit belief in a fixed human essence, or a dubious determinism that denies human freedom?[49] It does not. My appeal to human nature is non-technical and not problematic. By "human nature," I mean nothing more technical or questionable than a core of major powers, capacities, functions, and tendencies that are the result of natural human development. These capacities and needs, taken together, are the evolutionary and cultural heritage of humans as a species. This human nature stands behind our variations in lifestyles and helps to define human flourishing. There is a complex story to be told about how human characteristics have developed from genetic, evolutionary, and cultural factors. However, an ethical theory does not have to delve into these complexities. All that ethical theory presumes – with great plausibility – is the idea that the species has certain general patterns of development that play a role in our flourishing. Ethical flourishing is not a form of reductionism. It does not reduce the ethical view to a non-ethical scientific view, nor does it reduce ethical actions to neuronal firings.[50] Ethics is not a deterministic and causal effect of genes. Human action is a complex expression of genetic and biological material interacting with the physical and cultural environment.

Philosophically, my theory presumes what I call an open-ended human nature. Human nature is not static. It is not a fixed essence. It is a dynamic, evolving core of capacities that may set new goals for ethics and may alter our notions of human flourishing. Humans have reached the stage where they can even play a part in altering their genetic nature.[51] With humans, self-conscious rationality entered into nature. Humans became a species that could, as Kant says, "set its own ends" and now, today, can know and alter its physical nature. To acknowledge that I have a nature is not to deny my freedom. It is to realize that my nature gives me the possibility of freedom. I am free to the extent that I know my nature and can use it to achieve my goals. Dewey writes: "Nature's place in man is no less significant than man's place in nature. Man in nature is man subjected; nature in man, recognized and used, is intelligence and art." The bedrock value, as Mill states, is "the importance, to man and society ... of giving full freedom to human nature to expand itself in innumerable and conflicting directions."[52]

Liberals like Mill and Dewey, and contemporary liberals such as Rawls and Dworkin, are rightly nervous about prescribing one specific way of living well. However, this is not to say that humans do not share basic and universal capacities for flourishing. Our open-ended nature is an invitation to be inventive in ethics. It also makes life potentially tragic. Humans are never completed, and never wholly predictable. To be human is to bear the responsibility of completing one's own future.

Support for Theory

I contend that my theory is a plausible candidate for a flourishing theory of the good, with various forms of reasons. However, a philosophical conception cannot be verified conclusively once and for all by a set of facts. Its plausibility is due to its ability to meet holistically a number of general criteria for rational acceptance. The strengths and weaknesses of my theory can only be evaluated after we see how the theory is applied in the rest of this book and how well it responds to extended scrutiny by other inquirers over time. In the final analysis, readers must judge for themselves how well the theory expresses their idea of the good.

The theory is consistent with the evaluation criteria that were listed above. The theory enjoys the advantages of a natural, expansionist approach. It provides the ethical reasoner with a range of resources for evaluating beliefs. The theory is consistent with what we know about human development, and it incorporates insights from the history of ethical theory.

The theory gives us a target at which to aim, and the four levels indicate how our goods are to be integrated. The theory stands ready to be used by ethical reasoning to evaluate frameworks and eclectic thinking about situations, and to play a role in the construction of other, more specific, theories such as a global journalism ethics. I believe the theory captures our major intuitions about a dignified and flourishing life, and the goods named are the goods of common experience. If the theory is correct, it can serve as one of the two ultimate aims for ethics. We now turn to the second ultimate aim, the idea of well-ordered society.

WELL-ORDERED SOCIETY

Ethics requires a theory of the right to supplement a theory of the good because my pursuit of goods may conflict with your pursuit of goods. This is most evident when people act unethically and selfishly. Yet, even when people flourish, their flourishings conflict. Things are different with respect to *ethical* flourishing. My four-level scheme implies right and just relations among people. Achieving the common and public goods of my scheme, not to mention the ethical goods, requires right interactions. But what sorts of interactions? We need a theory of the right to spell this out. A theory of right is a distinct component of ethical flourishing.

I propose Rawls's conception of a well-ordered liberal society as a theory of the right for ethical flourishing. It is a society that embodies Rawls's notion of justice as fairness. I am interested in a theory of right for a liberal society because that is the society that many of us live in, and in which our journalism operates. I adapt Rawls's theory because his approach to ethics and politics, especially his notion of pursuing good in the right, is correct and has important implications for ethics in general, and journalism ethics in particular. In the following sections, I examine Rawls's theory of well-ordered society by describing his notion of liberal society, liberal citizenship, and liberal deliberation. Since Rawls's work is well-known, I only touch on ideas that I will use later to develop a global journalism ethics.

Well-Ordered

For Rawls, to speak of well-ordered society is not to speak about any sort of social order. It is to speak about an ideal, well-ordered, liberal democracy.

Societies are not well-ordered if tyrants impose cruel regimes of unfair laws for their own benefit. Society is not well-ordered because a powerful police maintains order. It is not well-ordered even if it establishes an efficient social system with a strong economy and low levels of crime.[53] It is not well-ordered if it is excessively liberal and allows individuals to pursue goods without concern for equality and justice. It is well-ordered if it brings into harmony the free pursuit of goods and the restraining demands of justice.

Rawls's conception of well-ordered society responds to a range of questions. What principles of justice are needed, and what sort of constitution is required for well-ordered society? What type of democratic citizens does a well-ordered society need? How do citizens deliberate about matters of fundamental justice? His answer is that a well-ordered society is "one designed to advance the good of its members and effectively regulated by a public conception of justice."[54] A liberal society is well-ordered only if the main institutions are organized in a just and democratic manner. In such a society all citizens share fairly the benefits of social cooperation. Principles of justice protect basic liberties for all citizens while assisting the least advantaged. Institutions honour these principles in their operations, policies, and rulings.

Rawls's theory also responds to problems within liberalism. Rawls believes that ideas of liberalism are inadequately formulated by utilitarianism, intuitionism, and libertarianism. Liberalism struggles to address the pluralism of modern society, where rival conceptions of the good life conflict. What is more, liberalism is a divided philosophy. Some liberals believe that liberty is the primary value; others argue for the primacy of equality. Justice as fairness, Rawls says, tries to "adjudicate between these contending traditions," to act as a unifying conception of social liberalism.[55] Rawls aims at empowering citizens through a better understanding of the "deep moral and political values that should regulate their social and political institutions."[56]

Cooperation and Conflict

Rawls is primarily interested in how society ought to be although, as a naturalist, he wants his ideas to agree with facts about humans and society. Rawls begins *A Theory of Justice* with the contractual idea of society as a system of rule-bound cooperation for mutual advantage. However, by cooperating, citizens do not abandon their own interests. In society, "a deep opposition of interests is presumed to obtain."[57]

Society consists of individuals-in-association who want to pursue their goods yet benefit from social cooperation. Questions of justice arise in the tension between self-interest and cooperation. To what degree can individuals pursue their goods without denying the rights of others to pursue their goods? Do the laws and institutions allow for a fair distribution of the benefits of social cooperation? Where pursuits of the good conflict, and where people question the fairness of society, there is need for a system of justice to maintain cooperation and prevent violence.[58]

Justice, Rawls says, is the "first virtue of social institutions." Laws and institutions no matter how efficient or well-arranged "must be reformed or abolished if they are unjust." A systematic theory of justice is needed to propose fair terms of cooperation – to specify the principles of justice.[59] The terms must result from a contract among citizens who deliberate in a free and equal manner. Rawls describes this contractual process in some detail.[60] Rawls uses a thought-experiment that imagines an "original position" where all groups in society consider the principles to govern their society. To ensure impartiality, each party works under a "veil of ignorance," which limits the sort of information they have about each other.

Rawls does not presume that such an agreement has occurred or will occur.[61] The original position is a device to help us identify what we regard – here and now – as fair conditions for contracting and fair restrictions on the reasons for various principles. Rawls uses the thought-experiment to put forward his two principles of justice, which provide "better understanding of the claims of freedom and equality in a democratic society than the first principles associated with utilitarianism, with perfectionism, or with intuitionism."[62]

Principle 1: "Each person has an equal claim to a fully adequate scheme of equal basic rights and liberties, which scheme is compatible with the same scheme for all; and in this scheme the equal political liberties, and only these liberties, are to be guaranteed their fair value." The basic liberties protected by principle 1 are: (a) freedom of thought and liberty of conscience; (b) the political liberties and freedom of association, plus the freedoms specified by the liberties and integrity of the person; and (c) the rights and liberties covered by the rule of law.[63] Since the basic liberties will conflict, none of them is absolute. The primacy and "absolute weight" of liberty applies to a mutually supportive family of liberties.[64] Rawls assumes the basic liberties will receive further specification by a country's constitution, legislature, and courts.

Principle 2: "Social and economic inequalities are to satisfy two conditions: first, they are to be attached to positions and offices open to all under conditions of fair equality of opportunity; and second, they are to be to the greatest benefit of the least advantaged members of society."[65] This is the "difference principle." It allows for inequalities, but only if such inequalities are necessary for improving the situation of the poorest or least advantaged.

Principle 1 takes priority over principle 2. Principle 1 secures basic rights and liberties for all. Principle 2 deals with the fair distribution of social advantages. Justice as fairness aims at a society where things are as good as possible for the least advantaged insofar as this is consistent with the basic freedoms of all. Together, the two principles express an egalitarian form of liberalism and justice.

The two principles are used to assess the fairness of society's basic structure. The basic structure is "a society's main political, social, and economic institutions, and how they fit together in one unified system of cooperation from one generation to the next." The institutions include the legal protection of freedom of thought, private property, and the family. This basic structure is the primary subject of justice because "its effects are so profound and present from the start."[66] To evaluate a basic structure, we ask: how does the structure assign basic liberties, rights, opportunities, and duties? How does the structure distribute the benefits of cooperation?

To summarize, Rawls's well-ordered liberal society is a system for fair cooperation reached through a free and impartial contractual process that affirms these two principles of justice. These principles determine the fairness of society's basic structure. Such a society allows the pursuit of goods within a public conception of justice, a conception where the principles are known to and affirmed by the public.

Well-Ordered Citizens

What sorts of citizens are needed to achieve a well-ordered society? What is liberal citizenship for democracy?

TWO MORAL POWERS

A liberal citizen in a well-ordered society is free and equal. Citizens are free because they can develop and pursue their conception of the good, and they are entitled to pressure their institutions to advance their conceptions of the good within justice. Citizens are equal because all have to "the essential minimum degree the moral powers necessary to engage in social cooperation over a complete life and to take part in society as equal citizens." To participate in society in this way, citizens must have two moral powers: the capacity to have a conception of the good, and the capacity to have a sense of justice. A conception of the good is an "ordered family of final ends and aims which specifies a person's conception of what is of value in human life." We discussed this notion of the good earlier in the chapter. The capacity for a sense of justice is "the capacity to understand, to apply, and to act from (and not merely in accordance with) the principles of political justice."[67] The capacity for a conception of good is a desire to advance my interests according (usually) to a rational plan of life. The desire for justice is not the pursuit of a particular worldly advantage. It is a desire to be a certain sort of person – an autonomous, reasonable agent living in a well-ordered society.

Rawls's conception of free and equal citizens is not intended to be a full conception of what it is to be a person. It defines only the "public, or legal, identity" of persons as citizens in society.[68] The conception goes back to the idea of a citizen in antiquity as someone able to take part in political life. The conception is consistent with, but may have little relation to, other conceptions of persons in psychology or philosophy.

Rawls contrasts this political identity of citizens with the larger ethical identity of persons. Citizens express their political identity by affirming "the values of political justice and want[ing] to see them embodied in political institutions and social policies."[69] Citizens express their ethical identity by pursuing non-political values embedded in their conception of the good, such as the values found in religious doctrines. The two identities are independent. If people change their moral beliefs or give up religion, they do not lose their political identity or their liberal rights.

REASONABLENESS

Rawls uses the distinction between the two moral powers to explain the important distinction between the rational and the reasonable.[70] People act rationally (and prudently) when they pursue their conception of the good through appropriate means, practical reasoning, and well-chosen plans of life. To know that someone is rational is not to know their ends but to know they will pursue their ends intelligently.[71] But something more is needed for people to act ethically. Like any capacity, we can use our rationality to act selfishly or brutally. Ethics requires us to act reasonably. Rawls defines the reasonable as the twin virtues of justice and tolerance: "First, the willingness to propose and honour fair terms of cooperation, and second, with the willingness to recognize the burdens of judgment and to accept their consequences." By the burdens of judgment, Rawls means that reasonable disagreement on values is always possible due to conflicting evidence, hard cases, and different experiences.[72] Tolerance of different conceptions of the good is required.

Ethics requires that we consult both the rational and the reasonable when we decide how to act. We recognize that the reasonable and the rational may conflict when we say, "Their proposal was perfectly rational, given their strong bargaining position, but it was nevertheless highly unreasonable, even outrageous." Therefore, ethics requires that we reconcile our rational desires with our commitment to what is reasonable. While we value our own rational interests, we also need to act from a sense of justice, to recognize other people's interests, and to tolerate other people's different views about the good.

The desire to be reasonable is buttressed by the assurance of reciprocity. In a fair society, we believe that all will benefit from being reasonable, and hence we are motivated to act toward others in a reciprocal manner. To be motivated by the expectation of reciprocity lies between our ability to be motivated by self-interest and by altruistic feelings. Reasonable citizens are neither egoists nor perfect altruists, neither saints nor sinners. They act from reciprocity. To act from a sense of justice without reciprocity would be psychologically difficult or self-sacrificial.[73] In a reasonable society, all citizens have goods to advance. Yet all "stand ready to propose fair terms" so that all may benefit. One might say that such citizens are, in moral personality, "well-ordered."

To act reasonably is to develop our moral capacities to the point where we act according to "full autonomy." Several concepts are involved here, all of which refer to some form of rational self-direction. Autonomy includes acting as a human agent, which is the most minimalist form of self-direction. To be an agent is to be capable of having a life, or one that you can call your own in some way. However, agency, in this sense, does not say much about the degree of control that one has, or how one came by one's beliefs and goals. Agency becomes rational autonomy when we rationally evaluate and decide to follow a plan of life where the choices and reasons for our choices are adopted in an autonomous fashion, apart from manipulation or the mere following of social norms. With rational autonomy we act from the norms and values that we affirm.[74] Nussbaum's list of basic capabilities and my four-level theory of goods encourage the development of a level of autonomy in people that is much richer than bare agency.

Rawls adds a moral component to rational autonomy. Autonomy is "full" or most fully developed when citizens consciously pursue their goods within justice. That is, citizens freely and consciously act in society from principles of justice, and they employ these principles when they debate the terms of cooperation. They express their nature as free and equal by acting from a "morality of principles" – the highest stage of moral development.[75] Citizens of well-ordered societies are persons disposed to exercise and reconcile their two moral powers. They do not pursue goods beyond the bounds of justice. They give priority to the right.

LIBERAL DELIBERATION

We have described the ideal of well-ordered society in terms of its just social structure and the moral capacities of well-ordered citizens. A third element, of special importance to journalism ethics, needs to be added. We need principles to guide how citizens communicate. How should well-ordered citizens discuss public issues regarding fundamental rights and duties?

Rawls defines a well-ordered democracy as such:

> The government is effectively under their (public's) political and electoral control, and that it answers to and protects their fundamental interests as specified in a written or unwritten constitution and its interpretation. The regime is not an autonomous agency pursuing its own bureaucratic ambitions. Moreover, it is not directed by the interests of large concentrations of private economic and corporate power veiled from public knowledge and almost entirely free from accountability.[76]

This definition assumes that there is a fair and effective process of deliberation by which citizens are informed of issues and are able to bring the government "under their political and electoral control." Contracting among citizens does not occur once, say in some founding of a constitution or in some original position. Contracting on laws and policies must go on every day as society evolves. Whether a society's basic structure is fair, and continues to be fair, depends on public deliberation about how the principles of justice are to be applied to new issues and new institutions. An ideal liberal democracy needs self-governing citizens who participate in reasoned, fair, and tolerant deliberation.

Political Liberalism

The question of democratic deliberation is acute in a pluralist, media-saturated world. There are two major problems. One is the fact of "reasonable pluralism" – the existence of a reasonable but different conceptions of the good within democracies due to a plurality of ethnic, religious, and cultural groups. A comprehensive view is a view about what is of ultimate value in life, or in some domain of life, as we find in religious, philosophical, or moral doctrines about the good life. Utilitarianism is a comprehensive ethical theory that specifies the moral criterion of right and wrong. Roman Catholicism is a comprehensive religious view that explains the purpose of life and prescribes principles and practices.

Reasonable pluralism is a sign of free society. Yet reasonable pluralism questions the stability of free society over time. It questions the possibility of common terms of cooperation. Rawls asks: "How is it possible that there may exist over time a stable and just society of free and equal citizens profoundly divided by reasonable though incompatible religious, philosophical, and moral doctrines?"[77] It is important to develop an answer because a clash of comprehensive views can lead to civil strife or the denial of rights.

The second problem is how we use the means of communication for fair public discourse and daily "contracting" on essential issues. The explosion of new forms of media, which began in the late 1900s, democratizes the means of communication. More people have the technology to directly participate in discussions of public issues through websites, blogs, social networking sites, and various forms of citizen journalism. Yet this democratization also has encouraged the proliferation of biased reports, uninformed commentary, unreasonable ranting, and propaganda. Is liberal deliberation possible in this type of public sphere?

Rawls's philosophy provides two conceptions to address these issues. One conception is political liberalism. The other is public reason. In his later work, Rawls reconceived justice as fairness in terms of a political form of liberalism. Rawls realized that justice as fairness in *A Theory of Justice* was flawed. The principles could be misunderstood as a uniquely true and comprehensive theory of the good life put forward to replace other comprehensive views among the contracting parties. But, in a pluralist society, justice as fairness cannot mediate between conflicting views if it is one of the competing comprehensive doctrines.

Therefore, Rawls, in *Political Liberalism* and other works, recharacterized the nature of contracting on fundamental issues as a political matter, not as a matter of comprehensive doctrines. The principles of justice must be understood (1) as terms of cooperation that do not depend on any comprehensive view whether it is metaphysical, religious, or philosophical; and (2) the principles are to be affirmed as the result of an "overlapping consensus" among reasonable citizens committed to a well-ordered society but who also continue to hold comprehensive views. In other words, citizens with different comprehensive views are able to agree on a core of political principles as a way to organize their pluralist, liberal society. The principles deal with political values such as justice, civil liberty, equality of opportunity, economic reciprocity, self-respect for all citizens, and informed public reasoning.[78]

Rawls's political liberalism retains the idea that we need to agree on just principles for cooperation. The goal is still a well-ordered society. However, the goal is not to prove or enforce the superior truth (or metaphysical correctness) of a comprehensive conception of the good. The goal is political and practical. The goal is an "overlapping consensus" on principles for organization of the political sphere of society. In a plural democracy, *no* comprehensive doctrine is an appropriate basis for liberal democracy. No such view will be accepted by the various comprehensive views. The principles of justice cannot depend on you accepting my comprehensive view about life. No consensus is possible on this basis.

The only basis for consensus is political liberalism. That is, we seek to identify just principles of social cooperation that are "freestanding." They are justified on politically terms alone, as terms of cooperation for a liberal society. What might those principles be? Rawls believes that if people seek an overlapping consensus, they will be disposed to affirm liberal principles of justice similar to those in *A Theory of Justice*.

There are several reasons why such principles might be acceptable. First, the principles, as free-standing, do not require anyone to accept the principles of other comprehensive views. They do not require anyone to abandon their comprehensive values as a moral guide for the non-political domains of life. Second, Rawls believes his two principles capture the fundamental values of justice in a liberal society and are reflected in existing political discourse. Citizens are already disposed to regard liberal principles of freedom and equality, for example, as a good way to organize their democracy in a fair manner. Three, citizens who hold a comprehensive view may accept freestanding liberal political principals because these principles express values that are already a part of their worldview. The reasons for accepting a liberal principle may be both political and religious. For example, Rawls notes how Martin Luther King Jr argued for civil rights as both politically right and commanded by God. Locke, in *A Letter Concerning Toleration*, defends toleration for political and religious reasons. He argues that God has given no human authority over another, nor can any human place the fate of their salvation in the hands of another. Therefore, Rawls allows the use of reasons derived from a comprehensive doctrine to support a principle, provided that in due course "proper political reasons" are presented to provide independent justification.

Ultimately, it is left up to citizens to decide how the proposed political principles relate to their comprehensive doctrines. The goal of political liberalism, psychologically and philosophically, is not to replace, reject, or give a "true foundation" for one's comprehensive views, which is "delusional."[79] The aim is to develop a political conception of justice as a sort of module, a self-contained political view that can gain the support of comprehensive doctrines. However, by overlapping consensus, Rawls does not mean a political agreement reached at any cost or by any means. The political conception is not the result of political bargaining among unequal groups. It is not a *modus vivendi* that balances the political forces. The principles must be affirmed because they are fair terms achieved through a free and equal contracting process.

Public Reason

Let's presume that plural liberal societies can reach a Rawlsian consensus on the principles of justice to govern their polity. Assume that they can accept Rawls's two principles of justice, specified above. Despite this consensus, a second problem, mentioned above, remains. How should citizens apply the principles to new questions? How should they deliberate and communicate about new issues, new political developments?

Political liberalism requires citizens to exercise "public reason," a restrained, reasonable form of deliberation about fundamental principles.[80] Public reason occurs when citizens, living with reasonable pluralism, reason about public issues in ways consistent with their commitments to reciprocity, civility, and impartiality. The exercise of public reason, and its communicative virtues, defines deliberative democracy. Rawls's public reason is a democratic extension of Kant's distinction of private and public reason, where the latter refers to giving reasons on public matters that would be regarded as reasonable, where the speaker acts like a "scholar before the entire public of the world of readers." This means that the public use of reason must be as impartial as possible, and at a distance from the speaker's particular interests.[81] Democracies need an idea of public reason to mediate among comprehensive views and to justify the state's use of force. Understanding how to conduct oneself as a democratic citizen includes understanding public reason. For Rawls:

> Public reason is characteristic of a democratic people: it is the reason of its citizens, of those sharing the status of equal citizenship. The subject of their reason is the good of the public: what the political conception of justice requires of society's basic structure of institutions, and of the purposes and ends they are to serve.[82]

Public reason is not identical with public discourse. Many forms of public discourse – discourse in public and among members of the public – fail to live up to the standards of public reason. The standards of public reason include certain attitudes and procedures, a certain content, and restrictions on the types of reasons.

The attitudes of public reason include those attitudes that define a reasonable, well-ordered citizen, such as the disposition to deliberate reasonably, aiming at justice and an overlapping consensus. Rawls's public reason also requires deliberation in an objective manner on the basis of "mutually recognized criteria and evidence." Without objectivity, we are merely "voicing our psychological state."[83]

In chapter 2, I discussed objectivity as a procedural stance that evaluated claims according to holistic, agreed-upon criteria. Objectivity in political liberalism is also a matter of common procedures. In this case, they are common procedures for assessing principles for a plural, liberal society.[84] In *A Theory of Justice,* the objectivity of claims is determined by the impartial contractual process in the original position. In *Political Liberalism,* objectivity is a fair contractual process aimed at consensus, interpreted politically. When citizens adopt justice as fairness, "we look at our society and our place in it objectively: we share a common standpoint along with others and do not make our judgments from a personal slant." Our moral principles are objective "to the extent that they have been arrived at and tested by assuming this general standpoint." In justice as fairness, we call upon practical reason to "express the point of view of persons ... suitably characterized as reasonable and rational." The outcome of public reason is not "true or correct" but rather "reasonable and legitimate law" binding on citizens by the majority principle. Rawls thinks that democratic citizens have an "intrinsic moral duty" to engage in public reason while holding officials to it. They fulfill their "duty of civility" and display "civic friendship."[85]

So, in the final analysis, when do objective reasons exist, politically speaking?

> Political convictions ... are objective ... if reasonable and
> rational persons, who are sufficiently intelligent and con-
> scientious in exercising their powers of practical reason, and
> whose reasoning exhibits none of the familiar defects of rea-
> soning, would eventually endorse those convictions, or signifi-
> cantly narrow their difference about them, provided that these
> persons know the relevant facts and have sufficiently surveyed
> the grounds that bear on the matter under conditions favorable
> to due reflection.[86]

Rawls introduces a significant limit on the subject of public reason and who the primary participants are. Rawls confines public reason to the discussion of the primary political values and principles that define citizens' social union. Public reason is about two things: "constitutional essentials" about the political values found, for example, in the US Constitution; and fundamental justice for the basic structure. Public reason is about a part of the public sphere, the "political public forum." One reasons about such topics from the principles of the social contract, such as justice as fairness.

Rawls limits public reason to the basic structure because he thinks the first task of political philosophy is to secure public reason as a norm for what is most important in political society, and then we can see if the norm can be extended to other areas. If we cannot secure public reason at the basic level, it is doubtful we can secure it elsewhere.[87]

Public reason also restricts how we reason. For Rawls, one cannot reason about fundamental issues by appealing only to personal or partial reasons. One can't deliberate about fundamental issues by using reasons that require others to accept one person's comprehensive view. Comprehensive doctrines should give way in public life when debating constitutional essentials and fundamental justice. Liberal public reason takes some issues off the political agenda. The existence of a Bill of Rights in political constitutions is a decision in the social contract not to renegotiate basic rights.

Rawls thinks the primary exercise of public reason in evaluating the basic structure and applying principles is carried out by judges, especially Supreme Court judges,[88] government officials and legislators, candidates for public office and their campaign managers,

especially in their public oratory, party platforms, and political statements. However, Rawls does recognize that other citizens can exercise public reason when they vote or discuss issues by imagining
themselves as ideal legislators.[89]

Why does Rawls stress public reason among judges and political
leaders? He thinks that we are more likely to approach the ideal of
public reason in special forums such as a supreme court. Rawls distinguishes ideal political discourse, guided by principles and reasonableness, from the less orderly and less principled discourse of what
he calls the "background culture" of civil society. This less principled discourse results from communications in the public sphere
and among society's many associations. Discourse in these domains
may not touch on fundamental issues; when they do, they may not
follow public reason. The restrictions of public reason do not apply
to the "non-public political culture," such as the news media, which
mediates the political forum and background culture.[90] In fact, laws
of free speech allow people to express themselves in self-interested,
uninformed, or biased ways. In later chapters, I will argue to the
contrary, that some form of public reason and objectivity should be
an ideal of journalism and other forms of public discourse.

Rawls intends his notion of objectivity to apply to practical
deliberations about what society ought to do, and how citizens can
achieve common goals. Rawls asserts the primacy of the practical in
shaping our conceptions in ethics and political theory.[91] Objectivity
consists of context-bound procedures for offering evidence, seeking agreement, and reaching goals. A conception of objectivity is
valid if it assists in the resolution of the practical problems it was
designed for. Rawls puts forward his conception of objectivity as a
set of procedures for exercising public reason and for seeking a just
liberal democracy.

GOOD IN THE RIGHT

Because my ideal of ethical flourishing is a combination of the good
and the right, I have spent considerable time describing my theory
of flourishing and Rawls's theory of just society, as forms of level
3 theorizing about aims. Having described the two theories, I conclude the chapter by explaining how they fit together to constitute
ethical flourishing.

The Priority Problem

The distinction between the good and the right is usually expressed as a difference between our relations with valued objects and our relations with people. The good consists of those things we value and care about – the ends that we pursue in life. The right is about my relations with other people, about doing the right action with regard to others. The rightness of an action is its acceptability, not only to me but also to those with whom I interact. The right includes questions of justice, duty, the obligations of social roles, and promises to others. The good refers to our pursuit of valued ends; the right refers to how humans treat each other as they pursue those ends. On this account, an action that harms you may be good for me, but wrong.

This distinction, however, can be misleading. The distinction misleads if it suggests that the right is concerned only with our relations with others and not with ourselves. We do interact with ourselves. We can treat ourselves wrongly or rightly. I can treat myself with disrespect, hate myself, enjoy a narcissistic fascination with myself, reflect on myself, subject myself to drug addictions, or ignore the development of my talents.[92] Also, the distinction is misleading if it suggests that what is right cannot be a good. The right can be a valued end of action. Justice and right relations with others are goods that many people care about. A just society is a great good.

This distinction leads to the priority problem. How are the good and the right related? Which is ethically more important? Is ethics is primarily about the good or the right? We seem to have to choose between opposing intuitions: "Surely," our intuitions say to us, "what is primary is to promote the good individually and collectively, even if we sometimes have to violate what is right." However, our intuitions about justice reply: "Surely, the most important matter is to secure basic rights and to insist on obligations."

As stated in chapter 1, ethical theories are distinguished by how they answer the priority question. Consequential theories affirm the priority of the good; deontological theories affirm the priority of the right in the form of duties and principles of justice.[93]

Both theories can marshal persuasive examples. For instance, consequential theories may argue that we need to severely restrict liberties in times of terrorism for the greater good. Deontological theories argue that liberties must be protected against those who would use our fears to compromise inviolable principles of justice.

What does "prior" mean in this context? "Prior" does not mean first in the order of time but first in the order of importance, theoretically and practically.[94] Theoretically, "prior" means most important in terms of logic or knowledge. Logically, a concept x is prior to concept y if y is defined in terms of x, or our understanding of y depends on our understanding of x. For example, "desire" is prior to "good" if we define "good" in terms of "what we desire." As a matter of knowledge, x is prior to y if our knowledge of y is based on our knowledge of x. In this sense, y is justified and grounded in x. For example, we justify a duty to keep promises by saying that it promotes utility. Utility is epistemologically prior to duty. One way of indicating which things are prior, epistemologically, is to distinguish instrumental from final goods. We show that x is prior ethically to y by showing that y is valued as a means to x. We justify y in terms of x. In ethics, priority is often described as a matter of having greater "ethical weight." To say that utility has greater ethical weight than duty is to say that, in deciding how to act, utility has first importance in reasoning. Utility overrides or trumps other principles, in case of conflict. We *first* consult x and make sure it is not violated.

Therefore, the priority issue is a debate over whether the good or the right is prior in two senses: (a) conceptual – whether the right is definable in terms of the good, or vice versa; (b) epistemically – whether the right is justified ultimately by the good, or vice versa. That is to say, whether the right or the good have greater ethical weight.

Theories of the good often argue for the priority of good, especially in the epistemic sense. The principles of the right may be regarded as civil laws and rules for coordinating social interaction and external relations among people that are justified by moral ends – the "intrinsic good of the ends they serve."[95] Liberal philosophers have used an instrumental approach to acknowledge justice and rights, but also to argue for their epistemic dependence on the good. To have a right, Mill says, is something so important that society's obligation to protect such rights assumes that character of absoluteness that distinguishes the feeling of right and wrong from that of expediency. Mill says justice is "the chief part, and incomparably the most sacred and binding part, of all morality." However, Mill also thinks that theories that make the right prior are wrong. The idea of justice as a distinct notion is "one of the strongest obstacles" to the principle of utility.

The demands of justice are based not on some notion of abstract right but because the goods of justice "stand higher in the scale of social utility."[96] For Mill, the good (as utility) is practically prior to the right and has greater ethical weight.

Some consequentialists, who are not utilitarians, have attempted to fit the right in the good by adopting "indirect" consequentialism, which promulgates that good consequences come from following the rules of justice. The rules promote the best objectively probable consequences. It sounds paradoxical, but the best way to maximize value is for people not to try to maximize value in every action. Rather, people promote good consequences by accepting restrictions on their actions and by honouring duties. Consequentialist Phillip Petit makes room for deontological considerations by arguing that if benefits genuinely accrue to someone as a result of respecting rights, then this benefit is dignity. Dignity assures persons of some "dominion" over their actions and protects them from being merely a unit of calculation in a larger benefit scheme. To recognize the benefits of dignity, consequentialists should acknowledge a "rights-restriction" on their thinking.[97]

In contrast, modern deontological theories, from Kant onward, have argued that the idea of right is a logically independent concept and aspect of ethical life; there is no defining of the right in terms of what is good. The principles of the right are also epistemically independent. They are not only of instrumental value but also are of intrinsic value. In addition, deontologists, such as Kant and Rawls, argue that the right is epistemically prior to the good. Ethics must recognize the right's greater ethical weight.[98] Kant states that the right is primary to "heteronymous" concerns about the consequences of our actions.[99] He writes: "The concept of good and evil is not defined prior to the moral law, to which, it would seem, the former would have to serve as foundation; rather the concept of good and evil must be defined after and by means of the law."[100] Rawls thinks a theory is deontological not because it denies the importance of consequences but because it makes the right prior. A theory is deontological if it does not make the maximization of good prior to the satisfaction of the principles of right. Rawls is mainly concerned to oppose maximizing forms of consequentialism, especially utilitarianism as found in the writings of Bentham, Sidgwick, and others. What is right is not what maximizes the general welfare or utility. Justice as fairness does not aim at or consider the net balance of utility or desire-satisfaction, and "there is no reason to think that just institutions will maximize the good."[101] Sandel characterizes this "deontological liberalism" as a view about what has primacy when we consider how best to arrange society. He writes:

> Society, being composed of a plurality of persons, each with his own aims, interests, and conceptions of the good, is best arranged when it is governed by principles that do not *themselves* presuppose any particular conception of the good; what justifies these regulative principles above all is not that they maximize the social welfare or otherwise promote the good, but rather that they conform to the concept of *right*, a moral category given prior to the good and independent of it.[102]

Why Is Right Prior?

I agree that the right is prior for several reasons provided by Rawls and others. One reason, mentioned throughout this chapter, is that a free pursuit of the good can be excessive and unethical unless restrained by principles of equality and justice. The rights of others may be denied, creating unequal societies. To say that people pursue their goods is not to say they pursue the common good. To restrain the good means to make the right prior, to make sure our pursuit of the good does not violate principles of justice. As Rawls says, it is impossible to deduce the principles of justice from only the principles of rational self-interest because "merely rational agents lack a sense of justice and fail to recognize the independent validity of the claims of others."[103]

Right is prior because the freedom to pursue one's interests without excessive government restrictions is only one side of the coin, when it comes to an adequate conception of liberal society. The other side is protecting others, especially the least advantaged, from being tyrannized by other citizens as the latter pursue their interests. One needs a socially just scheme in which such rights can be reconciled justly and directed toward the common good. The concept of right is not the idea of everyone having or claiming rights. The right refers to a just scheme of social cooperation that includes rights protection and adjudication. The right refers to right relations among citizens. Rawls's first principle of justice does not simply name basic liberties.

It also includes limits on the liberties. In *On Liberty*, Mill attempted to recognize such limits from within his utilitarian perspective by proposing that freedom is limited where it harms others. But Mill did not see that securing his famous "harm principle" requires the priority of the right. It requires a society that recognizes fair restrictions on what other can do to others, and this makes justice fundamental. If we regard the good as prior, and the development of right relations as merely instrumental to the good, harming others unfairly may be sanctioned if it promotes utility.

A second reason is that we need a theory of the right to mediate conflict in today's pluralistic societies among comprehensive views of the good. We need to heed Rawls's argument for political liberalism, which calls for principles of justice and social cooperation based on a sense of what is fair and right for all groups. In such a society, we need to first secure the fair terms of cooperation. We need to make the right prior.

A third reason is that the priority of the right is a better approach to the construction of an adequate theory of liberalism, justice, and society. If our aim is to construct an egalitarian liberal society, the priority of the right is essential. Considerations about the distribution of goods and the equality of rights cannot be added to our theory after we have maximized the good or as an attempt to correct liberalism, e.g., to reduce the excesses of the pursuit of the good. A theory that makes the right prior builds such considerations into a philosophy of liberal society from the start.

A fourth reason is that, from a contractual perspective, the priority of right is more likely to be affirmed by reasonable citizens of liberal democracies. Rawls correctly contends that contracting parties in the original position or citizens seeking an overlapping consensus would prefer the priority of the right to the maximization of the good as the primary principle for organizing social cooperation. In the original position, if one does not know one's position in society, it is rational and probable that one would prefer the priority of justice. The maximization of the good does not guarantee equal rights or fair cooperation. It is unlikely that contracting parties would adopt a utilitarian approach where the best social arrangements are whatever maximizes the good, whatever the distribution of goods happens to be.

A fifth reason is that the priority of the good violates our sense of the fundamental nature of the right and it seems to sanction unethical actions. There are well-known worries about how to reconcile the maximization of the good for the majority of citizens with the rights (and goods) of minorities. What if utility (or happiness) in a society was increased by restricting the actions of a minority, such as denying them religious liberty or freedom of expression? What if preventing homosexuals to live a life expressing their sexual orientation pleased a majority of citizens? Attempts to avoid such implications, such as Petit's dignity clause are ad hoc and unconvincing.[104] One alternative is to introduce principles of equality and rights on the same level as the maximization of the good. But that undermines the idea that the good is prior. Another alternative is to adopt a mixed ethical system where principles of the good and the right are said to be of equal importance. But such an ecumenical system fails to explain how we should reason ethically where the good and the right conflict.

Moreover, treating justice as instrumental makes our commitment to justice precariously dependant on circumstances. If the good is prior, then the "first virtue" of institutions is increasing the good, not justice. Fair cooperation and the fair distribution of social benefits is a secondary goal, a happy but contingent result for a society that makes the aggregate good its primary value.[105] But what if circumstances were otherwise? If our demands for justice interfered with a social engineering vision of society that encouraged us to use a number of far-reaching reforms to arrive at a more efficient society, could justice be ignored? One does not have to imagine an Orwellian society of enforced "happiness" to worry about making justice derivative.

A sixth reason is that the idea of a well-ordered society based on the priority of right is both an intrinsic part of ethical flourishing and instrumentally contributes to it. As I will argue below, to live in right relations with others (and to make it prior) is to join in a life of ethical flourishing. Living justly is an expression of ethical flourishing much like the blooming of a flower is an expression of a flourishing plant. Instrumentally, a well-ordered society supports the full development of human's moral capacities. Citizens develop as rational and reasonable social animals. I follow Kant and Rawls in making the full development of humans as free and equal citizens the ultimate point of rights and justice.

For these reasons, I concur with Rawls that a liberal society cannot be fair and egalitarian unless it protects basic liberties from compromise. The rights secured by justice "are not subject to political bargaining or the calculus of social interests."[106] This bargaining is what theories that maximizing the good do not do, or cannot do, in principle. The priority of right means that we give absolute weight to founding a society on principles of justice, whether or not they maximize or optimize utility. The priority of right is grounded in a prior and independent commitment to a just society.

Congruence

I have argued for the priority of the right in ethical theory; however, the priority of right does not mean that the right and the good are opposing ethical concepts, always and everywhere. It doesn't mean that we have a forced choice between what is good and what is right. It doesn't mean that we don't take the consequences of actions into account, or devalue the pursuit of the good. It does mean that the good and the right are related in a certain manner in ethical reasoning. One is prior to the other, and it is important that we correctly understand that relationship. One task of ethical theorizing is to explain how these two concepts, while independent and different, can work together within ethics to guide our reasoning and decision-making.

My view, again taking my cue from Rawls, is that the best understanding of the good in the right is to think of the good and the right as congruent. Two or more elements are congruent if they agree, are suitable, or are consistent in some manner. The good and the right are congruent if they somehow fit together in ethics. The ideal is a society that allows them to be congruent to the highest degree possible.

The right and the good are congruent if each element has an important role in ethical reasoning, and both are recognized as important elements in the good life. The right can be prior to the good and still allow the good such recognition. Rawls has already shown how congruence is possible. The first principle of justice gives absolute weight to a family of freedoms – freedoms for pursuing the good. It also protects these freedoms for every citizen. After all, this is a *liberal* theory. To make the good and the right congruent is to reconcile the rational and the reasonable in the lives of individuals and in society at large. The desire to be reasonable is buttressed by the expectation of reciprocity. Congruence expresses the Kantian thesis of the unity of practical reason whereby the reasonable and rational work together to do what is right.[107]

Deontological theories recognize the importance of the pursuit of the good, but they do not make it prior. Rawls argues that his theory of justice recognizes and allows for five major forms of the good: (1) the idea of goodness as rationality, or the individual's pursuit of their particular goods according to a rational plan; (2) the idea of primary goods, goods that people need to pursue their particular goods in almost any circumstance; (3) reasonable comprehensive goods, which are religious and philosophical conceptions of the good for life; (4) the good of the political virtues; and (5) the good of a well-ordered society. The five goods, suitably restrained by justice, define the concept of free and equal citizens pursuing good in democratic society.[108]

In justice as fairness, we do not begin by taking people's desires and inclinations as given and then seek to fulfill them. Instead, desires are restricted from the outset by the principles of justice. On this view "something is good only if it fits into ways of life consistent with the principles of right already on hand."[109] Despite these restrictions, Rawls does not envisage a grim life of absolute duties or a fanaticism of rules. He argues for the congruence of the good and the right. Not to allow a space for the pursuit of good would be a violation of liberal ideals and it would make the principles of justice unattractive to citizens. While justice "draws the limit, and the good shows the point," justice cannot draw the limit too narrowly.[110]

Moreover, the restrictions of justice apply only to a limited area of society. They apply to liberties, rights, equal opportunities, and the distribution of advantages. The pursuit of many goods does not raise questions of fundamental justice. Justice as fairness only aims "to approximate the boundaries" within which persons are free to seek the good.[111] Just institutions and political virtues should not only permit but sustain "ways of life fully worthy of citizens' devoted allegiance."

Congruence sets aside the common misunderstanding that a deontological theory that prioritizes the right doesn't or shouldn't consider the consequences of the theory or of our actions. The rightness of institutions and actions cannot be fully considered independently from their consequences. As Rawls bluntly states: "All ethical doctrines worth our attention take consequences into account in judging rightness. One which did not would simply be irrational, crazy."[112] Kant approached the question of priority in a similar manner, although his stern talk of duty and his worries about "inclinations" suggest a more repressive scheme. Kant allows that happiness ("heteronymous considerations") can be brought into ethical deliberation if duty and right are satisfied. A person is not expected to "renounce his natural aim of attaining happiness" but must "abstract from such considerations as soon as the imperative of duty supervenes." People must make sure their motives are not influenced by a desire for happiness.[113]

Rawls does not erect an implausible dichotomy between right and good. He does not force ethics to reason about actions either solely in terms of rights and obligations, or solely in terms of consequences and goods. For Rawls, it is a question of priority and overall fit. A deontological theory starts with the priority of right and then finds as much room as possible for the pursuit of goodness. Right and good are well-related only in a well-ordered society where justice is prior.

Ethical Flourishing Revisited

Ethical flourishing has been defined as the development of our capacities in an ethical direction. We now understand this idea as the establishment of congruence between the right and the good in individuals and society. We need both well-ordered persons and social structures where the right is prior in this liberal sense. When we pursue the good across the four levels and do so within the principles of the right, then we are pursuing ethical flourishing. Under such ideal conditions, humans fulfill their primary ethical impulses toward the good and the right. We fulfill our impulse toward the good in the highest ethical manner by seeking the flourishing of ourselves and others on all four levels. We fulfill our ethical impulse to realize right relations and justice. The good as flourishing and the right as well-ordered society, when brought together in one society, is the highest possible good for humans and the ultimate goal of ethics.

The capacities of central importance to a theory of ethical flourishing include the ability to conceive a rational plan of life, to have a sense of justice and to honour its principles, to act fairly and with reciprocity, to be concerned for others, and to be impartial in ethical judgment.[114] Ethical flourishing is the liberal, open-ended development of our capacities within the bounds of ethics. Ethical flourishing is the fullest development of the two moral capacities.

In summary, we can say that ethical flourishing is the development and expression of ethical capacities, individually and socially, so that we morally perfect ourselves within the bounds of ethics – bounds defined by our ethical capacities and principles. The goal is an ethical form of flourishing, a human goodness that combines duty and human development. The goal is an ethical approach to life that cares about well-ordered souls and well-ordered societies.

Some readers may wonder how my final conception of the ends of ethics ends up being a theory of the good after I have argued for the prior of the right. The air of paradox is removed once we realize that "good" is ambiguous – it can refer to two different levels of ethical experience. On one level we speak of our individual pursuit of our goods. The good in this sense refers to the various things that we care about and value. It can come into conflict with the right. My idea of ethical flourishing is not a theory of the good in this sense; it is not a theory about the many things that people pursue and value, and why they might do so. My theory of ethical flourishing is a broader theory of the more comprehensive and final good, which includes both the goods of rational autonomy and the goods of justice. The four levels list the capacities and goods that are developed in a good and just society. These are the goods that we experience to the highest degree if we are lucky enough to live in an ethically flourishing society. To enjoy goods across all four levels is to enjoy flourishing and, when combined with a well-ordered society, these goods become part of the experience of ethical flourishing. Ethical flourishing is an ultimate good that achieves congruence between our human love of flourishing and our love of right action or justice. Full ethical flourishing is rarely achieved since it requires a convergence of well-ordered persons and well-ordered social arrangements. It requires flourishing on four levels. It is a concept of ideal theory.

Ethical flourishing provides a deep metaethical reason for resisting the temptation to divide ethics into three rival camps – theories of the good, right, and the virtuous. As I said in chapter 1, none of these theories will ever be theoretically triumphant in this battle because they identify different and non-reducible (or eliminable) aspects of our complex ethical life. Ethical theory struggles to express the intertwining of justice and goodness. If this is what ethics is about, then our approach to reasoning should be holistic and congruence-seeking.

Living ethically differs from other forms of life and other forms of development. We recognize, as rational and natural beings, that we have an inescapable interest in our welfare plus an interest in what morality requires. As Kant repeatedly stressed, the goal of ethics is not our own happiness, as a feeling of contentment, or a life of pleasure and utility. The goal is not only the development of our physical and social capacities. The "real point" about ethics "is to promote our own moral character" so that we live as fully realized free and rational beings.[115] The entire and perfect good is virtue and happiness, where happiness is in "exact proportion to morality."[116] This is Kant's idea of the congruence of justice and the good. The aim of ethical flourishing is not simply the development of our capacities but their development so that we may be "worthy of the humanity that dwells within" us.[117]

Finally, my explication of the ultimate aims of ethics uses a method that I call "cumulative moral insight." The philosophical aim of ethical thinking is to grasp a clear and comprehensive conception of human goodness. It seeks a view of the ethically good life in the round. The view is a complex image in the mind of how many elements should be ordered into a whole. Ethical reflection culminates in a special integrative, insight that brings together a wide range of thoughts and truths. It constructs an image of what humans are at their best. It constructs an ethical identity for humanity.

The insight is an elusive and difficult goal approached by laborious reading in ethical theory, the refinement of common sense, reflection on the facts of human experience, and many other matters. It may be compared in some respects to Aristotle's notion of the mind grasping the universal in the particular. The rational defence of such an idea is a matter of reflective equilibrium.

CONCLUSION

We are at the end of the first section of this book. The section has presented my general theory of ethics: the nature of ethics as a human construction via practical reason, the three levels of ethical reasoning, and the ultimate aims of ethics as a congruence of the good and the right under the ideal of ethical flourishing.

In the next section, I will apply the results of these philosophical investigations to journalism ethics, showing how they redefine its self-conception and its basic principles. I will use the results as a conceptual platform from which to construct the foundations for a global journalism ethics.

SECTION TWO

Global Journalism Ethics

4

Global Journalism Ethics

When we theorize, we can discuss the fundamental ideas of our theory, or we can discuss how the ideas apply to various phenomena and contentious issues. To discuss the fundamental ideas is to examine the philosophical foundation of the theory. Some theories have weak foundations. The ideas are questionable or conflict. Some theories lack a clear foundation because the theory is new or needs to be extended to new phenomena. In many of these cases, a philosopher can help to create a stronger foundation by clarifying, organizing, and defending the basic ideas.

This chapter constructs a new foundation for journalism ethics by extending to global journalism the concepts introduced over the previous chapters. The topic is the *ethical* implications of global journalism. Many scholars investigate "globalization" as a trend in economics, trade, and culture. Others explore trends in global communication and journalism around the world.[1] Global journalism ethics uses this empirical data and theorizing as input for normative inquiry into journalism, asking: how do such empirical changes challenge existing journalism standards? How should ethics change if it is to take account of global news media?

My foundation is an extension of the concepts of naturalized, holistic ethics and ethical flourishing to global journalism. It is only a foundation. A full global journalism ethics, containing specific standards and detailed newsroom policies, is a more ambitious project. My theory is an act of ethical invention in an experimental mood. It establishes a beachhead on the difficult terrain of global journalism ethics.

The extension of the core ideas of the first section of the book will occupy the remaining three chapters. In this chapter, I describe the general shape of global journalism ethics. Chapter 5 describes how my global ethics applies to democracy. The chapter makes the promotion of global democratic structures one of journalism's new global duties. The final chapter, chapter 6, applies my foundation to a prominent and difficult question in global journalism – whether a global journalist should be patriotic.

GLOBAL ETHICS

Cosmopolitanism

Global ethics is global in three ways. First, it is addressed to citizens as members of a global humanity. Second, its main principle is the flourishing of humanity at large. A global ethics crosses borders by seeking fair terms of cooperation among peoples and nations. It proposes principles for citizens of the world. Third, global ethics seeks to be useful in shaping ethical deliberation about global issues. A global ethics provides standards for discussing global issues such as international relations, foreign aid, humanitarian intervention, human rights, war, terrorism and torture, climate change, extreme poverty, and other global inequalities.

Where should we start the construction of a global ethics? A good place is cosmopolitanism. Cosmopolitanism does not mean being sophisticated in the ways of the world; it is an ancient ethical theory. Cosmopolitan ethics asserts the equal value and dignity of all people, as members of a common humanity. Cosmopolitanism emphasizes universal principles of human rights, freedom, and justice. Brock and Brighouse write: "Each human being has equal moral worth and that equal moral worth generates certain moral responsibilities that have universal scope."[2] The nationality, ethnicity, religion, class, race, or gender of a person (or group) is morally irrelevant to whether an individual is a member of humanity and comes under the protection of cosmopolitan principles.

The roots of the modern cosmopolitan attitude go back to the Stoics of antiquity, the civic law of the Roman Empire, and the idea of a universal humanity in Christian humanism. Cosmopolitanism began with the idea that people outside my tribe or city – foreigners – were human like me. Therefore, I owe them certain decencies, such as hospitality or the privileges of citizenship. In philosophy, Kantian thought grounds a good deal of modern cosmopolitanism. Kant's categorical imperative enjoins us to universalize our maxims and to treat others as moral equals, as members of a "kingdom of ends." Kant's political writings envisage a world that seeks perpetual peace through a federation of free states governed by international law and respect for humanity.[3] Outside philosophy, cosmopolitan attitudes have influenced the International Committee of the Red Cross, the human rights movement, international law, and the establishment of the United Nations. In recent years, Nussbaum recommends cosmopolitanism as an antidote to parochialism in ethics.[4]

Cosmopolitanism is a thesis about ethical identity and responsibility. Cosmopolitans regard themselves as defined primarily by the common needs and aspirations that they share with other humans. This cosmopolitan identity is more important to their sense of self and ethical identity than facts about their place of birth, social class, or nationality. In terms of responsibility, cosmopolitanism "highlights the obligations we have to those whom we do not know, and with whom we are not intimate, but whose lives touch ours sufficiently that what we do can affect them."[5]

Cosmopolitanism has received increasing attention because of the debate over the role of the nation-state in a global world and the responsibilities of developed countries to the appalling poverty and illness on this planet. Cosmopolitanism rules out assigning ultimate ethical value to collective entities such as states or nations. It rules out positions that accord no value to some types of people or establish a moral hierarchy where some people count for more than others.

Cosmopolitanism is often misunderstood. The trouble arises over the imperative to make our primary ethical allegiance to a borderless, moral community of humans. Cosmopolitanism has been dismissed as an ethic that only a philosopher could love – some abstract principles about universal humanity. To the contrary, cosmopolitanism wears a human face. It is the ability to perceive our common humanity in the many situations of life. It is respect for humanity's rational and moral capacities wherever and however they are manifest. It is in our concrete dealings with others that we recognize humanity's vulnerabilities, and capacities, as well as its potential for suffering.

The cosmopolitan attitude does not deny or devalue cultural diversity or legitimate partialities. The cosmopolitan thinker is under no illusion that people will stop loving their family and country. The cosmopolitan attitude does not deny that particular cultures and traditions are valuable. Instead, the cosmopolitan attitude is concerned

with the *priority* and *limits* of our attachments. To say that our primary allegiance is to humanity is to say that more partial concerns
have a prima facie right to be recognized but may be trumped by
broader concerns. The claim of humanity acknowledges the stoic view
that we live simultaneously in two communities: the local community of our birth and a community of common human aspirations. It
insists only that, in negotiating our way between these two communities, we should not allow local attachments to override fundamental
human rights and duties. When there is no conflict with cosmopolitan
principles, life can be lived according to partial principles.[6]

While cosmopolitanism is clear in its general orientation, there are
difficult questions about what it requires. Today, many people would
agree, philosophically, with the idea of human equality. After all,
such sentiments are found in the USA's Declaration of Independence
and other basic political documents. But cosmopolitanism, taken
seriously, has difficult implications. It poses this tough question: if
you accept the principle of an equal and common humanity, how
does that fit with the fact that your family and country mean more
to you? Peter Singer has written that the way out of our modern
pursuit of self-interest is to embrace the idea of an ethical life with
its openness to others. This ethical life rejects an indifference "to
the vast amount of unnecessary suffering that exists in the world
today."[7] Yet here lies the rub: how much do we owe to strangers
and at what cost to near and dear? Does equal moral worth entail
that every human should have an equal share of the world's land?
Are comfortable North Americans ethically bound to contribute to
foreign aid to the point of damaging their ability to provide for their
children's university education?[8]

Despite uncertainties, there is a growing consensus among cosmopolitans that people everywhere should be able to meet their
basic needs and develop their capacities to some tolerable extent.
Today, the issue that engages cosmopolitanists and their critics is not
whether we have special relationships with friends, family, and our
country. The issue is to what extent citizens in one country owe assistance to citizens in other nations. One answer is weak cosmopolitanism: there are *some* extranational obligations. Another is strong
cosmopolitanism: our obligations are very strong and global. Our
fellow nationals have no special claim on us, and we have no right to
use nationality to determine our obligations or to guide discretion-
ary behaviour. The challenge is to construct an ethically legitimate

and detailed position between weak and strong cosmopolitanism.[9] In chapter 6, we will see that the limits of nationalism, or patriotism, are a central problem for journalists in a global world.

Cosmopolitanism as Ethical Flourishing

Cosmopolitanism, with its affirmation of humanity, is a general doctrine. How we affirm humanity can take many forms. I believe that cosmopolitanism, interpreted as ethical flourishing, is an attractive basis for global ethics and a global journalism ethics.

I construct a global ethics by linking cosmopolitanism with previous commitments to naturalized ethics and ethical flourishing. We make this link by "globalizing" these core concepts. Globalizing concepts means imagining how the ideas of well-ordered society and ethical flourishing would operate as principles for global ethics. We extend the scope of these ethical terms to the global stage. We go global, philosophically.

To use an analogy from music, the adoption of a cosmopolitan attitude transposes the ethical discussion into a new key, where familiar terms resonate with new meanings. My theories of the good and the right, originally formulated for a domestic stage – Western liberal democracies – become global ideas of the good and right. When we globalize our theory of the good, flourishing is no longer merely the promotion of flourishing in Canada or China. The goal is the promotion of the four levels of flourishing globally. We have a duty to improve the material, social, and political conditions that allow humans everywhere to rationally pursue their goods and enjoy the benefits of community and social respect. We have a duty to develop just and participatory political associations. The individual, social, political, and ethical dignity that we seek for citizens in our society, we now seek for humanity at large. Similarly, our theory of right envisages a well-ordered international community.

Ethical flourishing then becomes global ethical flourishing. It is a global congruence of flourishing across all four levels of the good within global justice, assisted by global democratic structures.[10] The ultimate aim is to increase the number of citizens of the world who are able to enjoy basic liberties and to flourish within the bounds of global justice. In later chapters, I will explain what such concepts as "global democratic structures" and "global ethical flourishing" mean, with reference to journalism ethics.

In a sense, global ethics is not new. Many philosophers, from early religious writers to Kant, have put forward ethical principles as universally binding on rational beings. Ethics has often been conceived of as "global" or universal because its principles apply to all. Moreover, my four-level theory of the good refers to capacities that belong to all humans. However, a global ethics is more than the idea of universal norms. The construction of a global ethics must be more explicit, detailed, and context-bound. To be sure, global ethics should use, where appropriate, ideas from the past: from Kant's categorical imperative to the insights of ancient cosmopolitans. But a global ethics must develop these ideas into a systematic global philosophy that applies to the new and difficult issues of a global, media-linked world. Furthermore, a global ethics must respond to a postmodern skepticism about the very idea of a global ethics.

GLOBAL JOURNALISM ETHICS

Why Global Journalism Ethics?

What does global ethics mean for journalism? It means using cosmopolitan values and globalized principles to reinterpret journalism ethics.

Historically, journalism ethics has been parochial with its standards applying to particular groups. Journalism ethics was developed for a journalism of limited reach. The evolution of journalism ethics enlarged the class of people that journalism was supposed to serve, from political parties to the general public. But even today, the news media's claim that it serves the public has limits. It is usually assumed that the public includes readers of local newspapers, audiences of regional TV news broadcasts, and the citizens of a country. Most of the four hundred codes of journalism ethics in the world today are for local, regional, or national media. Little is said about whether or not journalists have a responsibility to citizens beyond their town or country. Journalism ethics, it seems, stops at the border.

How valid is the idea of "ethics within borders" in a global world? Why not take the next step and define one's public as readers within and without one's country? Why not talk about a global journalism ethics? Responsibilities would be owed to viewers scattered across the world, and journalism standards would be redefined to promote a journalism for citizens across borders. However, the question can be turned back. Why should we consider taking this audacious step? Isn't ethics complicated enough without adding global concerns?

There are several reasons to go global. Journalism ethics should become globally minded because the news media, and the practice of journalism, is increasingly global. The facts are familiar: media corporations are increasingly global enterprises; new technology gives news organizations the ability to gather information from around the world; news reports, via satellite and the internet, reach people around the world and influence the actions of governments, militaries, humanitarian agencies, and warring ethnic groups. The reach of the Al-Jazeera and CNN networks, for example, extends beyond the Arab world and the US public. These developments have consequences for the ethics of journalism. With global reach comes global responsibilities. Journalism ethics will not be credible if it avoids engagement with these new complexities.

The need for global journalism ethics is due not only to technological innovation and new ownership patterns; it is due to changes in the world that journalism inhabits. Of primary importance is the fact that this media-connected world brings together a plurality of different religions, traditions, ethnic groups, values, and organizations with varying political agendas. Our world is not a cozy McLuhan village; our world is connected electronically like never before, yet this grid of connections coexists with a collision of cultures. Publishing materials deemed offensive by certain groups, as happened with the publication of the cartoons of Mohammed by a Danish newspaper, can result in violence that ripples across borders. In such a climate, the role of the news media must be re-examined. What are the ethical responsibilities of journalism in a radically plural world, no longer divided politically into two Cold War camps?

A global journalism is of value because a biased and parochial journalism can wreak havoc in a tightly linked global world. Unless reported properly, North American readers may fail to understand the causes of violence in the Middle East or of a drought in Africa. Jingoistic reports can portray the inhabitants of other regions of the world as a threat. Biased reports may incite ethnic groups to attack each other. In times of insecurity, a narrow-minded, patriotic news media can amplify the views of leaders who stampede populations into war or the removal of civil rights for minorities.

Therefore we need a global ethics as a bulwark against undue influence of parochial values and social pressures on journalism. We need a cosmopolitan journalism that reports issues and events in a way that reflects this global plurality of views; to practice a journalism that helps different groups understand each other better.

Journalism with a global perspective is needed to help citizens understand the daunting global problems of poverty, environmental degradation, technological inequalities, and political instability. These problems require concerted global action and the construction of new global institutions. Moreover, without global principles, it is not possible to criticize media practices in other countries, including draconian restrictions on the press.

We need a more cosmopolitan attitude in journalism for the same general reason we need it in ethics in general: to make sure we don't withdraw into an insular ethnocentrism as a response to the confusing, pluralistic world around us. A cosmopolitan attitude refuses to allow us to hunker down into "a narrow and minimalist ethics that refuses to confront the major issues."[11] My central claim, then, is that the globalization of news media requires a radical rethinking of the principles and standards of journalism ethics. A successful appreciation of the problems that face the world, and what actions are necessary, requires reporting from an informed and nuanced international perspective.

The construction of global journalism ethics is underway. Although a global journalism ethics does not yet exist, there are a number of international declarations of media principle that can act as a starting point. When we compare codes of ethics, we see similarities. In recent years, global media ethics has become a movement among scholars, producing a growing number of journals and books.[12] Ethicists have begun a search for the fundamental principles of a global media ethics.[13] These preliminary reflections allow us to indicate more exactly what a global journalism ethics amounts to: (1) a reinterpretation of journalism in terms of cosmopolitan aims; (2) the construction of new principles and norms for the framework as evaluative guides for global journalism; (3) the application of these ideas to the coverage of issues and events.

Journalism Ethics as Cosmopolitan

The invention of a foundation has two stages. (a) We adapt a cosmopolitan attitude to journalism, and we explain how it alters journalism ethics. One change is that journalists come to place greater emphasis on their responsibilities to people beyond their borders. (b) We adapt my ideas of ethical naturalism and ethical flourishing to specify the meaning of cosmopolitan journalism. Therefore, if you ask, "What is global journalism ethics?" the short answer is: a cosmopolitan journalism aims at global ethical flourishing. In this section we deal only with (a), the cosmopolitan attitude.

Cosmopolitanism has features useful to global journalism ethics. Cosmopolitans are right to regard themselves as defined primarily by the needs and aspirations that they share with other humans, such as a common aspiration to life, liberty, and justice. In a fragmented world, cosmopolitanism reminds us of what is fundamental ethically and what unites humans. As a war correspondent I was stirred by glimpses of that common humanity, as well as dismayed by what happened when we placed too much emphasis on the local, on "blood and belonging." Cosmopolitanism recommends a sensitivity to humanity to global journalists.

A second feature is the view that global concerns trump local concerns where they conflict. Cosmopolitan principles of human rights, freedom, and justice take precedence when they conflict with my own interests. This provides direction to journalists caught in the ethical maze of international events. When my country embarks on an unjust war against another country, I, as a journalist (or citizen), should say so. If I am a Canadian journalist and I learn that Canada is engaged in trading practices that condemn citizens of an African country to continuing, abject poverty, I should not hesitate to report the injustice. It is not a violation of any reasonable form of patriotism or citizenship to hold one's country to higher standards. The cosmopolitan attitude limits our parochial attachments in journalism by drawing a ring of broader ethical principles around them. When there is no conflict with cosmopolitan principles, journalists can report in ways that support local and national communities. They can practice their craft parochially.

THREE IMPERATIVES

The adoption of a cosmopolitan attitude changes journalism's ethical identity. The following three imperatives state the essential components of a cosmopolitan attitude in journalism.

ACT AS GLOBAL AGENTS

Journalists should see themselves as agents of a global public sphere. The goal of their collective actions is a well-informed, diverse, and tolerant global "info-sphere" that challenges the distortions of tyrants, the abuse of human rights, and the manipulation of information by special interests.

SERVE THE CITIZENS OF THE WORLD

The global journalist's primary loyalty is to the information needs of world citizens. Journalists should refuse to define themselves as attached primarily to factions, regions, or even countries. Serving the public means serving more than one's local readership or audience, or even the public of one's country.

PROMOTE NON-PAROCHIAL UNDERSTANDINGS

The global journalist frames issues broadly and uses a diversity of sources and perspectives to promote a nuanced understanding of issues from an international perspective. Journalism should work against a narrow ethnocentrism or patriotism.

THREE PRINCIPLES

These three cosmopolitan imperatives can be cashed out in terms of three principles to guide journalism practice. These principles are called "claims" to emphasize that they are components of a global social contract. If the news media do not observe these principles, the public has an ethical claim against them.

The first principle is the claim of credibility: all journalists (and news organizations) have the ethical duty to provide the public, wherever they live, with credible news and analysis within the limitations of newsgathering. This means that reports can be seen as credible to readers or audiences far beyond the country in which the journalist resides. To judge that a journalist, a news organization, or the news media as a whole is credible is to judge that they can be relied upon to provide accurate, reliable information. Credibility implies that news media have used the best methods of fact-gathering and verification to reach the most truthful account possible, given the constraints of deadlines, conflicting views, and incomplete information. Without credibility, public confidence in journalism erodes.

Journalistic credibility is a species of credibility in general. "Credibility" belongs to a circle of normative terms – trustworthy, believable, reliable – that applies to situations of trust where someone depends on another person or institution. To say "*x* is credible" is to attribute a disposition to *x* to provide believable information under certain conditions. The usual context for discussions of credibility is epistemological. Questions of credibility are questions about the evidence for a scientific claim, the methods and expertise of a professional, or the accuracy of witness testimony. Credibility is a social virtue because credible people meet expectations. A state of nature is a world without trust. Our need for credible media is part of our need for credible institutions.

The claim of credibility contains a subclaim, what I call "active credibility": the public has a right to actively test the news media's claims of credibility in general and for specific stories. The public should not be limited to passively accepting assurances of credibility; they should have the ability to question procedures so that they can arrive at a reasonable trust in a story or news organization. News media have a duty to facilitate the public's access to information on the evolution of stories, the nature and variety of sources, and possible conflicts of interest.

The second principle is the claim of justifiable consequence, which states that journalists should be able to justify the significant consequences of their actions according to their social contract. They need to include in their calculation the impact of their stories not only on compatriots but on people outside their country. This principle deals not with public expectations that journalists will provide credible reports but that they will consider carefully the harm caused by their reports. Journalists cause unjustifiable harm by publishing false reports or reports distorted by exaggeration and innuendo. Under the claim of justifiable consequence, ethical journalists claim that the consequences of their actions may be justified in three ways: (a) the consequences are insignificant, or ethically neutral (or permissible); (b) the consequences are beneficial to individuals or society; or (c) if the consequences are harmful, then they are necessary given journalism's social functions.

The claim of justifiable consequence in global journalism ethics recognizes the demand for professional responsibility across borders. Almost every profession, and every ethical and legal system, makes the avoidance of unjustifiable harm a basic obligation. All professions cause some harm as part of their normal activity. The physicians' ethical dictum, *primum non nocere* (first, do no harm), is inspiring but, in practice, physicians must harm, e.g., amputate a leg to save a life. Similarly, journalists publish reports on corrupt officials, incompetent professionals, and dangerous products. These stories harm some person or party. In many cases, the harm is outweighed by the benefits. In other cases, not publishing would be a greater harm, amounting to censorship or a failure to inform the public.

The claim of justifiable consequence does not state that journalists should avoid reports that cause harm. It talks instead of harm that is justifiable. Aware that harm cannot be avoided, journalism codes stress the principle of minimizing harm, such as reporting compassionately on families grieving from tragedy. Whether journalists cause justifiable harm depends to a great extent on how they construct their story. Almost any report can have justifiable or non-justifiable consequences. For example, reporting on a criminal trial harms the reputation of the defendant. The reporting, if factual and balanced, is ethically justified because of journalism's role in informing the public about the justice system. On the other hand, a reckless, inaccurate story about the trial is not justified. Issues of story presentation and justifiable consequence loom large in investigative journalism because investigations tend to produce extremely damaging stories, often through the use of deceptive practices such as hidden cameras.

The third principle is the claim of humanity. It translates cosmopolitans' ideal of a common humanity into journalism practice. It is the most important principle for the construction of a global journalism ethics. It deals with the fundamental allegiances of journalists, and their priority ranking. The claim of humanity is: journalists owe their primary allegiance to humanity, not parts of humanity. Journalists owe credible, justifiable journalism to all potential readers of a global public sphere. The claim of humanity extends journalists' loyalty from the public of their hometown and country to humanity at large. Loyalty to humanity trumps other loyalties, where they conflict.

The claim of humanity is the most controversial and ambitious of the three principles. Credibility and justifiable consequence are related to existing norms of truth-seeking and minimizing harm. The claim of humanity introduces a broader public to journalism and makes the strong claim that journalists have a duty to foreigners.

In addition to these three imperatives and three principles, adopting cosmopolitanism changes our understanding of other concepts. To start with, it changes the way we think about journalism's social contract. Cosmopolitan journalism's contract is not just with a particular society; instead, it is a multisociety contract. The cosmopolitan journalist is a transnational public communicator who seeks the trust and credence of a global audience. Also, the ideal of objectivity in news coverage takes on an international sense. Traditionally, news objectivity asks journalists to avoid bias toward groups within one's own country. Global objectivity would discourage allowing bias toward one's country to distort reports on international issues. The ideas of accuracy and balance also become enlarged to include reports with international sources and cross-cultural perspectives. Global journalism also asks journalists to be more conscious of how they frame major stories, how they set the international news agenda, and how they can spark violence in tense societies.

Finally, a cosmopolitan journalism rejects dangerous, inward-looking attitudes such as xenophobia and extreme patriotism. Journalism must not participate in demonizing other groups, especially in times of tension. It was disturbing to see how some news organizations during the Iraq War of 2003 so quickly shucked off their peacetime commitments to independent, impartial reporting as soon as the drums of war started beating. The duty of journalism in times of uncertainty is not a patriotism of blind allegiance or muted criticism. In such times, journalists serve their countries – that is, are patriotic – by continuing to provide independent news and analysis. This dogged determination of journalists to continue to bring a critical attitude toward their country's actions, despite the strong patriotic feelings of their fellow citizens, is an example of what the Spanish philosopher José Ortega y Gasset has called "criticism as patriotism."[14]

The cosmopolitan attitude does not imply that news organizations should ignore local issues or regional audiences. It does not mean that every story requires a cosmopolitan attitude. However, there are situations, such as military intervention in a foreign country, climate change, and the establishment of a fair world trading system, where we need to assess actions from a perspective of global justice and reasonableness. What is at issue is a gradual widening of basic editorial attitudes and standards – a widening of journalists' vision of their responsibilities. It asks them to consider their society's actions, policies, and values from a larger perspective.

Journalism Ethics Naturalized

The three imperatives and three principles provide the broadest possible characterization of the cosmopolitan attitude in journalism. The next step is to show how this general attitude can be specified further by my core ideas.

In chapter 1, I argued that ethics is a natural normative activity that helps humans solve problems, integrate values, validate frameworks, and live rightly. In journalism, as in any significant human activity, questions of correct practice arise due to conflicting values in the lived experience of responsible journalists. In light of such problems, journalists and ethicists are motivated to theorize for the same reasons that ethical theorizing occurs elsewhere. Journalism ethicists aim to integrate values into a consistent framework that helps adjudicate concrete disputes. They seek a reflective equilibrium among the normative concepts of journalism and their intuitions about concrete cases.

If ethics is a normative guidance system for people, journalism ethics is a normative guidance system for journalists, mediating between journalists' perception of a situation and their response. Our normative-guidance system in journalism can be crude or sophisticated, reason-guided or emotive, impartial or biased. The attempt by journalists to be ethical confronts the impediments due to our tragic human life and our composite nature. Responsible journalists, like all ethical people, struggle to be *steadfast* – to do what is right despite the pressure of internal desires and external forces to compromise their principles.[15] Virtue in journalism is as difficult as virtue anywhere.

The tenets of my naturalism apply to the norms of journalistic ethics and its methods of justification. The justification of principles and decisions in journalism relies on natural considerations – the consequences of actions, the requirements of agreements, the satisfaction of desires, and the flourishing of humans in this world. Journalism ethics is not grounded directly or solely on religious doctrine or tradition.[16] Journalistic principles may be supported by particular religious views. For example, the journalistic principle of minimizing harm to the subjects of stories could be accepted by many religious views. But, the primary justification of the principle must be based on naturalistic arguments true to the nature of journalism and about living well – and what sort of society we wish to construct. In this regard, journalism ethics must be a free-standing view similar to Rawls's notion of free-standing principles of justice.

Naturalized journalism ethics is best regarded as embracing constructivism and nonrealism. Ethical statements, judgments, and practical conclusions in journalism are not descriptions of fact that are true or false. They are human affirmations of value and practical proposals for good practice. Ethical judgement in journalism is an action-guiding choice based on ethical reasoning whose conclusions are judged reasonable or correct according to a set of norms and goals. Journalistic principles, such as objectivity or minimizing harm, are fallible, experience-based, general hypotheses about how to organize and integrate our practices so as to achieve the aims of journalism ethics.

Historically, journalism ethics is an ongoing invention of principles to respond ethically to new conditions. Journalism ethics eschews dogmatism. Journalism ethics should reflect the best available natural and scientific knowledge of humans, the best available knowledge of human interaction with media technology, and the best available knowledge of the economics and sociology of human communication.

The reflective engagement of journalists with their ethical problems should be holistic and eclectic, according to the three levels of reflection described in chapter 2. Holistic reflection in journalism ethics should aim at establishing reflective equilibrium in two ways: (1) an equilibrium among journalistic judgments about cases, the framework of journalistic principles, and the aims of journalism ethics; and (2) an equilibrium among the principles of the ethical framework of journalism. Also, reasoning about cases is eclectic. In chapter 2, I used the example of serious allegations against a politician to explain eclectic reasoning about journalism situations.

Promoting Ethical Flourishing

The cosmopolitan attitude is further specified by understanding the claim of humanity as entailing global ethical flourishing. The ultimate ethical aim of journalism is the ultimate aim of ethics. Journalism's aim is to serve humanity by promoting the four levels of flourishing and the principles of justice across borders. Global journalists, as global citizens, seek the individual, social, political, and ethical dignity for humanity at large. They use journalism's powers of investigation and communication for the development of just and participatory political associations. If we adopt a cosmopolitan attitude, the object of democratic journalism also changes. The goal expands beyond the promotion of a just liberal democracy, a well-ordered society at home, to an attempt to establish well-ordered global society, a global community marked both by the development of democracy abroad but also by the development of global democratic institutions and structures.[17] The topic of journalism and democracy is the concern of the next chapter. This chapter focuses on global flourishing through journalism.

Since journalism is a form of public communication, its contribution to ethical flourishing has to do with how it uses its communicative powers in the public sphere to advance ethical goals. Traditional normative approaches to Western journalism have described the goal of journalism more narrowly than ethical flourishing. The goal of journalism is usually described in political terms as serving the public or the public good. Serving the public good is explained in terms of the liberal theory of the press. For example, journalistic communication provides essential information to self-governing citizens, provides a "watchdog" on power, and provides a forum for the exchange of ideas. As we have noted, recent theorizing has added to these functions, such as empowering minorities or supporting caring human relations. The concept of the public good in these characterizations is my third level of the good – the political goods.

The political representation of journalism's ethical goal as a liberal democratic conception of serving the public good is correct as far as it goes, but it is incomplete. Journalism should serve other ends that are not strictly political such as the goods on the on the other levels of flourishing. I argue in the next chapter that the political dimension of journalism's activity is of great importance, but a full theory of journalism's ethics goal should start with the larger idea of ethical flourishing and show how the many forms of journalism can, collectively, promote this ideal. By using the four-level concept of the human good, journalists encourage a holistic evaluation of social policies while critiquing governmental, educational, and other initiatives that are defended by a single narrow criteria such as economic efficiency.

Applying the Four Levels

How can a cosmopolitan journalism contribute to something as philosophical and abstract as ethical flourishing in a well-ordered society? By contributing to human development across the four levels. I now describe how journalism can advance each level. To simplify, I divide the four levels into two tasks, the task of promoting the rational and the reasonable. The task of promoting the rational is the task of promoting levels 1 and 2 (individual and common goods). These two levels correspond to the capacity to carry out rational plans of life, which represents a level of enlightened prudence and sociability. The task of promoting the reasonable is the task of promoting a well-ordered society, which comprises levels 3 and 4, the public and ethical goods.

PROMOTING THE RATIONAL

Journalism promotes the rational good by inquiring into and promoting the individual and common goods, including Rawls's primary goods – the goods that all citizens must have to pursue other goods. Journalism provides valuable information about the world for the pursuit of rational plans by individuals, groups, and societies. Journalism also draws attention to the levels of physical, rational, and moral capacity provided by a society at a given time. Journalism can promote individual goods in at least three ways.

(1) *Provide information on (and an analysis of) world events and trends*. Journalism should be occupied with providing timely, accurate, and contextual information on political, social, and economic developments, from reports on new legislation and political instability to news of global trends in business and environment. This information is the basis for the deliberation of autonomous citizens.

(2) *Monitor basic levels of physical, individual, and social dignity*. Physical dignity: journalism has a duty to help citizens be aware of society's current ability to provide for all citizens a decent level of physical goods such as food, shelter, health, wealth, a reasonable length of life, and physical security through effective laws (and regulatory agencies) to protect the vulnerable.

Rational and moral dignity: similarly, journalism has a duty to provide the same information on, and public scrutiny of, a society's ability to assist citizens in the development of their rational and moral capacities. This duty requires journalistic inquiry into the educational system's effectiveness in developing rational and imaginative citizens, the capacity of the social fabric to develop citizens' emotional capacity through supportive communities, and the capacity of the public sphere to develop citizens' rational capacities through opportunities for philosophical, scientific, and cultural engagement.

Journalism has a duty to bring forward for debate the fairness of existing physical, social, and educational opportunities. By using a variety of metrics and by making cross-cultural comparisons, journalism can contribute to society's self-monitoring of its progress in these areas.

(3) *Investigate inequality*. Journalism has a duty to conduct in-depth investigative stories on people and groups who have been denied physical, rational, and moral dignity. It reveals whether gender, ethnicity, and other differences account for inequalities. By exploring below the surface of society, journalism promotes citizens' awareness of how egalitarian their society is, and the impact of policies on human development and dignity.

In addition to promoting individual rational plans of life and the development of individual capacities, journalism should promote the common goods. It has a duty to report on, analyze, and critique the ways in which citizens interact and create associations so as to enjoy the goods of social cooperation. The common goods of level 2 involve the sort of economic and social interaction that allows for capacity development and goods not achievable by individuals or small groups on their own.

Journalism should promote these goods in at least five ways:

(1) *Report critically on economic associations*. Journalism has a duty to report on and analyze how a free society allows citizens to participate and benefit from its various forms of economic association, including fair economic competition. It needs to monitor the use of economic power and its effect on egalitarian democracy and the principles of justice.

(2) *Assess the quality of social life*. Journalism should report on the types of social life, social and technological trends, and social possibilities available for citizens. It should inquire into whether such trends nurture caring relationships, meaningful collective activity, and flourishing communities.

(3) *Assist social bridging*. In a pluralistic world, journalism has a duty to act as a bridge between diverse classes, ethnic groups, religions, and cultures within and among countries. Journalism has a two-fold task to make visible, for consideration and critique, both the commonalities and the differences among citizens, and to encourage tolerant but frank cross-cultural discussion of issues.

(4) *Assist media literacy and the evaluation of media.* Journalism has a duty to inquire into the impact of journalism, media, and communication technology on society, and how new communication technology and new forms of journalism can be used to advance ethical flourishing and the social goods.

(5) *Use global comparisons.* Journalism has a duty to evaluate the level of human and social goods among countries and to investigative different approaches to major social problems. In this way, journalism is a force for progressive ideas and "experiments in living."

In summary, journalism promotes the rational good when it promotes a society where there is substantial individual and social dignity, where citizens have free and equal opportunity to pursue plans of life. Ethical journalism uses its communicative abilities to ensure that all citizens have an opportunity to pursue a fulfilling life characterized by social self-respect, equality, and dignity.

PROMOTING THE REASONABLE

Journalism can and should also promote the reasonable aspect of the human goods. To promote the reasonable means to nurture the development of morally reasonable citizens willing to discuss essential issues objectively and fairly and to nurture a society where the pursuit of the rational side of life is restrained within fair and effective principles of justice. Journalism promotes the reasonable when it promotes the political and ethical goods that form a major part of the four levels of the human good. Journalism can promote the political goods in at least four ways:

(1) *Critique the basic structure.* Journalism of the public good has a duty to inquiry into and to encourage deliberation upon fundamental justice. Journalism should report on society's basic structure and how well principles of justice are embodied by institutions, political processes, and the legal system. Journalism should address the fact of pluralism – how principles of justice relate to a plurality of comprehensive conceptions of life.

(2) *Monitor the basic liberties.* Journalism has a duty to promote and defend basic liberties and to ask to what extent citizens are able to enjoy the full value of basic liberties, such as freedom of speech, freedom of association, freedom from discrimination, and other constitutional protections. Are citizens able to exercise these

freedoms for the purpose of self-development and to enjoy the goods on levels 1, 2, and 3?

(3) *Encourage participation.* Journalism needs to monitor (and help to make possible) citizen participation in public life and their ability to have a meaningful influence on debate about government decisions. Journalism should engage in various forms of "civic" journalism that enhance public involvement in basic social issues and discourage public cynicism about civic engagement.[18]

(4) *Report on diversity and representation.* Journalism has a duty to insist on, and to help make possible, a diverse public forum with adequate representation of non-dominant groups. Journalism must be self-conscious about how groups can use language to manipulate, stereotype, and persuade citizens unethically. Through the media, powerful groups can dominate the public sphere.

Journalism contributes to the goods of level 4, the ethical goods, by helping to produce citizens with the ethical capacity and disposition to make ethical flourishing (including the public good) their primary aim. The role of journalism is to encourage citizens to seek goods beyond the goods of rationality or enlightened self-interest, or even loyalty to one's ethnic or religious group. Journalism needs to contribute to the public sphere in a way that promotes a primary loyalty to a just and well-ordered society.

Ethical journalism must be concerned with the development of the central ethical capacity: the Rawlsian capacity to be disposed, as individuals or as groups of citizens, to rationally pursue the good in creative, free, and self-fulfilling ways within the bounds of justice. Journalism must seek the congruence of the rational and reasonable as elements of ethical flourishing, to seek the good and the right in ethical flourishing.

In developing these levels, journalism has a two-fold task. One is to promote the free and creative self-realization of liberal citizens in the spirit of Mill. Journalism should promote liberal, autonomous persons fulfilling their capacities. Journalism should oppose social structures that would unduly limit creative plans of life. At the same time, journalism has a simultaneous commitment to liberal ideas of equality and justice. It should support not only creative, energetic individuals but also a reasonable citizenry and reasonable discussion in pursuit of just social arrangements.

Journalism, from an ethical perspective, is not only about free-doms and rights; that is, helping people to seek their goods. Nor is it just about supporting communal solidarity, justice, or "harmonious" structures.[19] It is about constantly seeking to *combine* the rational and reasonable, the pursuit of the goods and the just structures that allow and restrain such a pursuit. Journalism is neither about free speech nor any particular freedom or basic right; it is concerned with a family of rights and values, which include equality and jus-tice. Journalism ethics is neither libertarian nor communitarian; it is both. It seeks to support the good in the right and the right in the good. It should help societies deal with the precarious and difficult task of finding ways to balance these ethical ideals. In this view, jus-tice is a sort of freedom, or it is a condition of freedom.

UNIVERSALS AND INVENTION

Problems of Universals

So far in this chapter, I have putting forward a number of aims for global journalism in general. I have not dealt with the status of these values as universal principles. A skeptic could demand that I explain in what sense I understand these values to be universal. Given the diversity of forms of journalism and media cultures around the world, the difficult issue of universal values in journalism cannot be avoided.

Questions about universals are difficult because they involve three types of issues. One issue is philosophical. Must global journalism ethics solve the age-old problem of universals in ethics? The problem goes as far back as Plato's famous confrontation with the sophists of his time. What are universals? Do we construct or discover uni-versals?[20] Realists tend to favour the discovery approach while anti-realists tend to favour a constructionist approach.[21]

A second issue is sociological. To what extent do different cultures (or journalists) share ethical values? A third issue is political. What are the political and cultural implications of asserting universal prin-ciples? Societies have justified their imperial domination of other cultures by arguing that their values are universal. Critics of global journalism ethics worry that the proposed values will turn out to be the values of Western journalism, imposed on media systems with-out regard to cultural differences.

My invention approach to ethics and my modest relativism favours a constructivist approach. I cannot hope to solve the difficult issues surrounding universals in this chapter. However, I can explain how my global ethics regards universal principles and avoids various objections.

What Is a Universal Principle?

My ethical constructivism combines constructivism and universalism. It recognizes the important role of universal principles in ethics, yet it regards such principles as constructions of human valuing and reasoning. I have appealed to universal principles concerning human development as a part of human nature. I have proposed three imperatives as universal principles.

Universal principles are factual or normative. Factual universals are principles about the natural world, such as scientific laws or principles of human development. Normative universals take three forms. One form is a universal or "exception-less" fact about value. For example, anthropological inquiry may discover that, as a matter of fact, all members of a society or all humans share certain ethical values – without exception.

A second form of normative universal is what we might call a "rational normative principle." It is a principle that rational people *should* or *ought* to hold universally. It is a principle that is binding on all members of a group, such as an ethical principle of medicine or a principle regarded as binding on all humans, such as Kant's categorical imperative. A rational universal is not a factual universal since it does not presume or require that all members of the relevant group affirm it. There may be exceptions – dissenters who ignore or reject the principle. A rational universal is also not justified by an empirical survey of opinions but rather by reason or some form of normative argument. It is what Kant called a "fact of reason."[22] Reason (or some other faculty) says the principle is universal and binding, whether or not some individuals disagree. Dissention is usually explained as due to ignorance, irrationality, or unethical personality. The universal moral laws of society put forward by natural law theorists as rationally binding on all humans are examples of such rational universals.

A third kind of universals, a kind endorsed by my theory, are contractual universals. One can see a contractual universal as a kind of rational universal. Contractual universals are constructed and established by a contractual form of rationality. A contractual principle, such as Rawls's first principle of justice, is a universal principle arrived at by a fair and rational procedure for identifying, deliberating about, and affirming the principle. A contractual universal is advanced not as an established fact but rather as a practical hypothesis or proposal, to be fairly scrutinized and evaluated. To affirm a contractual universal is to claim that fair and rational deliberation shows (or could show) that the principle should be recognized and honoured by all parties.

A contractual universal is not a factual universal because its validity is not dependant on the fact that everyone embraces the principle, critically or non-critically. It resembles a fact of reason in requiring rational justification over and above the fact that (some or all) people accept it. The contractual universal is a "fact of reason" if "reason" refers to a rational procedures and methods of evaluation.

The "should" or "ought" of a contractual normative universal is not a metaphysical necessity. It is not absolute. The principle is not justified because it is in harmony with some external moral order, or justified by some other non-natural reason. It is the result of fair procedure of evaluation. The "should" of a contractual universal is the result of the imperfect evaluative procedures and rational restraints of ethics, as discussed in previous chapters. It is put forward epistemically as a reasonable proposal for guiding human interaction in some domain, or to guide human thinking about the ethical dimension of some practical problem. A contractual universal is a judgment, or proposal, of practical reason.

Contractual universals also display another important feature. They are proposed as basic principles that carry out an epistemic and social function. The epistemic role is that of an anchor for our ethical conceptual scheme and for our ethical reasoning. The social role is that of providing common ground for deliberation.

On my pragmatic approach, the most important feature of universals is not their ontological nature – whether universals exist in Plato's heaven or not – but whether the universal principle plays a pivotal epistemological role in ethical conceptual schemes. The issue about universals is not its nature or what type of entity the concept refers to, but rather the practical question of whether the principle can play a useful role in our reflective engagement with ethics. It is in this sense of a basic contractual universal that I propose, for example, the adoption of the claim of humanity, the idea of ethical flourishing, and the three imperatives of a cosmopolitan attitude.

A universal contractual principle is not discovered by some philosophical insight into the nature of reality. A universal contractual principle is constructed and then established among reasonable people through ethical argument and reasoning. We need a normative argument as to why a certain principle should be accepted as a basic action-guiding tool.

To say that x is a universal normative principle is a covert way of saying it *should* be a universal. It is to say that x is justified or normatively worthy of being affirmed as a universal principle in the conceptual scheme of group y, according to our best normative arguments. We need to show that a principle is worthy because the fact that some principle is affirmed or that some value is shared is insufficient to establish the validity of a normative universal. Widely accepted values may be problematic. For example, we might discover that all cultures have high degrees of tolerance for violence against women. Is this a universal we wish to enshrine in our ethics? What if we find a consensus among journalists that their primary role is to support their country, right or wrong, in times of war, and that role trumps objectivity and truth-testing? Is this a principle we wish to affirm? A principle should be considered basic because it plays a *normatively justified role* in our ethical thinking and decision making.

What is this normatively justified role? Proposed principles can be affirmed as worthy universal principles only if they are capable of playing expressive, epistemic, and pragmatic roles.[23] A candidate plays an expressive role if the role expresses a key element in our ethical vision of how humans should live together. It expresses such a central element of our ethical identity that we consider it worthy of being universally affirmed. For instance, the principle of liberty expresses a crucial element of the liberal's worldview, and the moral dignity of humans is fundamental to Kantian ethics. A principle serves an epistemic function if it is of sufficient generality and logical fecundity that it supports the more specific principles and norms of our ethical framework.[24] For example, a bedrock belief in the perfection of human capacities implies the development of our rationality through education.

Finally, a principle plays a pragmatic role if it is useful in deliberation. A principle that is universally affirmed but is of little use in helping us deliberate about situations would be superfluous. We use basic principles to clarify and address issues in practice, to balance values, and to support more specific professional standards. For example, the idea of social responsibility in journalism is basic for many ethicists not only because the principle resonates with their worldview but also because, pragmatically, it helps them deliberate about issues. Similarly, we might use Kant's categorical imperative, to never use humans merely as a means, as a guide in sorting out journalistic issues such as protecting confidential sources or minimizing harm to the sources of stories.

To summarize: to say that x is a universal principle is to make the normative claim that x is worthy of being affirmed by all relevant people; to say that x is worthy of being affirmed is to be ready to provide a persuasive normative argument for why this principle should play a basic role in our ethical framework. The argument must show that the candidate principle satisfies, to some tolerable degree, the role criteria just named.

Therefore, ethical constructivism is compatible with the existence of universal principles, if universals are understood as normatively justified affirmations of basic values and action-guiding principles. Ethical constructionism is compatible with the attempt to develop universal principles, regarded as fertile hypothesis about how to better organize conduct in a domain. For its part, a global journalism ethics proposes a set of normatively justified basic principles, or contractual universals. Global journalism ethics seeks to express universal principles.

Invention or Discovery

My discussion of contractual universals as "facts of practical reason" implies a view about whether principles are invented or discovered. Despite my support for invention, I reject certain ways of thinking about the invention-discovery distinction because they oversimplify the relation of normative and factual ways of reasoning.

What I reject is a traditional realism in metaethics. This realism creates a false dilemma: either ethical principles and values exist independently in reality apart from the human mind and its inventive capabilities or there *are* no valid ethical values or principles. Everything in ethics is radically subjective or relative. I believe there is a way to recognize both invention and discovery in ethics while avoiding simplistic dualisms.

My constructivism asserts that universal ethical values are not discovered; they are values that are formulated, evaluated, and affirmed. They are ontologically dependant on the human mind and practical reason. This view of universals is consistent with the possibility of an empirical discovery that all people share some values. This discovery would not show that these values are independent of the human creation of values. It only shows a convergence of value judgments. All or many people have come to affirm this ethical statement or principles. My naturalized ethics is well-positioned to explain this sort of agreement on values. Given a common human nature and a common world, we should expect to find agreement on some values and principles, and also disagreement.

Naturalized ethics can reject the idea that universals are discovered in the world while recognizing the importance of facts about ethical values around the world. Natural knowledge about the world plays an important role in suggesting what sorts of things should be valued and proposed as ethical principles. The discovery of major trends and scientific laws should inform ethical thinking and theory. Sociological discoveries about shared values suggest that these values are useful to many types of human conditions and should be affirmed as basic principles for ethical reasoning.[25]

This method of constructing ethical notions from natural facts and discoveries was the method that I used to construct the idea of ethical flourishing from natural facts about human development and flourishing. Reflecting on the nurturing of human capacities, I constructed, affirmed, and argued for ethical flourishing as a basic value concept. I did not discover ethical flourishing or invent it out of nothing. Using our best available natural knowledge, I constructed an ethical concept that I *proposed* as a basic principle.

Factual universals are discovered. Contractual universals are constructed. The materials of construction are often suggested by natural knowledge. Factual universals highlight aspects of human behaviour and human society that are worthy of being affirmed ethically across borders. There is a place in ethics for discoveries about ourselves and the world, but this doesn't mean that discoveries are identical with ethical constructions. For example, I may come to see the value of the development of human capacities and I make them basic principles of my ethical theory. But I do not confuse the fact of these capacities with their value for me and ethics. To adopt the ethical stance is to bring to bear on our natural experiences and

knowledge a different form of reasoning and experience characterized by invention, valuing, and normative reasons.

Combining invention and discovery in ethics allows me to look
favourably upon a recent trend in the study of universals. This trend
is the search for universal values rooted in some deep, universal facts
about humans. It seeks universals in fundamental human experiences
and action, and in the presuppositions of human communication or
reasoning. Kwasi Wiredu, for example, finds "cultural universals" in
communication and elsewhere.[26]

A related approach regards value systems as different expressions of a certain type of universal called a "protonorm." Clifford G.
Christians holds that that global ethics must be grounded in universals, such as the sacredness of life, which is honoured in all cultures.
For Christians, these universal values are protonorms – fundamental
commitments grounded in who we are as humans-in-relation. They
are the values of "universal being." The implication is that these universals are not constructed but discovered. They are not hypotheses
but fundamental presuppositions of human living and communication prior to their articulation as explicit principles and theories.[27]

My inventionism thinks that the protonorm approach to universals is valuable, even though I do not think that it shows that these
protonorms, as they stand, amount to a discovery of universal ethical principles existing "out there." It may be a discovery of a universal in nature but, in my view, to become an ethical principle we
need a normative argument as to why it is worthy of being a basic
principle. Protonorms point to important aspects of human life that
suggest candidates for contractual universals. Just as facts about
human flourishing moved me to construct ethical principles around
flourishing – to propose them as worthy of being basic principles –
so can the inquiry into protonorms of communication and culture
indicate possible new and inventive principles for global ethics. I do
not confuse the fact of the protonorms with my decision to place
ethical value on the protonorms, or to formulate them as candidates
for basic ethical principles.

A positive feature of the protonorm approach is that it avoids the
idea that universals are transcendent of all particulars. It avoids the
criticism that universal principles ignore or abstract from important local contexts and variations. Universal values as protonorms
are embedded in human action and communication. They can be
expressed in many ways by different cultures.[28] In a plural world,

a theory of universals needs a way of thinking about the construction and applications of universal principles as an intimate dialogue between the general and specific, the global and the local. For example, there is much work to be done in showing how universal principles in journalism ethics, from objectivity to freedom of expression, can be sensitive to local variations in journalism culture and media systems.

The same challenge of the relation of the global and local confronts the theory of human rights where we attempt to apply universal principles to varying cultural and political situations. Ivison has proposed an "emergent universalism" where aboriginal and other cultures enter into a rich dialogue with liberal universal notions of human rights. Through this dialogue we come to new understandings of how universal notions are related to, and can be defined by, these "local" practices.[29]

My naturalism, therefore, encourages investigations into common aspects of human nature and society. Ethical construction is not creation *ex nihlo*. It benefits from well-conducted research into common values held by people, cultures, and codes. When constructionists look for values and principles, they look not only into the solitude of their own minds but to facts about shared values and facts about the common human condition. For example, Martha Nussbaum developed universal principles for her cosmopolitan ethics by looking to human capacities in development literature.[30]

We should adopt more complex ways of thinking about inventing and discovering. Traditional notions of discovering ethical principles and values "out there" are based on an incorrect view of objectivity in ethics that requires correspondence with fact rather than a fair process of evaluating our values. Traditional notions of discovery obscure the important point that basic values can be challenged and, at times, should be reformed. Often in ethics, the proposed universal principle is not accepted by all so the point of the discussion is not to announce the "discovery" of some principle but to argue persuasively for its rational affirmation. In global journalism ethics, for example, we may propose new values that are embraced by a minority of forward-looking journalists, such as the idea that journalists should "act as agents of a global public sphere." We may propose a controversial basic principle, e.g., that journalists should abandon their patriotism, or limit it, in times of war. We should recall that there was a time when the idea of journalists as objective was a novel and controversial proposal. It was not discovered and then adopted. In such circumstances, we do not discover or "find" such principles but, rather, construct them and put them forward as a hypotheses or conjectures on how a changing domain of activity should be ethically guided. We propose and evaluate these principles as worthy of common affirmation and engage in the rhetorical process of building agreement around new ideas.

My answer to the question "Are values made or discovered?" follows the answer provided by Putnam: "We make ways of dealing with problematic situations and we discover which ones are better and which worse."[31] Ethical inquiry, like all inquiry, should straddle dichotomies, bringing together the empirical and normative, mind and world, value and knowledge, discovery and interpretation. The project of ethics should be guided by a sophisticated epistemology that avoids dualisms and finds a role for discovering and inventing. The question "Are values made or discovered?" is a *bad* question if it presumes a dichotomy in ethical inquiry between empirical and interpretive activities, between objective facts and subjective values.

Critical Perspectives

The preceding section explains my position on universals as elements of ethical reasoning and knowledge. What about political concerns about the misuse of universals for imperial or colonial purposes? I believe my appeal to universals and the broad ideals of my ethical theory are global and non-imperialistic. As noted, the aims allow for wide variation in the expression of human capacities on four levels. The cosmopolitan attitude and principle are values and aims that could be adopted by many forms of journalists, codes of ethics, and media systems. The contractual approach of evaluating universals in journalism (and ethics) encourages non-imperialistic, non-dominating discussions and the widest inclusion of different voices.

Ideas about ethical flourishing and well-ordered society cannot be easily turned into Western imperialistic or ideological weapons. To the contrary, cosmopolitan journalism and its global ethics encourage the sort of "de-Westernization" of journalism and media ethics called for by critical and postmodern theories of media.[32] Such theories ask: how can discussion around a global ethics be open to many perspectives, including non-Western values? Critical theories warn that Western ideas of enlightenment and reason can be used to justify imperialistic and colonizing purposes. Fourie writes: "It [the postmodern view] starts from the view that institutionalized knowledge and theories about issues such as race, class, gender, sexuality, and the media are/were subject to forces of colonialism."[33]

My foundation for global journalism ethics can take these criticisms on board, since it sees the widening of the conceptual base of journalism ethics and the cultural widening of its practices as part of the transformation of the field. One implication of critical and postcolonial theory for journalism ethics is that scholars should consider other ethical foundations. For example, some writers have examined whether the African tradition of ubuntuism should be the fundamental ethical value for African journalism, since ubuntuism's communal values are more in line with African society than with the Western ideal of a free press. De-Westernization also means using cross-cultural comparisons when discussing the principles of media ethics, and giving due weight to African, Indian, and Eastern ethical systems. A global journalism ethics should favour cross-cultural approaches to media studies and the teaching and practice of journalism.

Another implication is that journalism ethics should place more emphasis on the representation of others since misrepresentation can spark wars, demean other cultures, and support unjust social structures. Such issues go beyond factual accuracy and fairness. They require journalists to have a deeper cultural knowledge and a deeper appreciation of how language can distort "the other."[34] Paying attention to issues of representation means questioning everyday news practices that exclude less powerful voices. It means defining "news" to include issues of social justice and their historical context, not only daily events and facts. It means seeking a greater diversity of sources in stories, and telling such stories from the perspective of non-dominant groups. Paying attention to issues of representation also means questioning the everyday news practices that routinely exclude less powerful voices. This means defining "news" to include issues of social justice and their historical context, not just daily events and facts. Again, these new or different practices should be part of the cosmopolitan reconception of journalism ethics.

I do not wish to give the impression that the incorporation of new paradigms and critical ideas into global journalism ethics is easily accomplished. There is serious theoretical work to be done. It is one thing to say that these implications are consistent with my foundation and quite another to show in detail how such ideas can find a clear and "radicalizing" presence in a cosmopolitan theory of journalism. A foundation for global journalism ethics must formulate its principles and aims so that it expresses sincerely a true global perspective, not a colonial or national perspective disguised as a global philosophy.

CONCLUSION

The chapter has outlined the approach, content, and aims of a global journalism ethics that adopts cosmopolitanism and the core ideas of my ethical approach. The next two chapters put "meat on the bones" of this outline. Chapter 5 explains how journalism can promote global democracy while chapter 6 develops a theory of patriotism for global journalism.

5

Global Democratic Journalism

The care of human life and happiness and not their destruction is the first and only object of good government.

Thomas Jefferson[1]

In this chapter, I develop one component of my global journalism ethics as outlined in the previous chapter. I explain in greater detail how journalism can honour in its practice the theory of right of chapter 3, which is the aim of well-ordered society. In particular, I explain how global journalism should serve the political goods, or the goods of democratic and just political association, one of the four levels of flourishing.

The chapter has four parts: an overview of the links between well-ordered society and democracy; the idea of a public and the public good; the notion of global democracy; and how journalism serves a democratic public.

DEMOCRATIC PUBLIC

Political Goods

A normative theory of democracy describes how democracy should be structured to promote flourishing and justice. Therefore, normative democratic theory is part of a conception of the right. The theory explains how right relations among people are best embodied in a historically contingent political entity – a democratic society. Normative democratic theory is the political aspect of a theory of right. The idea of right relations among citizens goes beyond the idea of correct political relations among citizens. Although questions of what is right is associated with civil society and its laws, there are questions concerning what is right among the members of a family, private association, or church.

I believe that the form of government that best serves ethical flourishing in general, and social justice in particular, is a well-ordered liberal democracy. An egalitarian liberal democracy is the political structure of a well-ordered society. To promote this well-ordered society is to promote the political goods of level 3 of ethical flourishing, the political goods of democratic self-governance.

In chapters 3 and 4, there were two discussions that are relevant to a democratic theory for global journalism ethics. One was chapter 3's elaboration of ethical flourishing as the congruence of a Rawlsian well-ordered society with a four-level notion of the human good. The other was chapter 4's discussion of how journalism can promote the rational and reasonable aspects of citizens and their polity.

Recall that I have defined a well-ordered society in terms of a well-ordered liberal democracy. The former consisted in a transparent democracy where government is under the effective control of citizens, not political leaders, bureaucracies, or powerful corporations. Institutions are regulated by fair terms of cooperation, and the basic structure follows egalitarian principles of justice. The principles are justifiable by contracting in an "original position" or by reaching an overlapping consensus on political free-standing principles amid different comprehensive views. This well-ordered democracy also has free and equal citizens. Citizens are disposed to be reasonable when dealing with fundamental issues. To be reasonable is to be disposed to discuss fundamental issues under the objective standards of public reason.

In chapter 4, I suggested some ways in which this abstract description of a just society can be understood in terms of concrete political activities and goods. I said that the political goal of journalism is to add political dignity to individual and social dignity. Journalism on the third level of flourishing is focused on the political structure of society. It is not enough for journalism to provide information for individual plans of life or to support community. It is not enough that journalists publish sports scores or today's stock market results. It is not enough to follow the latest entertainment trends. Democratic journalism has to consider the overall political structure of civic life and the civic character of its citizens. Journalism investigates the justice of the state according to Rawlsian concerns about constitutional rights and liberties, the clarity and application of principles of justice, and the distribution of social advantages. Journalists at this level ask whether their country (or another country) is a well-ordered society. Journalism must conduct difficult investigations into what lies below the surface of the daily news – the economic and political structures that are the framework for our lives.

This approach to democratic journalism attempts to define more clearly the common idea that journalists should serve the public good. To be theoretically adequate, the approach needs to say more about how it conceives of "the public" and the "public good." There exists a good deal of skepticism about such concepts in today's pluralistic world. The next section defines these key terms before addressing the question of the aim of political journalism in a cosmopolitan mode.

Political Association

A "public" is the creation of a certain form of political association. Thus, to understand the idea of a public we need to understand the nature of political association. Society is the origin, location, and support system for innumerable types of human associations, from families and private clubs to religious organizations and scientific societies. Humans gain their identity and morality from being in society and its different forms of association. They have, as Rawls says, "no prior identity before being in society." But we should not understand society as simply a means to individual needs and goals. Rawls thinks it is trivial to say that humans need society to learn language, participate in science and culture, and so on. More interesting is the fact that humans in society develop intrinsic social values. They have shared final ends, common activities, and institutions valued for themselves. Humans need one another as partners in ways of life that are engaged in for their own sake. The enjoyments of others are necessary for and complimentary to my own good.[2]

Within society, there are many forms of social unions where people share (1) final ends and common activities valued for themselves and (2) rules on how the final ends should be achieved.[3] Having the same desire is not enough. During the US Civil War, Grant and Lee both desired to hold Richmond but they were not members of the same social union. In fact, conflict may arise when people desire the same things, such as money, power, or status. Members of a social union must also agree to follow fair rules, or "an agreed scheme of conduct in which the excellences and talents of each are complimentary to the good of all." Rawls writes: "The essential thing is that there be a shared final end and accepted ways of advancing it which allows for the public recognition of the attainments of everyone."[4] Artistic associations and scientific research projects are examples of associations that are social unions entered into freely, as are friendships, churches, political parties, and private clubs. Even games, such as baseball, can be seen as a social union devoted to shared ends and norms. The shared end of all players is that there should be a fair and excellent game, and this requires that the game be played according to the rules. For some social unions, the ends and norms may be the ends and norms of comprehensive views. The norms of a community of monks are set by their comprehensive religious view of life. Members of some associations, such as small communities or families, establish emotional ties that support the unity of the association and cause them to care more for each other than for strangers.

Society is system of cooperation among these many social unions, "a social union of social unions."[5] It is the most inclusive social union, with distinct ends and means. Societies also are the location of political associations. The political association of society as a whole applies to all citizens and defines their political interactions. The political association includes more specific political associations such as political parties.

A well-ordered democracy brings the many social unions together in a specific manner. It provides a framework within which social unions (for example, associations, families, communities) can fairly pursue their goods. The public is a special form of association. The public is the most inclusive group of all – the association of citizens. Democratic political society is a special way of integrating and unifying people as citizens. It is the broadest category of denizens of a society.[6]

Political association is a general form of association that abstracts from specific similarities and differences among social groups. The members of a political association belong to different and more particular associations, from golf clubs and stamp collecting fraternities to religious and ethnic groups. The members of these particular groups are members of the broader political association. They live under and share a set of political principles, power-sharing structures, and political aims. The rules of political association – for example, the constitution and the rules of law – are intended to supersede the rules of other forms of association when they conflict and when questions of control and power are concerned. Among these citizens, some people act as political officials and are organized into institutions for carrying out the laws and goals of political association and performing the various functions of government. These officials and their institutions are the state. Their role is to advance the goals of political association. Officials and institutions are individual and corporate agents who do political business for others.

Political association is association for the sake of ordering and controlling the relations among these social unions. Political association deals with the use of coercive state power, basic rights and privileges, laws and their enforcement, the distribution of resources and advantages, and the basic structure of society. Therefore, political association is about power, social control, and mechanisms for the resolution of disputes. Political association seeks to manage and control actions that have a political interest, in much the same sense in which Mill and Dewey spoke of public actions as actions in which society has a legitimate interest in controlling. Politics is the often familiar practices by which power among social unions is obtained, exercised, shared, and validated. Political association is not needed in every form of association. Some associations, such as a family, are too small to need the formal mechanisms of political association found in large states.[7] But even relatively small social unions need structure to organize the effort of members and to encourage an interest in their goals. As Dewey says, associations generate an interest in the management of affairs for a common good.[8]

Political association is needed when there is a need to organize citizens across many social unions, that is, to organize large numbers of people within a region. Where the actions of individuals or groups affect each other, politics – the negotiation of interests and rights – begins. The origin of politics is the same as the origin of justice, as we saw with Hume and Rawls. A lack of sufficient human beneficence and resources, combined with differing interests among people, calls for a political structure and rules of justice to allow cooperation.

Therefore, we can define a political association as a group of people within a society who live under a set of political rules and institutions for the purpose of coordinating and controlling the activity of their more particular associations and interests. "Political" refers to the political relations among citizens. "Political goods" are the goods that come from the proper political management of their social unions.

Political associations are distinguished by their political ends and their means of accomplishing them. Different forms of political life reflect different ways of structuring power relations among citizens. A democratic constitution, for instance, summarizes what those relations should be in terms of fundamental principles and institutions. Historically, societies have set up many forms of political association for the sake of social control, ranging from tribal chiefdoms, absolute despots, and aristocracies to constitutional monarchs and various kinds of democracies.

The Public

The idea of a public is political in two senses. A public is political in terms of its origins. It only emerges from the establishment of a certain political association in a society. It is also political in its meaning and particular form in a society. That is, the political structure of a society determines what being a public means for citizens. Who is a member of the public, what privileges accrue to being a member of the public, and so forth are defined by specific forms of political association.

I reserve the term "a public" for citizens of a society who have the capacity and opportunity to be members of a democratic political association in ways that are both participatory and just. A true public exists, and true public goods are enjoyed, only where a flourishing democracy exists. The meaning of "a public" has to do with these capacities for meaningful and reasonable democratic action.

Therefore, the reference of "a public" is not the members of any political association, even if such members sometimes act in public, because such membership is not sufficient to amount to a well-ordered, flourishing, democratic society. A king, a despot, or an oligopoly of aristocrats may claim that they and their officials constitute a state and represent the public. Also, there have been empires which existed politically due to the forced rule of taxes and soldiers, and the words "state" and "the public" are used. In these societies, the characteristic signs of a public are absent.[9] The vast majority of members of society have little or no say in the political process, the relations among social unions are unjust, the institutions are closed to participation by many, and the goals of political association are only nominally in the public good. The real goal is the benefit of the few. It does not matter if the members of such societies appear to give tacit consent to their political associations insofar as they go along peacefully with current arrangements. A public is citizens who give explicit and free agreement to a political structure that they recognize as fair to all. Where there is no public, the members of society may be a mass, a multitude, subjects of a king, or a people.

Historically, there have been other examples of a public, such as the public of ancient Athens and Rome. A democratic public incorporates many of the features of such older forms, the right to active participation in decision-making and the right to hold public office. But a democratic public exhibits additional features such as extending membership in the public to the widest possible number.

The public is defined by two features. First, a public is a political association where members enjoy active and meaningful participation in the political processes. Members of the public have substantial representation in government and they can have significant influence on discussions on essential matters. To act as a citizen is to be engaged in issues about the common good, the means to that good, justice, and the direction of the commonwealth. I do not act as a citizen (or member of the public) simply by consuming goods, running a business, or enjoying a private moment with my family. To belong to the public is to belong to society's broadest association – a public that is concerned with how citizens govern and are governed, according to the standards of a well-ordered liberal democracy.

Second, a public seeks influence in a certain manner that demands virtue and fairness. The public is a political association where members ensure that their active participation contributes to a fair association for all members. Members of a public are disposed to be reasonable in the exercise of their influence and in their participation in the political process. While they may pursue the interests of their own group or causes, this pursuit does not take precedence over the public good of all, where the two pursuits conflict. Members of this ideal public see voting as a duty to support not just candidates that might provide them or their special group with money or services but also candidates who are best equipped to serve the public good of all.

Ideally, the public consists of Rawlsian citizens. They are free and equal citizens who seek a well-ordered society by developing and fusing their rational and moral capacities. Rawlsian citizens support a well-ordered, flourishing society. A public consists of active and reasonable citizens committed to reciprocity and fairness in the society's basic political structure. Active citizens avoid the passivity of political subjects. Political activity by itself is not sufficient for well-ordered democracy since citizens may be only rational and motivated to act unjustly by their own interests.

The goal of an active public should be human flourishing within an increasing democratization of society. The members of the public, then, have a democratic duty to take an interest in their political process and to help assess and improve their basic political and social structures. The citizen's duty is to engage in fair public deliberation on important issues, allowing minorities and other viewpoints to be heard. Like the journalist, a member of the public has a duty to approach issues from the public stance, not merely from the perspective of their own interests.

In my theory, the concepts of the public and well-ordered democracy are inseparable. Members of the public are members of a participatory, egalitarian, democratic association under fair principles of justice that encourage ethical flourishing. Under the first feature, participation, members of the public are not simply subjects of the king, members of families, consumers of goods, and workers in the economy occupying various social and economic classes. Despite their differences and their different associations, they are united in being members of a political group. They are citizens engaged in self-governance through the discussion of public issues and participation in public affairs. Under the second feature, fair association, citizens are conceived as rational and morally autonomous agents who are able to consider the public good in addition to their self-interests.

To be a member of a public is to be a certain type of citizen. We may, with Walzer, define a citizen as "a member of a political community, entitled to whatever prerogatives and encumbered with whatever responsibilities are attached to membership."[10] Citizenship was a primary value for the stern communitarianism of Sparta and the radical citizenship of revolutionary France. Citizenship is a necessary but not sufficient condition for being a member of a public. One must be a citizen who is free and equal and able to enjoy the democratic political goods.

Historically, citizenship, as an ideal, contains two ideas that do approach the conditions required for people to be Rawlsian citizens. One idea is that of self-sacrifice for the public good. True citizens are supposed to place great weight "both to their moral principles and to the interests of others."[11] If the ends of public and private life conflict, allegiance to the public good prevails. A second idea is citizenship as "self-government within the law." Citizenship as self-government is prominent in republican thought. It warns that citizens will maintain their liberties under an "empire of law" only if they are devoted to the public good.[12] Riesenberg notes that, ethically speaking, citizenship is "the constant advocacy across the centuries of selfless service on behalf of society." Citizenship is that highest of human achievements, to be capable of taking on the "role of a political being, to act in the ennobling sphere of ethical politics."[13] The emergence of citizenship is the emergence of a new political loyalty that takes precedent over other loyalties of self-interest, tribe, faction, or family. Rawls (and I) would add the norms of democratic citizenship to these two worthy aspects of the ideal of citizenship. To be a member of a public is to be a citizen who is motivated to act in the ways of the reasonable, as described earlier. Of course, we should not forget that citizenship has been used historically for partisan political purposes counter to the public good. Entrance into the circle of citizenship meant privileges and rewards. Political leaders used membership in the class of citizens to gain support among certain classes of society, to exclude threatening groups, to mollify restless factions, and to satisfy private ambition. Although citizens were supposed to seek the common good, they also sought the personal rewards of citizenship.

My approach to the idea of a public is normative and ideal. It views the members of society as citizens, as members of a political association that implies certain rights and duties, privileges, relationships of power and the power to coerce, institutions, and laws. It combines the common idea of democracy as governed by "the many" with the idea that the "many," to be a public, must have additional characteristics. This liberal conception of a public contrasts with citizenship in societies where many people are slaves or where many people are the restricted members of a hierarchical social order such as a caste system. Liberal democracy is a form of political association that seeks to allow active and free flourishing of individuals with a share in governing through a fair and just form of participation through deliberation.

Therefore, democratic political society is a special way of integrating and unifying people as a public. A well-ordered democracy provides a framework within which social unions can live together as they pursue fairly their own goods, but also a way in which they can work together to support a common political structure. This concept of the public is an abstract and sophisticated kind of political relationship, establishing itself relatively late and sporadically in history, and requiring the existence of a number of demanding social and political conditions.

Public and Private

The concept of democratic public implies a public area of society, as distinguished from a non-public or private area. The area consists of those political actions and interactions of members of the public, and the actions and operations of political institutions. However, the public-private distinction that forms part of our conception of a public is not identical to the way that people use "public" and "private" in ordinary life. For example, we may use public to refer to something that anyone can easily access and observe, e.g., the side of my house that faces the street. It is not private like the bedroom washroom inside the house. At first glance, it is not obvious how this public-private distinction might be related to the idea of a public.

The distinction of the public and private is a family of distinctions drawn for different reasons and different purposes. Public is opposed to private in general. Yet public is also contrasted with such terms as secret, arcane, personal, and private interest. The public-private distinction takes four forms: political, informational, spatial, and the arcane. The political, informational, and spatial are the most important categories for our purposes.

To take a couple of least important distinctions, we can say that the public is opposed to the private as the arcane (or esoteric) in the sense that some information may not be accessible to the public because it is very technical or requires special knowledge. The topic is not public in the sense that it is not a matter of common sense or general knowledge.

The spatial distinction refers to public and private spaces. Public refers to spaces that are open and easily accessible by any citizen, while private refers to spaces that restrict access and make public observation difficult, such as the interior of monasteries. The informational sense refers to the access, control, and use of information. Public refers to information widely accessible and private means information that has serious restrictions on its access and use. Public information can also be contrasted with secret information – private information that some person or agency actively ensures is not shared with others. In contemporary society, the increase in media technology and the need for information has placed the informational distinction at the forefront of debates about the protection of private or personal data.

The spatial and informational senses play a role in creating and maintaining a domain of society where citizens can exercise their political rights and participate in deliberation and decisions. They are, in effect, necessary conditions for the existence of a public domain. The spatial public-private distinction is important for a public domain because it limits intrusions into our private spaces. To have privacy or some private spaces with limited access is one of the requirements of a liberal democracy. If all space in society were public or open to all to observe and access, then the state or any person (or group) could intrude into every part of one's life. In contrast, it is important that buildings for the conduct of the public's business must be public in the spatial sense. Courtrooms need to be open to the view of any citizen, as do parliaments.

The informational distinction is also important to a democratic society and a democratic domain. Citizens cannot act as a self-governing public without having reasonably open access to information about their society and government and, simultaneously, protections against the misuse of private information about themselves. Many liberals believe that a society is not truly protective of its members unless it has substantial protections for private information and for private spaces.

The democratic public sense of the public-private distinction includes the spatial and informational senses, but it gives the distinction an additional meaning – the idea of actions *of* a public and actions *for* a public. What is public in this sense is not only spaces or forms of information easily accessible to government and citizens; it is certain types of activities of a democratic public, as opposed to non-public (or private) actions. Public actions are distinguished from private actions when individuals are not acting as members of a public. In this case, citizens act as private individuals or as members of some other form of association.

The public sense includes whatever is important or useful to the political association of a public. Therefore, the public domain includes:

(1) *Physical objects, resources, or services built, maintained, and used for the benefit of all citizens, such as highways, natural resources, and schools.*[14]

(2) *Political offices, official state positions, and public roles.*

For instance, an individual acts as a public official in the justice system while at work, but enjoys a private life at other times.

The public sense distinguishes between those who work directly and explicitly for the public and its good and those who do not. The former are the public officials, politicians, and institutional bureaucrats who work for (and implement) the mechanisms of the state in the name of the public. Contrasted with these public figures are "private" individuals who do not hold a political or government position of responsibility. The complexity of this political sense of the public domain, as referred to be (1) and (2) is evident in the concept of *res publica* (literally, "a thing of the people") in Roman antiquity. *Publica* derives from *populous*, whose etymology refers to a physically mature male, the age of puberty, or the pubic region. Another meaning is that of a fruit full of sap or juice. Initially, *res publica* meant the body of men capable of serving in the army and the property of the army, especially the land it conquers and holds in common. Eventually, *res publica* came to include most citizens.

(3) *Activities that fall under the proper concern of state authorities and the laws, such as illegal acts.* The public domain also includes the legitimate use of state power to regulate such activities and to control the actions of groups where they impinge on other groups. These public activities are distinguished from private activities that are not the proper concern of the state or its public officials. The public sense contains the liberal idea of a private sphere where private individuals can hold their own beliefs and pursue their own interests, goods, and tastes unimpeded by public authority or law.

(4) *The institutions, forms of communication, and procedures by which the public is informed about public issues and participates in their discussion.* Journalism is part of the public domain, as are elections and debates in parliament.

(5) *The common good and the political aims of the public as a whole, and whatever affects the public good, as distinguished from private interests.* Therefore, "public" in the political sense

can refer to something as concrete as resources held in common
and to something as abstract as the principles of a constitution.

PUBLIC GOOD AND COMMUNITY

Public Good

The public good is the good of the public, where "public" refers to
the special political association described above. The public good
is the common good of this group of citizens. More specifically, the
public good is those actions and policies that help a public come into
existence and flourish as a democratic political association. What is
needed primarily are political structures, mechanisms, and opportunities organized in such a way as to encourage the two features of
the public: active participation and reasonable influence.

The public good consists of the goods that are made possible by
just political structures and institutions. The goods include political
and legal freedom and being able to enjoy the full value of basic liberties while enjoying meaningful participation in political life. These
goods are achieved by political arrangements that allow the public
to engage in fair and inclusive discussion, constitutional protections
against state torture, rule of law, a fair distribution of resources, and
tolerance of reasonable comprehensive views. The value of the public good is the value of political dignity.

This conception of the public good is normative because it describes
how citizens ought to act in concert to achieve political goods. In
their acts and their opinion-making (and exchange of opinion), citizens need to display their reasonableness as well as their rationality.
The human good is not reducible to the actual preferences or desires
of self-interested individuals or the maximization of utility, as pleasure or happiness.

Public Interest

Why have I chosen to use the term "public good"? rather than "public
interest"? I prefer the public good because it makes it clear that we
are discussing the actions of the public from an ethical perspective.
The idea of interest, with or without the adjective "public," has its
origins in the notion of private and potentially unethical interests that
could conflict with the common good. Public interest can be used as a

stylistic substitute for the public good as long as it is clear that what is at issue is an ethical understanding of what democracy requires.

Historically, our oldest conception of the good for societies or groups is that of the common good as whatever goods and goals a group of people happen to share.[15] Members of a group were presumed to have common goals in the way that rowers of a boat have common goals. The members combine their efforts to bring about some external state of affairs, such as the building of a bridge, aqueduct, or temple; they work together to avoid famine, extinguish a fire, or defeat an invading army.

"Public good" developed out of "common good" as a political interpretation of the common good, as the good of a politically active public. It referred to the good of a political association. Societies came to praise the great good of their political constitutions, the good of efficient government, common principles of law, and the right to influence decisions of society. These political values were held in common. Cicero writes: "A republic is the property of the public. But a public is not every kind of human gathering, congregating in any manner, but a numerous gathering brought together by legal consent and community of interest."[16]

The classical ideals of the public good and the active citizen – *homo politicus* – declined during the Dark Ages and amid the hierarchical social structures of medieval Europe. Held describes the change as a transition from citizens as *homo politicus* to *homo credens* of the Christian faith. The citizen of active judgment was replaced by the "true believer" who obeyed divinely sanctioned authority.[17] Medieval thinkers thought that citizens should be virtuous and care about the common good but, in such a society, only the king and his favourites had political rights and were politically active in any meaningful sense. The rest of the people had duties to obey. The concept of the public good was replaced by a religious interpretation of the older idea of a common good. Humans, as citizens, should obey government and work for the common goods of society; however, the highest common good was service to God and God's heavenly city of saints. Caring for the common good was a Bible-supported injunction to care for others. By caring for the common good, persons modelled their actions on the creator's, who cared for all. Political legitimacy required a right relation to God and toward God's church.[18]

The idea of a civic public with a secular public good returns with the revival of republicanism in Italian city-states of the Renaissance and ends with the establishment of limited monarchy in England by the late seventeenth century. Contractual ideas support liberty for citizens, religious tolerance, and political equality.

The transition from "public good" to "public interest" begins in the eighteenth century as naturalism combines with a scientific approach to ethical and political problems. Originally, having an "interest" referred to subjective or individual values. The term was contrasted with the public or collective good. Interests gave rise to factions and narrow partialities that threatened the good of society. Today, we understand interest as something that makes a difference. Interest is not only a psychological feeling or curiosity in something, in the sense that I find something interesting. An interest is "something being done, enacted, or brought about, or maintained. It is an interest in action of some kind."[19] This sense of interest has been well-stated by Lever, who defined interest as "having an interest in something when changes in its state could affect us advantageously or disadvantageously."[20]

This understanding of interest helps to broaden the concept, but it says nothing about whether the interests are ethical. The very real possibility of these interests conflicting with the public good remains as much a problem for normative political theory today as it was centuries ago. Today, officials and politicians still serve their private good by stealing from the public purse. Corporate greed can benefit certain businessmen but work against the good of many citizens. Given the gap between the public good and "interest," how did the term "public interest" arise and, in many cases, replace the older term, "the public good"?

In the eighteenth and nineteenth centuries, the gap was bridged by developing a theory of the good that defined "good" psychologically and individually as what is in one's interests or what someone desires. An interest was good for someone. The next step is to define the common good as what serves the interests of most people in society. We call this aggregate of interests the "public interest" and use it to replace the "public good." In this way, the objective connotation of "what is good" – a goodness that transcends individual views – is replaced by the subjective notion of "what is in my (or someone's) interest."

Political and scientific motivations lay behind this translation of the public good to the public interest. The phrase "the public interest" was embraced in the eighteenth century when the goal of politics increasingly came to be interpreted as the satisfaction of individual interests.[21] Public policy was to be judged according to the desires of individual members of society, not by elevated philosophical or normative criteria. Something was significant if it affected one's interests, and public policy had to be formulated and judged by the de facto interests and demands of individual citizens. Since interests were factual "givens," the translation suited a method of settling public issues by appealing to the plain facts of existing interests that were available to observation, surveys, and other empirical methods.

The French materialists of the Enlightenment opposed older religious interpretations of humans by arguing that humans were moulded by their environment and physical nature, not by some immaterial soul or spiritual forces. The only innate tendency of humans was to seek happiness, defined as one's own self-interest. Since humans couldn't be motivated to go against their interests, moral and religious preaching was futile. Instead, the materialists stressed that the common good of society could only be reached through laws and education. Laws should reward behaviour conducive to the common good and punish selfishness. Education should teach humans to see that acting in the common good is actually in their long-term self-interest. It was hoped that conflicts between interests and the public good could be ended and social life harmonized through social engineering based on knowledge of humanity's true goods. For example, the eighteenth century philosopher Claude Helvetius created an outcry with his publication of De l'esprit (On Mind) in 1758 because of its atheistic, utilitarian, rationalistic, and egalitarian ideas. Helvetius believed society could channel and manipulate human desires and self-interest toward useful social habits that promoted the common good. He advocated substituting the language of interest for the language of social condemnation used by the social critic and religious preacher.[22] Jeremy Bentham adopted "public interest," which he defined as "the interest of the community." This phrase meant "the sum of the interests of the several members who compose it."[23] Interests, and their management and aggregation, was becoming everything in politics.

My conception of the public and its good is a successor of historical conceptions of the public as active, starting with homo politicus of Athenian direct democracy and Roman republicanism. It incorporates the contract tradition's emphasis on the importance of participating in a public that influences decisions. But my conception is normative, not psychological, in the eighteenth-century sense. I do not define the public good as an aggregate of current desires or interests. The public good is not about protecting liberties to pursue one's own interests. The public good is political goods that citizens should desire and pursue to bring about a just society.

Community

My conception of the public good is political and relatively abstract. The public good consists primarily of certain principles and ideals for reasonable liberal citizens. It does not refer to concrete ways of living together. It does not refer to richly textured and particular social activities, rituals, loving relationships, and communal bonds. My conception is not opposed to feeling and intimate association; to the contrary, it recognizes more emotional aspects of society in the levels of ethical flourishing.

My conception does hold, however, that on the political level, the most important forms of association are relationships based on liberal-democratic principles and ideals that are formulated, affirmed, and applied by reasonable members of a public. The source of unity for this political association is a fair contractual agreement on the terms of social cooperation. Liberal political society is not conceived of as a social group defined by concrete relationships and friendships. Democracy is not a tightly knit village, where personal relationships, tradition, and fellow-feeling substitute for formal principles and political institutions.[24] What democracy depends on is whether citizens are motivated to be reasonable, act reciprocally, and care about the common good.

There are several reasons for not identifying modern political society with a community. Modern society is too large, complex, and impersonal to be a community with close personal relations. There will be close ties among groups of citizens and between overlapping areas of society. There may be widespread feelings of patriotism to the country. But it is unrealistic to expect that all (or most) members of the society have personal attachments to each other similar to those found in small communities. In today's society, people are often strangers to each other and do not participate in common activities. Citizens of democracies are not, and do not need to be, brothers, comrades, fellow Christians, fellow Irishmen, or even close friends. This does not deny that we can experience a moral emotion at being part of a society of fellow democrats or even a cosmopolitan citizenship of humanity. We cannot count on warm feelings, based on close or constant interaction, to ground our support for well-ordered society.

There are occasions when we feel a strong emotion toward others as fellow citizens, such as national celebrations. These occasions are increasingly few in number in contemporary society. In recognizing others as citizens, we often recognize the rights and dignity of people whom we dislike or with whom we feel no personal bond.

A democratic public or a political society also differs from communities such as the congregation of a church by not being united by a comprehensive doctrine. The basis of the unity is political. Ideally, a democracy supplies a mediating framework for just and peaceful coexistence amid conflicting comprehensive views. People have deep conflicting interests that, in many cases, cannot be settled by appealing to friendship or kindness. In such a society, politics should be based on principles, objectivity, and public reason. With Dewey, I see democracy as a precondition for the richest kind of communal life and human flourishing. But democracy is *not* community.

The ends of democratic political society differ from the ends of other associations in terms of what persons are cooperating *as* and what their cooperating *achieves*. An ideal democratic society is characterized by people cooperating as free and equal citizens with fundamental rights. They seek a just basic structure with institutions realizing the principles of justice. The end of political society is political justice whereas in an association people cooperate to achieve whatever moved them to form the association in the first place. Citizens of well-ordered democracy do not affirm the same conception of the good but do affirm the same conception of justice. Associations are allowed to pursue their own ends and offer different privileges to members, if they don't conflict with justice. In our current world, this form of political unity is the best we can hope for.

The public of a well-ordered democracy is similar to what Ronald Dworkin calls a "liberal community." Dworkin's liberal community is a political association of reasonable citizens embracing common principles of justice.[25] The communal life of liberalism is limited to political activities, such as legislation, adjudication, enforcement, and other functions of government. If a liberal community has success in such acts, then it also improves the lives of citizens. Liberals feel their own lives are enhanced or diminished insofar as they live in a just or unjust society.

Our efforts to separate democracy and community should not lead us to think of democracy as the political form of a private society where communal bonds, government, and the public good play a minor role.[26] A well-ordered democracy is not a *modus vivendi* or contract for solely personal interest. The private ends of individuals are independent of each other and potentially in conflict. Competitive economic markets are a paradigm example of a private society. It is also possible that an entire society takes on the qualities of a private society. In private societies, institutions have no value in themselves. Participating in institutions and doing one's public duty is often regarded as a burden. Individuals evaluate their society and its arrangements as a means to their private aims; it is not necessary to consider the goods of others. In a private society, individuals prefer the most efficient scheme that gives them the largest share of resources, wealth, property, assets, or other goods. In a private society, the division of social advantages is determined by a contingent balance of power. By good fortune, it could happen that a private society results in a fair distribution of rights and advantages. Private and collective interests align themselves only to the extent that the state can arrange matters so that it is in the interests of individuals to act in a socially beneficial manner. Private society is not held together by a public conviction that its basic arrangements are just and good in themselves, but by the rational calculations of citizens.

Global Public Good

So far, the discussion about a public and the public good has assumed that the public in question is the citizens of a nation. What does this aim of political association look like when the concept of the public good is globalized?

The global public good remains a political conception. It refers to those actions and policies that would help publics around the world to come into existence and flourish as democratic political associations. What is needed are political structures, mechanisms, and opportunities organized to encourage a global expansion of the two features of the public: active participation and reasonable influence. The goal is the development of global democratic institutions and structures.[27] In sum, global public good is the promotion of political dignity across borders.

These goods are to be achieved by many means, including constitutional protections against state torture and methods to protect human rights and prosecute violators. It includes the rule of law domestically and internationally and a fair global distribution of the world's wealth, technology, and resources. The extent to which these goods can be accomplished will be affected by many factors. Different societies will implement democracy in different ways. These institutional arrangements may not be liberal democratic in the fullest sense. It may be that certain cultures can only approach the level of what Rawls calls a "decent" society with liberal leanings. However, there are limits to that variation. I would argue that a country lacks any significant notion of the public good if its arrangements do not respect human rights and civil liberties, do not promote regular government consultation of the public, do not enforce the rule of law, and so on.

The global public good means justice within countries and among nations, cultures, and peoples. The focus is on democratic structures for the promotion of just international relations and the rights of global citizens. However, it is often remarked that the idea of someone being a citizen or having rights requires the existence of a country that defines and enforces the rights of citizenship. Therefore, it is argued, there is no such thing as a global "citizen" because there is no global equivalent of the nation state. We can still make sense of the notion of a global public and global justice if we think of human rights and principles of justice as emerging from our participation in a "global political structure."[28] Increasingly, the relations among nations is structured by a growing number of international agencies and bodies such as the World Trade Organization, the World Bank, the United Nations, the International Monetary Fund, and the International Criminal Court; multinational free trade agreements; and multination political bodies such as the European Union.[29]

The task of ensuring that such international political structures are efficient, just and democratic is enormous and important. The norms, aims, and practices of these transnational agencies have dramatic impact on the lives of citizens around the world. In addition, economic and technological globalization means that the actions of citizens in one country have an effect on citizens of other countries, and vice versa. Therefore, global democracy and global justice are matters of making this global political structure more democratic and more equitable.[30] We are global citizens in this developing sense, as members of a global society where no one person or country can solve global problems. Therefore, we all have a responsibility, as societies and as citizens of these societies, to work together to improve and reform the global structure and its agencies.

The political aim is not a warm and friendly global community but a well-ordered global society based on principles and the global public good. We need a world of well-ordered societies that follow international law and support human rights through fair and effective global institutional structures, from a revived United Nations and a restructured international banking system to effective international criminal courts.

JOURNALISM AND DEMOCRACY

Whom Does Journalism Serve?

The topic of democracy is important to journalism because the ethical basis of journalism is service to the public or the public good. Journalism's best practices, its norms, and its ideals are ultimately justified by appeal to the creation, maintenance, and promotion of a democratic public sphere. Journalism, because of its direct and powerful influence on public deliberation and the information base of citizens, needs to be acutely conscious of the special ways in which it can serve the public good. Although journalists frequently fail to live up to these ideals, the goal of public service is important to inspire good journalism and critique media performance.

Given our discussion of a democratic public, we can clarify what serving the public means today, as one part of journalism's larger duty to serve ethical flourishing. Whom ought journalism serve politically speaking?

Journalism ought to serve individuals and groups of society in their roles as citizens, as a collective public. The public consists of all individuals who are part of society's cooperative political enterprise, which aims to encourage human flourishing within an increasing democratization of society. This is the public that journalism serves. Journalism should support the public good as the good of active and reasonable democratic citizens.

A journalism of the public good is a journalism of social justice, a daily inquiry into society's basic structure and basic liberties, and the levels of political participation among all citizens. Journalism has a duty to insist on and help make possible a diverse public forum with adequate representation of non-dominant groups. Journalism should support the practice of public reason. A journalism of public reason supports objective, informed discussion on essential issues in ways that respect all participants and the principles of justice. Journalism should encourage the development of citizens with a well-ordered personality that combines the rational and reasonable, and is willing to limit their pursuit of goods.

A journalism of the democratic public good should be distinguished from other notions about whom journalism serves. The democratic idea is easily confused with other conceptions. A communist or authoritarian model of the press will interpret how journalists serve society differently from a liberal model. The democratic model is distinguished by its claim that journalists' primary responsibility is to serve the public (and its democratic life), not the state, not a government policy, not an institution, such as the military or police. Journalists' primary responsibility is not to serve people as consumers. Serving the public is about creating a news media system, or news media space, that encourages a critical, open public sphere of diverse, often unpopular, views. Journalists serve the public by helping a reasonable, informed, inquiring public to exist.

The idea that journalists serve society can be interpreted in ways that encourage the silencing of critical voices. For example, in Southeast Asia and other regions, the developmental journalism paradigm began among journalists in the late 1960s. Developmentalism was to be authentic expression of indigenous culture and protection against manipulation by former colonial masters.[31] Developmental journalism was contrasted with a Western liberal press model, with its principles of independence, objectivity, and neutrality. On the face of it, developmental journalism has noble goals: to use media to develop countries with weak economies and serious social problems; to build social solidarity; and to allow people to take control of their lives. In the 1980s and 1990s, however, leaders of Southeast Asian countries, such as Indonesia, Malaysia, and Singapore, attempted to harness the media for their own interests in the name of nation-building and economic development. Serving the nation through developmental journalism meant pointing out corruption among minor provincial officials, but not corruption in the highest places. It meant downplaying or ignoring government mistakes in economic or social planning; not damaging social solidarity by embarrassing reports of inadequate health services or violations of human rights. It meant editors taking advice from political leaders on what coverage was in the national interest.

For a journalism of the public good, the problem with the developmental model is not the goals of development or social solidarity. The problem is how the press is expected to serve those ends. To serve the public according to democratic journalism, three elements must be present: (a) a notion of serving the public that is *not* reducible to the interests of the current government or special interests; (b) the adoption of an independent, impartial stance by journalists, which creates a critical distance between reporter and story, and between reporter and state official; and (c) the use of the press to create a critical, deliberative, public sphere. Without these factors, serving the public is reduced to the rhetoric of uncritical patriotism; the idea of media-supported social solidarity becomes the idea of not challenging the status quo. Journalism of the public good insists that, in the long-run, social goals are best pursued by allowing the media to construct a critical and open public space for deliberation.

Journalism should be, as Carey said, a "particular kind of democratic practice."[32] Public journalism is the organized, socially recognized activity of communicating to the public for the public, from the impartial perspective of the public good, democratically understood. Journalists should speak to the public in a manner different from partisan communicators such as the social advocate, the lobbyist, or public relations expert. This form of public journalism amounts to "journalism communication done on behalf of the public interest, by people who are relatively independent of special interest."[33]

Service to a democratic public fulfills journalism's social contract. Journalists have a duty to improve the informational and deliberative health of citizens as public health officers are responsible for the physical health of citizens. Journalists support the public's informational health by carrying out five democratic functions: (a) providing essential news for the public in an independent, accurate, and comprehensive fashion; (b) acting as a watchdog on abuse of power and as a voice for the less powerful; (c) creating a forum for the deliberation of public policy from a variety of views; (d) providing fair representations of groups and minorities, as befits a pluralistic society; (e) writing stories in a manner that encourage citizens to engage the issues and avoid a passive or cynical attitude; and (f) promoting the general welfare of citizens and their long-term task of developing a more just and equitable society.

My stress on serving the public good, as a political duty, raises questions about journalism's obligations with respect to the other levels of ethical flourishing, such as the individual and social goods. The answer is that journalism's ultimate goal is the promotion of the human good in the round. It should promote the various goods that secure rational, moral, and political dignity, as aspects of ethical flourishing. Given the interdependency of these parts of the human good, it is difficult to say that journalism should support one level more than another.

However, if pressed, I would argue that journalism must make promotion of the political goods, or the public good, primary. Journalism has a special and distinct influence on people as citizens and their political goods as a whole. Journalism has a historically grounded interest in dealing with issues of basic rights such as free expression and in exposing manipulators of public opinion. As public communication, journalism is inherently directed toward issues that affect the public good. In other levels of the good, there are many experts and educators who can analyze and promote the relevant goods. For example, teachers, spiritual leaders, and many others have competency in developing the individual goods (or rational and moral dignity) of society. To be sure, journalism indirectly affects people's self-development at the individual and social level; but, when it comes to the public good, journalists have a direct impact since public goods rely so heavily upon the way information is made available and distributed across society.

At the political level, journalism deals not so much with the activity of specific communities or private societies but with the political structures that mediate tensions among far-flung citizens. It is inquiry into what is right and fair among disagreeing citizens who may be strangers to each other. This level of journalism investigates the justice of the state according to Rawlsian concerns about constitutional rights and liberties, the clarity and application of principles of justice, and the distribution of social advantages. At this level, journalism asks whether its country (or another country) is a well-ordered society. Therefore, it can be claimed that journalism's first concern should be the vigour of the public and their good.

A journalism of ethical flourishing and social justice recognizes that many forms of journalism are necessary to serve the public good. It proposes an ecumenical notion of journalism. A healthy and vigorous public sphere requires the journalist to take on many public roles: objective informer, investigator of abuses, informed analyst and interpreter of events, reformer. At the same time, all such communication should minimize harm and nurture caring communal relations among citizens. What all forms of responsible journalism have in common are principles of truth telling for the public good.

Global Democratic Journalism

When we globalize this conception of "political" journalism, the result is a cosmopolitan journalism that seeks political dignity for humanity. Global democratic journalism finds concrete ways to carry out the three imperatives of cosmopolitan journalism; it becomes a journalism of social justice at a global level.

Global democratic journalists use their powers of investigation and communication for the development of just and participatory political associations everywhere. Journalism supports those actions and policies that help publics around the world to come into existence and to flourish as democratic political associations. Global journalism seeks the expansion of democracy abroad and the development of global democratic institutions and structures.

Global democratic journalism is a critic of the global political structure. It is a watchdog on human rights, basic liberties, state torture, lapses in the rule of law, and unfair distribution of resources. Global journalism asks: are citizens in different parts of the world able to exercise their basic freedoms for the purpose of self-development and to enjoy the human goods? Can they participate in public life and in the decisions that affect their lives? Global journalism helps the world to address urgent global problems, from climate change to the control of AIDS. Reporting on these issues must be informed and multiperspectival; it should put pressure on those who are reluctant to act for reasons of self-interest or narrow national interest.

Global democratic journalism acts as a bridge of understanding between cultures and nations. It encourages citizens to seek goods beyond the goods of rationality or enlightened self-interest, or even loyalty to one's ethnic or religious group. Global democratic journalists insist that disputes within countries and between countries are adjudicated in terms of the basic principles of justice and international law.

Global democratic journalism investigates itself. It inquires into the impact of journalism, media, and communication technology on various regions of the world. Global journalism supports diverse media systems that adequately represent non-dominant groups. Journalism needs to be self-conscious of the methods and manner by which we communicate in society, the role of media, and related issues about the freedom and diversity of the public sphere.

Global democratic journalism should push for the development of human capacities around the world across two stages of development. The first stage aims at a decent and minimally flourishing life where physical needs are primary. The second stage aims at an ethically flourishing life by developing all four levels to the maximum. In this way, journalism can see itself as promoting ethical flourishing even in countries where the practical reality makes the pursuit of the "higher" goods difficult or impossible. As a journalism of capacity development, journalism can oppose abuses of democratic power and alert citizens to failures to secure decent standards of the human good at home and abroad.

Journalism and Public Reason

In addition to informing and investigating, global democratic journalism promotes the public good by supporting the exercise of public reason by journalists, officials, and the public. Good journalism deliberates and allows others to deliberate. "Deliberation" in this context has been described by Michael Walzer as "a particular way of thinking: quiet, reflective, open to a wide range of evidence, respectful of different views. It is a rational process of weighing the available data, considering alternative possibilities, arguing about relevance and worthiness, and then choosing the best policy or person."[34] Using his definition, we can say that the goal of journalism of the public good is informed public opinion formed under the demands of public reason and democratic deliberation. Globally, journalists should assist the exercise of public reason on global issues among participants in different countries.

On this view, journalism's contribution to reasonable citizens is as important to journalism ethics as the historically privileged value of a free press – the freedom to publish opinions in almost any manner or tone. If journalism's goal is well-ordered society, the form and quality of journalistic and public deliberation on essential issues is an important issue for journalism ethics, not just the accuracy of the content of journalism reports. Journalism is more than the exercise of free speech; it is an exercise of democratic speech, of just, respect-ful, and equal speech directed toward the ultimate aims of human justice and goodness.

A journalism of public reason supports objective, informed dis-cussion on essential issues in ways that respect all participants and the principles of justice and acknowledges the fact of reasonable plurality and the burdens of judgment. Journalism should oppose a manipulative media world and transform the public sphere into a more rational arena. Ethical journalism allows a reasonable public to come into existence.

Journalism should avoid reducing itself to sensational and parti-san opining that lacks respect for other views and does not seek a fair, inclusive consensus on essential issues. Within the news media there is a dire need for journalists who can write from such a per-spective. Journalism, rather than focusing on individuals motivated by extreme passions and greed, should write about individuals with the capacity to act virtuously and with a sense of justice. Journalism should not be attracted solely to citizens who love combative and extreme debate and are clever enough to know what will attract the news media's attention. It should highlight debate among peo-ple capable of offering reasonable, alternate views, who can adopt impartial ethical perspectives on issues, and who are willing to delib-erate according to public reason.

In an era of hype, edgy commentary, and partisan hot talk, it may seem that the purposes of news media are simply to blow off steam or to find others who hold similar views. It may seem that the pur-poses of media are to send verbal volleys at political enemies from the isolation of their ideological silos. While I support the legal right for robust free speech, ethically I think that a country whose pub-lic discourse is predominately intolerant and ideological is headed for serious trouble. How we speak to each other in democracies is almost as important as what we say. Democracy needs not just many actors, but actors willing to stop talking and to listen.

I don't expect discussions in news media to be a logician's model of rationality and objectivity; but there has to be *some* degree of rationality and objectivity at the heart of our news media system. We will never solve urgent issues by polarizing discussions where it is winner take all, or by deliberately misrepresenting those who disagree with us. Democracy will always be a messy process, but it may not survive a large-scale corruption of the means of communication.

As I wrote in *The Invention of Journalism Ethics,* journalism at its best is the lifeblood of democracy. It is the way in which a society informs and reforms itself. Journalism cannot play that role except in a society that is tolerant and deliberative. When open and honest communication wanes, journalism can become the art of the demagogue and despot. It can become the propaganda tool of powerful interests who subvert popular self-governance by manipulating the channels of information. Journalism is debased if it falls into the hands of unethical media owners and journalists, or when editorial resources are squandered on entertaining stories. Journalism falters when it fails to question the powers that be and when budget cuts strangle investigative journalism. Journalism degenerates when the business of journalism overwhelms its democratic functions, seeking profit through every cheap trick in the history of popular printing – jingoism, sensationalism, and fearmongering. Five centuries after the first newspapers, journalism still struggles to avoid debasement, let alone live up to its democratic duty.

CONCLUSION

This chapter has discussed how journalism can contribute to the third level of ethical flourishing, the promotion of the political goods at home and abroad. Using a Rawlsian notion of the public, I argued that journalism serves the public good by serving the creation, maintenance, and promotion of democratic political associations.

Combining the discussions in chapters 4 and 5, we have a foundation for global journalism ethics. Chapter 4 described how journalism could contribute to each level of flourishing, while this chapter described journalism's democratic role.

In summary, my proposal for a foundation for global journalism ethics consists of (1) the adoption of a cosmopolitan attitude and its three imperatives and principles, (2) the elaboration of the cosmopolitan ethic through the four levels of ethical flourishing, and

(3) the redefinition of journalism ethics around the promotion of these four levels.

Much more could be said about this foundation of global journalism ethics, not to mention its more detailed application to the many problems of journalism ethics; but that is a task for the future. I have provided an outline that indicates both the nature of the foundation and why I think it is a plausible and attractive theoretical structure.

I conclude the book in the next chapter by considering how the foundation addresses a major problem for global journalism – patriotism. It explores the tension between love of country and love of humanity.

6

Patriotism and Global Ethics

In this final chapter, I examine how my global journalism ethics treats the partiality of patriotism. The first test of a global ethics is how it approaches the issue of patriotism and other partialities that challenge a cosmopolitan commitment to humanity.

I discuss to what extent patriotism and journalism are compatible, and I develop a theory of moderate, democratic patriotism. I then consider a global patriotism for global journalism. The result is a philosophical theory of patriotism for journalism in a global age. The theory provides a framework to help journalists understand how they can be patriotic citizens without violating principles of responsible public journalism. It does so by setting ethical limits on the love of country and by identifying a distinct and appropriate object of patriotism for democracy and democratic journalism.

I have been thinking about patriotism and journalism for some time. I keep coming back to it, unable to put the problem to rest. Why this attraction? Personal experience, for one thing. As a war correspondent in the 1990s, I came under pressure to be patriotic when reporting on Canadian soldiers or peacekeepers in the former Yugoslavia and elsewhere. The patriotism that sought my allegiance was almost invariable narrow and anti-democratic: I should not embarrass Canada by reporting on mistakes in the field; I should not quote soldiers puzzled about their mission; I should do "feel-good" pieces about soldiers watching hockey via satellite in warring Bosnia. Then came the Iraq War. I was dismayed as major news media dropped any pretence at objectivity to beat a patriotic drum. I rebelled against such claims of patriotism then, as I do now. In a democracy, any patriotism worth its name must be more nuanced, more ethically defensible, and more attuned to our global world.

Another reason I am interested in patriotism is because the topic challenges cosmopolitan thinking on several levels. Patriotism represents a deep emotional attachment to one's country, and that attachment has often trumped ethical commitments to the fate of citizens in foreign lands. The challenge is historical, psychological and ethical. There are ethicists who argue that one's primary responsibility ought to be to one's compatriots. Our ethical duties to those beyond our borders are not more important than our duties to family, neighbours, and fellow citizens at home. At best, the claims of foreigners are a matter of benevolence that is ethically commendable but not required. This type of ethical thinking questions cosmopolitan ideas about acting as global citizens with a primary allegiance to humanity.

This presumed primacy of patriotism affects journalism ethics. Can journalists be patriotic without compromising the principles of their profession, which call for impartial, truthful, and fair reporting? If the claim of patriotism on citizens trumps the claim of cosmopolitanism, then journalists, as citizens, should make patriotism a more important matter than the imperative that they act as agents of global citizens. This form of thinking appears to imply that journalism's primary duty is to promote the national interest in times of war or international disputes. News organizations would with good conscience, abandon objectivity and fairness in times of conflict. If required, journalists would be patriotic by practicing a muted, uncritical journalism that supports the government or military.

I develop my response to these challenges across several sections of the chapter. In the first section I define patriotism and explicate the idea of moderate, democratic patriotism. In the second, I explain how to evaluate claims of patriotism. In the third section, I discuss how a democratic patriotism is compatible with the tenets of ethical, democratic journalism. I recommend a moderate patriotism for democratic community, a rational and ethically restrained form of patriotism compatible with the ethical norms of democratic journalism.

In the final section, I raise doubts about the theory I have constructed. I question the adequacy of this traditional, nation-based notion of patriotism for a global world, a cosmopolitan ethics, and an evolving cosmopolitan journalism. I suggest that the next task is to transform this domestic idea of patriotism into a global patriotism for humanity. I consider a global patriotism devoted to global democratic community, a loyalty that takes priority over nation-based patriotism where the two conflict. Nation-based forms of patriotism remain ethically permissible insofar as they do not conflict with the demands of global patriotism. The domestic version of patriotism is a temporary placeholder until we can articulate and implement global journalism ethics.

The analysis arrives at the following conclusion: ethical journalists can be patriotic only under strict conditions – if patriotism is defined along moderate, democratic lines. Journalists can be patriots only if they are moderate, rationally constrained patriots serving their country and humanity by fulfilling their distinctive social role as critical informers of democratic citizens. They can be patriots only if they evaluate claims of patriotism according to the principles of inclusivity, rational restraint, and public scrutiny. When journalists serve a different form of patriotism, they violate their ethical role in an open democratic society.

FORMS OF PATRIOTISM

Patriotism is a contested value. Some people praise patriotism as a primary civic virtue that overrides other virtues. Critics reply that patriotism is aggressive and xenophobic. More than 100 million people were killed in patriotic wars during the last century. Tolstoy wrote: "Seas of blood have been shed over this passion [of patriotism] and will yet be shed for it, unless the people free themselves of this obsolete relic of antiquity."[1] Therefore, is patriotism an unruly emotion or an essential civic attitude? Do appeals to patriotism carry ethical weight and, if so, how much? Patriotism is not a "local" ethical problem that fails to engage other issues. To evaluate patriotism we need a theory of partialities and a method of adjudication for conflicting loyalties. In dealing with patriotism, we encounter difficult questions about our obligations to others. Patriotism is a problem for journalism ethics because patriotism entails duties of citizenship, and journalists *are* citizens. If patriotism demands that journalists not inform the public about a military mistake, does that violate the journalist's duty to report truthfully? Another source of trouble is that both patriotism and journalism ethics demand that journalists serve the public. Once again we face the question: what does serving the public mean?

Much debate about patriotism, yesterday and today, goes along three lines. One debate is over what patriotism requires. Some writers argue that patriotism must be an attachment to concrete and parochial objects that are seen as mine, such as one's native soil, and one's people and customs. Others argue that patriotism is (or should be) a love for more abstract principles of political liberty which belong to all. Still others argue it is time to move away from national patriotism toward a cosmopolitan allegiance to humanity.[2] A second line of debate is to what extent patriotism is rational and can be restrained by rational principle. A third line of debate is the ethical priority of patriotism.

Political and Communal Patriotism

Historically, we can distinguish forms of patriotism as mainly communal or mainly political. Communal patriotism is love of a pre-political community: a loyalty to one's tribe, land, village, language, or customs. Communal patriotism is concrete, emotive, and folksy, based on direct personal ties to specific peoples and places. Communal patriotism is pre-political because it existed before the modern state with its complex political structures. Even if political association exists, the focus of communal patriotism is the non-political features of social life, such as language and custom. Political patriotism, in contrast, is love of one's country political values, structure, and ideals.

Forms of patriotism are communal or political depending on which aspect receives the greatest emphasis. Pure forms of political or communal patriotism are rare. Communal patriots usually favour certain political structures; political patriots praise the constitution *and* the beauty of their country and its traditions. Cold War patriotism, Western or Soviet, was more than a communal love of one's land; it was patriotism fired by political ideology. Even in Western democracies with strong constitutional traditions, patriotism is not purely political but contains communal love of land and people.

Political and communal forms of patriotism may favour different forms of society and government. Political patriotism can take many forms – as many forms as they are political systems. Political patriotism may support an authoritarian or republican form of government. Authoritarian patriotism is patriotism to an authoritarian form of political association. It stresses the need for law and order. It believes that a stable society needs an affection for, and strict obedience to, authority as embodied in monarchy, aristocracy, or military elite. A republican patriotism is a commitment to the political structure that protects freedom under the rule of law. It is more liberal and individualistic, praising the republic's constitution and its free citizens. For the Rawlsian liberal, political patriotism is allegiance to one's country primarily because it exhibits the features of a well-ordered society – a just structure of rights, freedoms, institutions, and laws. Political patriotism is loyalty to a constitution, to the rule of law, to the rights and freedoms of citizenship.

Communal forms of patriotism may be devoted to the establishment of an organic society where the primary value is social solidarity, not individual freedom. Communal patriotism may be the love of a utopian society – a classless, communist society, or a totalitarian society unified under a powerful leader. Such communal ideals usually favour some political structure. In this way, political and communal patriotism converge into a full political and social perspective.

The two forms of patriotic attachment have evolved and mingled across history.[3] In antiquity, the patriotism of the Athenian city-state or Roman republic joined a communal love of *terra patria* (land of the fathers) with a political patriotism directed at *res publica*, which secured the common good. To be historically accurate, we should say that the political sense was built upon the communal sense of common soil, language, birth, and customs. In ancient Greece, with the emergence of the city-state, *patria* acquired a political sense but it remained anchored communally in the soil, tribe, and a relatively small community. Patriotism to the city-state is patriotism to a relatively small and concrete entity where the effect of citizens' actions on others could be perceived and appreciated. In such a society, the line between the communal and the political blurs, since the city-state develops a patriotism by remembering the city's special religious mysteries, its own gods and heroes. The city-state is still a sacred land or soil.[4]

Even in ancient Rome at the height of its empire, the Romans never lost the communal sense of being Roman, which included many traditions and rituals, including the sacred founding of the city. The enlargement of Rome from city to empire created changes to its notion of patriotism and citizenship, but the communal sense was never lost. Cicero expressed clearly the idea of a political patriotism devoted to the republic. "One fatherland embraces all our loves; and who that is true would hesitate to give his life for her, if by his death he could render her a service?"[5] Yet Cicero would never lose his communal patriotism to the small town and surrounding land in which he was born, even if he was grateful to Rome, which adopted him as a citizen: "We consider both the place where we were born and the city that has adopted us as our fatherland."[6]

The republican *patria* has several interesting features. The republic commands a particular type of love and respect, a *pietas,* or *caritas.* Love of country, like love of one's family, is expressed in acts of service and care. It is an inclusive and non-aggressive love in which our affection extends beyond family to embrace all fellow citizens. Patriotism was closely associated with acting bravely and impartially for the common good and a just country. Patriotism is the ultimate political virtue because its object is the political entity, the republic, which is the common good of all citizens. Gradually, the political sense of patriotism, the laws and institutions of the city, came to be independent from more communal loyalties such as the customs of the people.

Amid these forms of patriotism was the broadest form of all, the philosophical ideal of a duty to all citizens of the world as members of humanity, a notion put forward by individuals as different as Diogenes the Cynic, the stoic philosopher Seneca, and Cicero. We are told by Diogenes Laertius that Diogenes the Cynic declared he was a citizen of the world. When asked why he had no love for local customs and his country, Diogenes the Cynic replied: "My country is there," his finger pointing to the heavens.[7] Some writers warned that patriotic declarations can be insincere rhetoric. Marcus Aurelius said that when men speak like patriots they speak like actors.[8]

In the Dark Ages and medieval Europe, republican patriotism weakened due to the decline of central government and the rise of a religious perspective on the aims of life and community. The rise of Christianity redefined patriotism as the love of a supernatural God and God's heavenly community of souls. Worldly patriotism was legitimate insofar as it approximated Christian love and charity for others, and advanced the common good. Augustine, in *City of God,* bequeathed to the Middle Ages the idea of a supernatural and an earthly *patria.*[9] For Augustine, love of country was a form of compassion that encouraged us to see love of family within a larger love for the republic. Yet patriotism is not the final loyalty. *Patria* in Augustine and the texts of Church Fathers and canonists is the primary spiritual attachment to the "heavenly city" – a *patria paradisii.*[10] The martyr's sacrifice for the city of God is higher than the pagan soldier's sacrifice for worldly honour and his republic.

For medieval jurists, *patria* was the duty to honour the monarch's public persona, which physically represented the state and God's divinely appointed ruler. The feudal system encouraged vassals and knights to die for their lords, to honour bonds of fidelity and faith. The feudal system did not promote the classical idea of republican duty. Crusaders were urged to die to obey God's divine plan and save their souls. However, the ideas of republican patriotism survived in scholastic philosophers such as Aquinas who, in *Summa Theologia*, refers to Cicero's idea that love of country was a form of piety expressed "in acts of loving care and benevolent service for the fellow-citizens and the friends of the country." Such affections prompt citizens to serve the common good.

The ancient political patriotism began to recover with the rise of Renaissance city-states in Italy. Writers from Bruni to Machiavelli revived the idea of political patriotism as an attachment to polities that secure the civic good. Civic humanists and theorists of self-government stressed the love of republic on two grounds.[11] Patriotism was a rational love since it is rational for citizens to love "sweet liberty" in a city free from the control of a monarch. Patriotism was a duty of service to one's country because citizens owe their country a debt of education and nurturing that cannot be completely repaid. Alamanno Rinuccini wrote in his *Dialogue on Liberty* of 1479 that citizens need fortitude to stand up to tyrants since liberty is a property of a strong mind that refuses to obey others "unless his commands are just and legitimate and serve a useful purpose."[12]

For the quattrocentro humanists, the patriot who serves the common purpose is opposed to the corrupt citizen who favours his own or his party's interests; anyone who refuses to serve one's country is a fool and an immoral person. Yet, even in the fifteenth-century, patriotism in city-states such as Florence involved more than a commitment to a republic of free citizens. Patriotism had a communal aspect. Florence patriots praised the city's military and cultural superiority, the nobility of its ancestors, and the purity of its language. Florence claimed that the city was so extraordinary that it was "worthy of attaining dominion and rule over the entire world."[13] The writings of Leonardo Bruni in the early 1400s state that Florence was open to all who wished to serve the city and enjoy its freedom. But there is also an exaltation of Florence's pure language and unique splendour.

Niccolo Machiavelli made patriotism the dearest thing to his heart. Machiavelli repeats Cicero's theme: "I have always gladly served my country even when it was onerous and dangerous, because no obligation is greater than that that we owe to our country."[14] His patriotism was broader than the patriotism of Florence, encompassing a love for the regeneration of Italy. One of the purposes of Machiavelli's *Discourses* is to encourage the youth of Florence to imitate the virtue of the Romans. By *virtu*, Machiavelli meant patriotism, a love of common liberty that made citizens generous and capable of seeing their private goods as part of a common good, and willing to fight for the common good. He writes that the ancient Roman people were enemies of kings and lovers of glory and the common good. Patriotism was the reason that the Romans stayed free for centuries. If *patria* dissolves into tyranny, then citizens no longer do their duty. When love of country fades, virtue becomes brute force. It eventually destroys liberty.

In the sixteenth and seventeenth centuries, the language of patriotism underwent significant change. In some countries, patriotism became fidelity to a powerful monarch. Patriotic identification with a leader had been present in previous commitments to emperors, barbaric chieftains, and feudal lords. However, this patriotism was to an absolute monarch barely distinguished from the country or the emerging entity called the state. The doctrine of "reason of state" held that a citizen's highest obligation was is not to the *patria* as a republic but to the state personified by the monarch.

Critics of republican *patria* sought to disconnect *patria* and liberty. Love of country, free or not free, was more important. Citizens were not capable of virtuous deeds and therefore unfit for republican self-government. Republican and liberal notions of patriotism were dangerous ideas for powerful monarchies and hierarchical society. For example, the neo-Stoic Justus Lipsius, in *De Constantia* in 1584, argued that love of country was a dangerous passion for stable monarchies. It contradicts the rule of reason and must be opposed to maintain social order. A republican patriotism must be distinguished from a "natural patriotism" which is "a secret bond of nature" – an affection for one's native soil that has a special "place of memory."[15]

A similar conservative patriotism was put forward in England by Robert Filmer in his *Patriarca* of 1680, which Locke attacked in the first of his *Two Treatises of Government*.[16] For Filmer, a true patriot had to be a royalist since *patria* is a community founded on the power of the "fathers." The power of the prince was the same

as the power of a father over children; the king held the title of
Pater Patriae and could command absolute fidelity. Disobedience,
then, was unnatural and amounted to treason and impiety. Thus, the
language of patriotism was emptied of republican content.[17]

Eventually, this conservative loyalty to the person of the king would
come up against the political patriotism of reformers who sought a
commonwealth. Patriotism of a republican kind was promoted by
popular movements such as the Levellers, and was defended by anti-
royalists in England in their battle with Stuart kings. The rivalry was
evident in the Filmer-Locke debate. During the English civil war,
a political patriotism offered powerful motivation and ideas. The
patriot was a soldier who fought for common right and liberty with
a duty to advance a "communitive happiness" because "no man
is born for himself alone." In 1660, when John Milton attempted
desperately to help preserve the English republic against the return
of the Stuart monarchy, his political writings spoke of "our old
Patriots," the members of the Rump Parliament who abolished king-
ship.[18] For Milton, there needed to be established a commonwealth
grand council that consisted of "chosen Patriots [who] will be then
rightly called the true keepers of our libertie."[19]

In the eighteenth and nineteenth centuries, new forms of political patriotism appear with the modern nation-state. In Diderot's
Encyclopedia, patria was defined, not as a place of birth, but as a
"free state" whose laws protect liberty and happiness and allow citizens to participate in public life. Republican patriotism, especially in
England and the United States, took on a liberal and then a democratic cast, as the object of patriotism moved from a love of liberal
society, governed from above by the best liberal minds to an egalitarian patriotism that was loyal to the self-government and well-being
of the masses. Political patriotism referred back to constitutions
established by revolution in the USA and France.

At the same time, a romantic version of communal patriotism
arose in the late 1700s, especially in Germany. Romantic patriotism
stressed the uniqueness of one's *volk* and its land, language, customs,
will, and solidarity. The fascination with race, language, and differences would lead to nineteenth-century nationalism, an extreme
form of patriotism. A communal love of country as the love of the
unique spirit of a people or its language was exploited by political leaders. Both liberal and Marxist writers failed to foresee the

power of nationalism.[20] However, Mill did warn that the "principle of nationality" did not mean "a senseless antipathy to foreigners; or a cherishing of absurd peculiarities because they are national."[21]

The history of patriotism in the nineteenth century is the history of how the emotional power of patriotism was used to support an extreme nationalism and imperialism. Nationalism, as extreme patriotism, turned a national, patriotic sentiment into collective self-worship. At the same time, patriotism was coming under criticism from the "internationalism" of the developing communist movement.[22]

These trends continued into the twentieth century. Liberal-democratic forms of patriotism were aligned, ideologically and militarily, against fascism and communism. Fascism took the communal ideal of organic solidarity to a new level, combining a utopian vision of a totalitarian culture with total government control, extreme authoritarian government, and the sophisticated manipulation of patriotic emotions. As humanity hurtled toward two world wars, claims of patriotism became mixed with populist appeals to racial superiority and the "myth of a people."[23] Loyalty to one's nation meant unity and purification through the expulsion of Jews and ethnic minorities.

After the Second World War and the Holocaust, writers such as Habermas argued that only a non-communal, political form of patriotism could be valid. It must be a "patriotism of the Constitution" based on universal political principles of liberty and democracy embodied in the constitution of the Federal Republic of Germany.[24]

One reaction to Habermas was that a theory of patriotism must combine the communal and political. Rusconi criticized Habermas for trying to disconnect citizenship and nationhood. One becomes a citizen within and by means of a national history and culture. A democratic nation is therefore based on bonds of citizenship created by a common ethnicity and culture. It is both "demos," voluntary membership in a political community, and "ethnos," attachment to shared historical and cultural roots.[25] Viroli argues that we need a language of patriotism that connects with the attachment to one's cultural identity.[26] We need to translate belonging to a common culture into a common culture of citizenship. Without a political culture of liberty, ethnocultural unity generates love of one's uniqueness. Democratic politics does not need ethnocentric unity; it needs citizens committed to the way of life of the republic.

Structure of Patriotism

To clarify this complex topic, we need to identify the structure of all forms of patriotism and the structure of an ethical theory of patriotism. Patriotism is a group loyalty that involves an attitude directed, in varying strengths and in various ways, at a valued object. Therefore, an ethical theory of patriotism is a normative theory with three elements: (1) a description of what that attitude should be; (2) a description of what the object of patriotism should be; and (3) criteria for evaluating claims of patriotism in specific situations. One's normative theory will depend on one's ideals, such as freedom and democracy. My interest is in constructing a normative theory of patriotism for democratic journalism.

Nathanson provided a useful analysis of patriotism as an attitude. All forms of patriotism have a "positive commitment to act on one's country's behalf in ways that one would not normally act for other countries." Nathanson defines patriotism as "a special affection for, identification with, and a concern for one's own nation and a willingness to act on its behalf." The attitude of patriotic loyalty differ across several dimensions, such the object of loyalty, the strength and scope of the loyalty, the basis for the loyalty, and the attitude toward other loyalties.[27] Nathanson uses these dimensions to distinguish moderate and fanatical loyalty. Fanatical loyalty focuses exclusively on one object as a supreme duty that always overrides other loyalties. It is the ruthless pursuit of a goal. Fanatical loyalty takes an intolerant view of other loyalties.

We can conceptualize these distinctions as occupying a continuum with extreme patriotism on one end and a rejection of patriotism (or weak patriotism) on the other end. Moderate patriotism lies between these extremes. Extreme patriotism includes: (1) a special affection for one's country as superior to others; (2) an exclusive concern for one's country's well-being and few constraints on the pursuit of one's country's interests; and (3) automatic or uncritical support for one's country's actions. Extreme patriotism prepares the ground for extreme nationalism. In contrast, moderate patriotism consists of: (1) a special affection for one's country; (2) a desire that one's country flourishes and prospers; (3) a special but not exclusive concern for one's country; (4) support for a morally constrained pursuit of national goals; and (5) conditional and critical support of one's country's actions.[28] Moderate patriotism is moderate loyalty to one's country. For moderate patriots, their country is one of several objects of loyalty. This loyalty is limited, presumptive, and subject to scrutiny. Moderate patriotism is moderate because it acknowledges limits to patriotic partiality. It eschews exaggerating the uniqueness and superiority of one's country as a basis for aggressive attitudes. It respects the interests of people in other countries.

Moderate patriotism is the basis for my concept of democratic patriotism. Democratic patriotism is a form of moderate patriotism. It shares with moderate patriotism a moderate attitude toward the object of its loyalty – one's country. However, democratic patriotism is distinguished by adopting a more specific object or goal for patriotism. It provides a political interpretation of love of country. The object of loyalty is an ideal political association that is republican in its stress on liberty and democratic in its egalitarian stress on civic participation and equality. Democratic loyalty is republican in being a love of the republic as an association of free citizens motivated by the public good.[29]

Democratic patriotism is rational love of a democratic society that seeks to realize the human good on all levels.[30] Democratic patriotism is not identical with love of a leader or even the state since democratic community may or may not be served by any government, leader, policy, or state institution. This love can be divided into three types. First, a love of democratic political structure: the principles, institutions, and laws that secure liberties and self-government for citizens. Second, a love of meaningful political participation by informed and deliberative citizens. Third, a love of the diffusion of liberal-democratic values into the non-political activities of the public sphere, from education and scientific inquiry to the professions. Democratic patriotism recognizes more parochial values such as the love of family and ethnic traditions. But the values of democratic community are primary.

This democratic patriotism is inclusive, restrained, and open to evaluation. It is inclusive because it includes the liberty of all citizens within a nation. It is restrained because its commitment to moral dignity excludes xenophobic hatred toward other peoples and aggressive forms of nationalism. It is not the love of membership in an exclusive or superior group. This commitment is not dogmatic. It is open to evaluation with regard to how it is applied in any situation. It is open to the force of reasons and facts.

Moreover, democratic patriotism includes other values, such as the requirements of international law and fair relations among countries. Citizens of other countries have a right to construct their own democratic communities.

In one sense, democratic patriotism is an artificial passion created by certain historically contingent social structures. In another sense, it is a passion rooted in the human capacity for a sense of justice and goodness. Democratic experience provides principles of solidarity among citizens that go beyond their shared language and location. Solidarity is based on principles of common human rights, capacities, and aspirations. If democracy is the goal, what type of patriotism promotes this ideal? It is, I contend, a moderate patriotism that asks a country to live up to democratic criteria that define and restrain patriotic emotion.

My theory of democratic patriotism is a political form of patriotism that emphasizes rational principle and ethical ideal. It is similar to Viroli's notion of patriotism, noted above, as a political patriotism that incorporates and channels the strong emotions of communal patriotism to a love of democratic principle. A purely emotive, communal love of one's country is a potentially dangerous loyalty, vulnerable to excess and the rhetoric of demagogues. However, my theory recognizes the psychological and historical importance of communal factors in the special affection of patriotism. It is not possible (or necessary) to deny personal affection for one's country. The goal is to develop a strongly supported (and well understood) moderate discourse of patriotism that prevents extreme patriotism from claiming to be the "real" patriotism. The theoretical task is to develop a framework that allows us to systematically integrate these communal values with ethical and political principles. The social challenge is to develop a civic culture that transforms communal loyalties to group or neighbourhood into a more encompassing, ethical loyalty to the common good and ultimately all of humanity. This encompassing loyalty is a love of one's country as a democratic political community, which is part of a human community.

EVALUATING PATRIOTISM

I have sketched a notion of democratic patriotism that restrains patriotism in general. How should we use this notion to evaluate claims of patriotism in specific circumstances? To evaluate patriot-

ism in a consistent manner is an example of a larger ethical task –
to evaluate consistently our conflicting partialities. In this section, I
suggest an approach to evaluating partialities like patriotism.

Partialities

Partialities can be good or bad. Partialities can motivate ethical
action, such as acting generously toward a friend. Partiality can
prompt a father to dive into deep water to save his drowning child.
John Cottingham has argued that agent-related partialism and philophilic partialism are ethically valuable.[31] Agent-related partialism is
a preference for one's goals and a proper concern for one's welfare
and enrichment. Philophilic partialism is a partiality to loved ones
or friends. Some partialities express special relationships that entail
duties, such as the duty of parent to child. In deciding whether to
promote the interests of person x, I assign a certain ethical weight to
the fact that x is my loved one.

However, there are questionable forms of partiality. An extreme
loyalty to Canada may cause me to be callous toward the AIDS
epidemic in Africa. Andrew Oldenquist argues that group affection
and loyalties bind people together into "moral communities."[32] Not
always. Blind loyalty to a tyrant or ethnic group can lead to geno-
cide. To be a committed person sounds admirable, but I may be a
committed neo-Nazi. Josiah Royce said loyalty to a cause gives individuals a unifying identity. But loyalty should be to a good cause.[33]

In evaluating partialities, we should adopt what I call the attitude
of "mitigated impartialism."[34] Mitigated impartiality recognizes
the presumptive ethical weight of partialities. Mitigated impartialism stands mid-way between two incorrect views about partialities:
impartialism and partialism. Impartialism is the claim that ethics
requires us to allocate our time and resources without preference to
our own goals, and without displaying favoritism to those people
near to us. Partialism is the thesis that "it is (not merely psychologically understandable but) morally correct to favor one's own."
Partialism runs into problems, such as how to select good partialities from bad. Impartialism struggles to recognize legitimate claims
of partiality, such as parents' love for their children. In deciding
between x and y, impartialists are wrong to say, "I should assign
no weight to the fact that x is 'my own.'"[35] Mitigated impartialism
recognizes that partialities may have ethical weight; however, the
ethical weight is determined by systematic evaluation.

To evaluate partialities such as patriotism, we need to systematically incorporate partialities into our ethical thinking. But how? We evaluate partialities, such as patriotism, by applying the attitude of mitigated impartiality combined with a framework of restraining principles. Mitigated impartiality, as we noted, recognizes the presumptive ethical weight of partialities. Our framework, meanwhile, can be expressed as a series of questions about the patriotism being advanced. Is it fanatical or immoderate? Does it violate ethical principles? What are the consequences of being patriotic or loyal to x in situation y? Does honouring this partiality entail (or violate) rights and duties? What primacy should this claim of patriotism have vis-à-vis other partialities and other values? Does this claim of patriotism violate the ethical standards for some public office or public practice? What is the object of this patriotism? Is it allegiance to the commands of a charismatic leader or is it love of democratic society? We ask whether the claim of patriotism is compatible with more general principles of rational and ethical behaviour. On this analysis, a claim of patriotism upon citizens is reasonable and has prima facie ethical weight if and only if:

1. *The claim of patriotism is inclusive*. It respects the rights and freedoms of all citizens within a nation. Patriotism has no moral force when it supports actions that favour a subsection of citizens or the repression of a subsection of citizens.

2. *The claim of patriotism is restrained*. It is not xenophobic toward other peoples, and it lacks the aggressiveness often associated with nationalism and extreme forms of patriotism. The policy must be consistent with fair relations among countries and not violate principles of international law and human rights.

3. *The claim of patriotism must survive sustained public scrutiny and investigation*. Patriotism should be what Scanlon calls a "judgment-sensitive attitude" that is open to the force of reasons and facts.[36] Such evaluation can only be made in a public sphere that is open and informed by an impartial free press.

We can apply this approach for evaluating the ethical weight of patriotism to journalism. Again, we can ask: does the claim of patriotism ask journalists to be uncritical or extreme in their patriotism? Does it ask journalists to violate general ethical principles, right or duties, or to violate a principle of the profession of journalism? Does it ask journalists to promote a just liberal society, the political object of democratic journalism? Is the claim of patriotism compatible with the stated principles of inclusivity, rational restraint, and public scrutiny? By adopting this holistic form of evaluation, journalists would erect a critical, ethical barrier against the emotive pressure of extreme claims of patriotism. Neither journalists nor citizens in general are ethically required to respond to the claims of patriotism if they fail to satisfy the criteria embodied in these methods of evaluation.

"Genuine" Patriotism

Before I consider the compatibility of this democratic patriotism with ethical journalism, I will entertain two objections to my moderate patriotism. The first objection questions my claim that ethical deliberation has room for claims based on partiality. In this view, ethical reasoning must transcend the partial perspectives of prudential and other forms of thinking. Moreover, ethical principles must be universal. An ethical judgment must be supported by impartial deliberation and impersonal reasons. In Rawls's *A Theory of Justice*, deliberators screen out the influence of partialities by choosing principles from behind a "veil of ignorance." A rational and impartial spectator "assumes a position where his own interests are not at stake."[37]

The objection is correct in stressing that ethical deliberation is impartial and that ethics contains universal principles. It is, however, a misunderstanding of impartiality and universality. It wrongly assumes that impartial reasoning cannot contain premises about partialities. We've seen that this is false. Special relationships are a source of ethical duties and therefore are legitimate premises for deliberation. Even if ethics is based on universal principles, such as all people have equal dignity, we can still recognize the prima facie weight of special preferences. What is important is that the reasoner can look at an appeal to a partiality in an impartial manner by weighing a claim of partiality against other values and principles. It is also false that the actions (or duties) of partial relationships cannot be universalized so as to become ethical principles. Among the Ten Commandments, "Honour your father and mother" is a universalized partiality. All children owe honour to *their* parents. To take another example, from "I ought to take care of my child," one can universalize to the valid rule: "Everyone ought to take care of their own children."[38]

There is, however, a second source for this mistaken view. Ethical and religious discussions sometimes portray partialities as psychological obstacles to ethical behaviour. Partialities are desires that cause us to abandon our ethical duties for pleasure or gain. Consequently, ethics requires that we determine and carry out duties impartially, without the distorting influence of inclinations and passions. In Kant's ethics the only thing that has unconditional moral value is a will that acts according to duty alone.[39] Taken to extremes, the idea of partialities as obstacles can lead, as in some versions of Christianity, to a view of partialities as sinful cravings.[40] But a repression of partialities is neither possible nor desirable. Partialities can be good, and they perform important psychological and ethical functions in our lives. We do not need people to become pure altruists; what is required is that persons bring an ethical framework to the evaluation of their partialities.

The second objection concerns the nature of patriotism. The argument is that a moderate, principled patriotism is too rational or abstract to be a genuine patriotism. This objection assumes that patriotism is essentially communal and due to particular facts about one's birth and history. In "Is Patriotism a Virtue?" philosopher Alasdair MacIntyre argues that a moderate, rational patriotism is an "emasculated" patriotism that attempts an "incoherent" mix of partiality and impartial ethics. Another philosopher, Andrew Oldenquist, has argued that genuine loyalties should be defended even if they conflict with universal principles. He distinguishes between "loyalty patriotism" and "impartial patriotism." Only the former is genuine. Loyalty patriots are influenced by the thought that *their* country is at stake; impartial patriots consider this fact irrelevant. They support their country only because it meets certain criteria.

Both criticisms force us to choose between a pure (or strong) communal patriotism and an "emasculated" patriotism that is a hybrid of partiality and principle. The history of patriotism, outlined above, shows this to be a false dilemma. Communal and political elements have evolved and mingled throughout history. MacIntyre himself acknowledges that the political and communal elements combined in the French and American revolutions.[41]

Furthermore, it is false that political forms of patriotism ignore the fact that what is at stake is *my* country. A moderate patriotism recognizes this obvious fact – it is part of the definition of patriotism. But it insists that such identification be shaped and restrained by other values. Finally, these two philosophers fail to address the implications of their view. If genuine patriotism is based on tradition and communal elements, how can patriotism avoid irrationality or extreme nationalism? Neither philosopher addresses Habermas's concern about patriotism after the Holocaust.

THE COMPATIBILITY PROBLEM

Assume that, as a citizen, I commit myself to democratic patriotism, its restraining principles and methods of evaluation. Also assume that I am a journalist committed to ethical standards and democracy. How compatible are these commitments? I contend that moderate democratic patriotism is largely compatible with (and supportive of) the aims of democratic, ethical journalism.

My model assumes that the journalist has a democratic role that is different and more specific in its duties than that of the citizen. The rights and duties of a democratic citizen per se are very general. All citizens have the right to vote, influence public policy, engage in political activity, live under the rule of law, and so forth. However, democracy needs, in addition, certain types of citizens – public persons – to fulfill various democratic duties, such as politicians, judges, heads of institutions, and journalists. The role of journalists is to promote ethical flourishing in an open democratic society.

Given these principles – a commitment to moderate patriotism, deliberative democracy, and democratic journalism – we can draw two substantial conclusions about journalism and patriotism. One, the principles of democratic journalism are largely compatible with the principles of democratic patriotism because both share the goal of democratic community. An individual can be both a democratic journalist and a patriot of democratic community, although the journalist may serve democratic community in distinct ways. Democratic journalism and democratic patriotism share a substantial overlap of values such as freedom, openness, and tolerance. The democratic patriot and the democratic journalist will be on the same side of a number of public issues: both will support accurate, unbiased information; free speech; a critical news media; and a public sphere with diverse perspectives. Both will favour the protection of liberties, transparency in public affairs, and the evaluation of appeals to patriotism.

Second, extreme patriotism is largely incompatible with democratic journalism because it tends to support editorial limits on the press, or it exerts pressure on journalists to be uncritical, partisan, or economical with the truth. Journalism's commitment to moderate democratic patriotism implies that journalists must reject pressure to depart from its public role by practicing a more guarded, narrowly patriotic journalism. Journalism's democratic values come under severe test when a country decides to go to war, to deny civil liberties for security reasons, or to ignore the constitution in order to quell domestic unrest. The duty of journalists to critique a country's leadership may be very unpopular among some citizens in times of war. The publication of a government's human and civil rights abuses may lead to accusations that the press is aiding the "enemy."[42] Nevertheless, the public journalist is still duty-bound to resist such pressures and not fear social condemnation.

Even in times of uncertainty, journalists have a duty to continue to provide news, investigations, controversial analysis, and multiple perspectives. They should not mute their criticisms, and they should maintain skepticism toward all sources. Journalists need to unearth and explain the roots of their country's problems and coolly assess alleged threats. If journalists abandon their democratic role, they will fail to help the public to rationally assess public policy. The journalist's well-meaning desire to be patriotic may, in fact, assist the manipulation of public opinion by not questioning the powerful emotions of patriotism.

In a similar vein, Deni Elliott has argued that we need to distinguish between a "nationalistic" and a "patriotic" press: "Patriotic journalism is journalism that keeps in mind what citizens need to know to make educated decisions for self-governance. Nationalistic journalism, on the other hand, is journalism that echoes what authorities want to say or what citizens want to hear. The difference between patriotic journalism and nationalistic journalism is the difference between 'reporting' and 'repeating.'"[43]

As discussed in the previous chapter, the democratic idea that journalists serve society is easily confused with other conceptions, including that journalists serve their country by adhering to a narrow or extreme patriotism. The notion of a democratic journalism based on a moderate, political form of patriotism prevents this confusion by insisting that journalists serve their country by serving a democratic public.

GLOBAL PATRIOTISM

My analysis has found substantial compatibility between a certain conception of journalism, democratic journalism, and a certain conception of patriotism, moderate patriotism. The analysis assumes nation-based concepts. I have presumed, up to this point, that patriotism is loyalty to a country, and journalism's duty is to serve the democratic public of that country. But is a nation-based notion of patriotism still adequate in a global world with global media? I suggest that the answer is no. Just as the concept of whom journalism serves needs to be globalized, so does the idea of patriotic journalism need to be globalized.

If this is true, why bother to theorize about a moderate domestic patriotism for journalism? Why not simply construct a globalized concept of patriotism? There are several reasons. In terms of theory-building, it is helpful to start with existing notions and to then extend them, rather than attempting to invent from scratch a completely new notion. Invention usually proceeds through extension by way of analogy, metaphor, and the gradual enlargement of existing notions. To construct a new concept without reference to the old one risks constructing a concept that has little bearing on the phenomena and problems that needed explication in the first place – that is, our ordinary experience of patriotism within nations. Another reason is that a global journalism ethics is not yet in existence, and journalists today continue to face problems surrounding domestic forms of patriotism. Therefore, we still need a clear and restrained form of domestic patriotism to address these problems.

These reasons also explain why I do not abandon the idea of patriotism altogether and why I do not argue that journalists should simply reject the idea that they should be patriotic. As my analysis has shown, this is psychologically unrealistic and unnecessary. The attitude of mitigated impartiality is based on the recognition that patriotism is a recurring and inescapable partiality for humans, now and for the foreseeable future. Such partialities have some ethical weight. It is perfectly reasonable to expect people who live in a country and contribute to its communal life to develop a partiality toward their country.

The best approach is to ethically restrain the limits of patriotism and to show how citizens should evaluate the claims of patriotism.

We need to find a middle position between two types of society. One type is a society of citizens who care nothing for their country because of a philosophical commitment to a totalizing cosmopolitanism, a cosmopolitanism that requires citizens to place no (or little) importance on the interests of their country or compatriots. This is a false cosmopolitanism that damages the real cosmopolitanism, which is about balancing the local and the global. Another type of society is a society that cares little about the interests and good of others beyond its borders and is prone to unjust actions toward other societies due to an aggressive and uncritical patriotism. Philosophically, we need a conception of patriotism for a society between these extremes.

PATRIOT OF HUMANITY

The best way to explain how to globalize domestic patriotism is to return to the structure of moderate patriotism. Earlier I explained patriotism as a group loyalty that involves an attitude directed, in varying strengths and in various ways, at a valued object. A global concept changes the attitude and the object of patriotism. What remains the same for domestic and global patriotism is an ethical commitment to a moderate and ethically restrained patriotic partiality. We remain committed to a systematic evaluation of claims of patriotism. However, with global patriotism, we alter the attitude. The attitude becomes the cosmopolitan attitude described in the last few chapters. Global patriots adopt a new ethical identity; they see themselves as global citizens and, as journalists, as agents for global citizens and a global public sphere. With this attitude comes the various imperatives and principles of my cosmopolitanism. Citizens continue to live in their respective countries, to feel affection for those who live near them, and worry about citizens within their borders. They worry and care in a different psychological and ethical manner. No longer is the fact that such people live within my borders considered to be the sole or primary ground for caring for them. Rather, under cosmopolitanism, I see such "domestic" care as one particular expression of a universal concern for all people. Domestic patriotism is grounded in my claim of a common humanity. As Appiah states about African identity: "We will only solve our problems if we see them as human problems arising out of

a special situation."[44] Similarly, we will not resolve the most fundamental problems among countries until citizens see such problems as
differences arising among a common humanity, to be adjudicated as
"human problems" arising out of special situations.

This alteration in ethical identity and attitude has important practical consequences. It means that, when are attempting to decide
if policies or actions are ethically justified, we place our domestic
patriotism within a prior and more fundamental patriotism to something larger; that is, we give our patriotic attitude a new "object."
Global journalism ethics is the embrace of a new object for patriotism – a global patriotism to humanity and its ethical flourishing.

Now that we have constructed a cosmopolitan notion of ethical flourishing, it is not difficult to state what a global patriotism
entails. It entails that we should make primary our commitment to
ethical flourishing across borders. We are to evaluate international
issues and policies by reference to this ideal. We can add to the
ideal the principles that we find in human rights treaties and other
expressions of cosmopolitanism. It follows that journalists, as cosmopolitan agents, should consider the promotion of global ethical
flourishing as the object of their patriotism. In this way, journalists
too are global patriots.

If our ethics is cosmopolitan, then patriotism to one's country has
a diminished role to play in our ethical thinking and actions. Global
patriotism is not a superfluous philosophical attitude. It is an attitude that is essential for the future of our common humanity on our
troubled small blue planet. As noted, our allegiance to a borderless
human community rules out assigning ultimate ethical value to collective entities such as states or nations. Cosmopolitanism does not
deny that people can have legitimate feelings of concern for their
country or compatriots; it only insists that such feelings must not
violate the universal principles of humanity and human rights. If we
adopt a cosmopolitan attitude, the object of democratic journalism
becomes not only the promotion of national democratic publics but
also global democratic structures. Nation-based forms of patriotism
remain ethically permissible in journalism insofar as they do not
conflict with the demands of global media ethics and its cosmopolitan patriotism.

We now can see more clearly the importance of the "claim of
humanity" for journalism. It is the central ethical concept around
which journalists should construct their ethical identity.

CONCLUSION

We come to the close of this book, but we are far from closing the book on global journalism ethics. These chapters provide a foundation – the basic philosophical concepts to begin the invention of a detailed and theoretically solid global ethics.

The construction reformulated existing concepts through philosophical reflection and argument, and through a consideration of the new conditions of journalism today. This volume combines the right and the good into a fuller philosophy of journalism ethics and extends this philosophy to construct a global journalism ethics.

This foundation is put forward in a pragmatic spirit as a set of principles that have the potential to advance a cross-cultural dialogue on global journalism ethics. I believe I have proposed principles that have a reasonable chance of being accepted by people (and journalists) from different cultures, or at minimum provide the first formulation of adequate principles.

My foundation is not neutral. It is developed from a liberal democratic perspective. It borrows from Western philosophical traditions such as contract theory, constructivism, and cosmopolitanism. One objection might be that these traditions cannot be used in a foundation for global ethics because they are of Western origin.

My response would be that the Western ideas I have used are not strictly and exclusively Western for they are expressed in non-Western cultures. For example, cosmopolitan ideas can be found in Confucianism and Eastern philosophies. My ethical contractualism is inclusive and seeks a dialogue with liberal and humanitarian forms of thought from any and all cultures.

Contractualism is broad enough to allow a discussion among diverse approaches in journalism and social philosophy. True, it is not open to every form of political and social thought, such as totalitarianism and extreme nationalism, but no theory can be open to every viewpoint.

Further, the objection that a global theory must have ideas of global origin, and therefore not of Western origin, is not a coherent notion. Any approach to global ethics will have to borrow ideas from somewhere. A global ethics cannot be constructed by using ideas and approaches that have no history. All ideas have a history. Global ethics cannot be the evaluation of principles from a detached "view from nowhere." There is no such thing as a perspectiveless theory, at least not in ethics and politics. What a global approach requires is a cosmopolitan allegiance to humanity. A global approach requires forms of thought that are open to other views and a rich dialogue among many forms of thought. What is crucial is not where ideas come from but where they lead us. What promise does an approach or an idea portend for the task at hand, and is it open to change and challenge? Can it sufficiently learn from and incorporate ideas from other approaches?

Given this ideal of a global journalism ethics, what are its realistic chances of being achieved in journalism? As an ideal, it will never be achieved, at least not in full. Realistically, the practical goal of constructing a global journalism ethics cannot be that, within the short or medium term, all journalists and journalism organizations in the world will adopt one code of global ethics. That is too much to ask of any ideal conception or ethical theory, let alone one dealing with the practical and diverse business of journalism. It may be that, in the end, journalists will accept the need for global ethics but hold a number of different conceptions of what a global ethics entails, differing on some principles and applications. These variations in realizing global ethics would not, on my approach, invalidate global ethics. Instead, it would be in line with my notion of universals expressing themselves differently across cultures. Variations in global ethics may be considered a good thing, especially by those who get nervous when people speak of all journalists agreeing on any idea or doctrine.

If a full consensus among all journalists on one unique code is not the practical goal, what is? I think we have to start with more modest, intermediate goals. First we should adopt the more realistic goal of achieving a gradual widening of the ethical attitudes of increasing numbers of journalists. The goal is the gradual adoption of a cosmopolitan attitude that works as a force for improving global media and reducing the dangers of parochial journalism. Then, we can see to what extent regional and international associations of journalists wish to consider and formulate the first drafts of global codes of ethics and how they might be implemented. At the same time, we can encourage journalism organizations, media ethicists, human rights workers, and others to continue to hold media practices up to the liberal global standards found in this book and others. Coalitions of journalists and citizens can work together to maintain constant pressure on media organizations to view their work, and the consequences of their work, from a global perspective. In this manner, we will be sowing the seeds of a global ethics attitude. This is the first practical step in making cosmopolitanism a significant part of journalism culture and ethics.

As we take practical actions to embed global ethics in journalism, it is important to remember that the project must be a combination of the practical and the theoretical. We cannot ignore one or the other. A global journalism ethics will not emerge from theory alone, even if the theory is a brilliant philosophical work of invention. Any proposed theory will have to be seen as useful and important by working journalists. Nor will global ethics emerge solely from more practical activities, such as workshops and conference discussions among working journalists where participants attempt to formulate a code of international standards. Without the support of theory to guide code writing, such codes and well-meant declarations are likely to be inadequately grounded in philosophy and ethical theory.

Practically speaking, an adequate global journalism ethics will require the convergence of both types of activities. Agreement will only emerge out of dialogue among increasing numbers of journalists and the public, and such agreement must be rooted in philosophical argument and theory.

My hope is that this volume can contribute to both sides of this construction. I encourage others to improve, clarify, and critique my scheme. These are the ways of ethical invention. The success of philosophical labours cannot be known directly or immediately. Only time will tell if these ideas are useful for redesigning journalism ethics. In the end, my approach may be shown to be a false step toward a global journalism ethics. However, even a failure or a partial success may be of help to a community of scholars and practitioners who care deeply about democratic public journalism.

Notes

INTRODUCTION

1 Rosen, *What Are Journalists For?*
2 MacIntyre, "Is Patriotism a Virtue?" 3.
3 Dewey, *Reconstruction in Philosophy*, 22.

CHAPTER ONE

1 Ortega y Gasset, *Meditations on Quixote*, 37.
2 Blackburn, *Being Good*, 1–8.
3 Gibbard, "Wise Choices, Apt Feelings," 56.
4 The idea of doubt and conflict as the origin of serious thinking as put forward by Dewey in *Reconstruction in Philosophy*, 80–3.
5 Lukes, *Moral Relativism*, 62–3.
6 Scanlon, *What We Owe Each Other*, chapter 4. See Lukes, *Moral Relativism*, 63.
7 Adams, in *Finite and Infinite Goods*, 18, talks about the seriousness of normative discourse. Also see Hare, *The Language of Morals*, 142–4.
8 Marcus Singer used the term "moral fanaticism" to refer to "the idea that no action is indifferent or trivial" (*Generalization in Ethics*, 184).
9 MacIntyre, "Epistemological Crises, Dramatic Narrative, and the Philosophy of Science," 8–16.
10 Audi, *Practical Reasoning and Ethical Decision*, 1–2.
11 Horgan and Timmons, "Introduction," *Metaethics after Moore*.
12 Lukes, *Moral Relativism*, 123.
13 This categorization is close to other schemes, such as the distinction between metaethics, normative ethics, and practical ethics, in LaFollette, *Blackwell Guide to Ethical Theory*, 1–3; and the division of ethics into metaethics and normative ethics, as in Brink, *Moral Realism and the Foundations of Ethics*, 1–2.

14 Smith, *The Moral Problem*, 2.

15 Ivison, *Rights*, 22.

16 Ibid.

17 Rawls, *Lectures in the History of Moral Philosophy*, 3–4.

18 Ibid., 10.

19 Hume, *A Treatise of Human Nature*, 477–501. The subtitle of this work is *Being an Attempt to Introduce the Experimental Method of Reasoning into Moral Subjects*.

20 Ibid., 484.

21 Ibid., 495.

22 Rachels, "Naturalism," 74.

23 Broad, "Some of the Main Problems of Ethics," 103.

24 Moore, *Principia Ethica*, 10.

25 Ibid., 147.

26 Hurka, "Moore in the Middle."

27 Ayer, *Language, Truth and Logic*, 103.

28 Hudson, *Modern Moral Philosophy*, 1.

29 James, "The Moral Philosopher and the Moral Life," 614.

30 See Korsgaard, *Creating the Kingdom of Ends*, ix.

31 Blackburn, *Ruling Passions*, 68–9.

32 Blackburn, "Relativism," 39.

33 Berlin, "Prologue," *Political Ideas in the Romantic Age*, 11.

34 Rawls, *Lectures on the History of Moral Philosophy*, 244–5.

35 Rawls, *Lectures on the History of Moral Philosophy*, 245.

36 Darwall, *Contractarianism/Contractualism*, 1.

37 Scanlon, *What We Owe To Each Other*, 5.

38 Habermas, *The Inclusion of the Other*, 33.

39 Korsgaard, *The Sources of Normativity*, 35.

40 Ibid., 36–7.

41 See Nietzsche, *Beyond Good and Evil*.

42 Dennett, *Freedom Evolves*, 15

43 What the is-ought distinction in ethics overlooks is that the same combination of normative and factual premises occurs in science. Scientific reasoning cannot proceed purely from facts to scientific conclusions. Among the premises of a scientific argument are normative premises about the correct norms and methods of scientific procedure.

44 Hume, *A Treatise of Human Nature*, book 3, part 1, 469–70.

45 Rawls, *Lectures on the History of Moral Philosophy*, 51.

46 Dennett, *Freedom Evolves*, 2.

47 De Waal, *Primates and Philosophers*.

48 Dennett, *Freedom Evolves*, 202.
49 Korsgaard, *The Sources of Normativity*, 17.
50 Schudson 1978; Mindich 1998.
51 Peterson, "The Social Responsibility Theory of the Press."
52 Commission on Freedom of the Press 1947, 21–8.
53 Christians and Nordenstreng, "Social Responsibility Worldwide," 4.
54 Darwall, *Contractarianism/Contractualism*.
55 Klaidman and Beauchamp, *The Virtuous Journalist*; Kovach and Rosenstiel 2007.
56 For examples of proactive and restraining principles, see major codes of ethics such as the code for the Society of Professional Journalists in the United States, at www.spj.org, and the code for the Canadian Association of Journalists at www.caj.org.
57 Black, Steele, and Blarney, *Doing Ethics in Journalism*, 29–30.

CHAPTER TWO

1 My "reflective engagement" is close to the idea of moral engagement that is found in Bracci and Christians, *Moral Engagement in Public Life*.
2 My theory assumes a continuum of actions increasingly under the control of reasoning. At one end there is hardwired reflexive behaviour, e.g., I duck a brick thrown at me. Next is learned or habitual behaviour, such as locking my car's doors. Then there are actions influenced by practical thinking and, finally, actions due to explicit deliberation.
3 The example is used by Audi, *Practical Reasoning and Ethical Decision*, 3–4.
4 Most logicians would not claim that the way that people reason in ordinary life models the forms of argument found in logic textbooks. But the correspondence can be reasonably close and, where successful, logical analysis expresses the overall intent and reasoning of the reasoner. See Groarke et al., *Good Reasoning Matters*.
5 Aristotle, *Nicomachean Ethics*, 1139a23–b5, 1023–4.
6 Audi, *Practical Reasoning and Ethical Decision*, 96.
7 Ibid., 6.
8 Stevenson, *Ethics and Language*, 1
9 This example is not hypothetical. In 2003, I helped the Canadian Association of Journalists formulate a special code of ethics for investigative journalism as an extension of its existing general code.
10 Eclecticism was a mode of thought endorsed by Kant and some of the most significant German thinkers of Kant's generation. In France, Diderot

praised the "eclectics" in the *Encyclopaedia*. Eclectics were independent thinkers in service of humanity who were subject to no ideology. They investigated all doctrines and accepted things only on their "reason" and experience. See Kuehn, *Kant: A Biography*, 179.

11 Ross, *The Right and the Good*, 30. My eclecticism goes beyond Ross's view. I place eclecticism within a theory of reasoning that details how such weighing occurs. I provide a scheme and a model for such reasoning, a set of criteria for evaluating frameworks, and the method of reflective equilibrium. These concepts will be explained later in this chapter.

12 Aristotle, *Nicomachean Ethics*, 1140a24–b12, 1025–6.

13 Black, Steel, and Barney, *Doing Ethics in Journalism*, 29–30.

14 Practices, from journalism and games to art and scientific inquiries, are "forms of systematic human activity, each with its own goods internal to each. Practices develop through time in directions dictated by the conceptions of achievement internal to each, the achievement both of the goods specific to each particular type of practice and of excellence in pursuit of those goods" (MacIntyre, "Colors, Cultures and Practices," 46).

15 However, I disagree with MacIntyre's realism, his notion that the avowal theory is wrong and moral claims must be seen as descriptions that are literally true or false (MacIntyre, "Moral Relativism, Truth and Justification, 58, 61–6).

16 Darwall, *Contractarianism/Contractualism*, 1.

17 As Taylor writes about frameworks: "To think, feel, judge within such a framework is to function with the sense that some action, or mode of life, or mode of feeling is comparably higher than the others which are more readily available to us" (*Sources of the Self*, 19, 31).

18 In *Political Liberalism* (9, 13), Rawls moves from justifying principles of justice by an appeal to individuals using reflective equilibrium to a public process in which citizens seek an "overlapping consensus" on principles. Reflective equilibrium becomes a method of evaluation in a political process.

19 Rawls, *Political Liberalism*, 23.

20 Rawls, *A Theory of Justice*, 19.

21 Rawls, *Political Liberalism*, 8n8.

22 Nussbaum, *Frontiers of Justice*, 299–300.

23 Rawls (*A Theory of Justice*, 20) writes: "There are questions we feel sure must be answered in a certain way" such as that religious intolerance and racial intolerance are unjust. These convictions are "provisional fixed points which we assume any theory of justice must fit."

24 Elgin, *Between the Absolute and the Arbitrary*, 198.

25 The example is taken from Wilkins and Coleman, *The Moral Media,* 143. In this example, the analysis and evaluation are guided in part by the code of ethic of the Society of Professional Journalists. Other codes could be used for these two stages.

26 For a discussion of top-down and other reasoning methods, see Audi, *The Good in the Right,* 162–5.

27 Sidgwick, *The Methods of Ethics,* 11.

28 Mill, "Utilitarianism," 63.

29 Ibid., 64, 82.

30 Postema, "Bentham's Utilitarianism," 40.

31 Mill, "Utilitarianism," 66, 90–1.

32 The metaphor of an arch is from Quine, *Word and Object,* 11.

33 Ibid., 3.

34 Darwall, "How Should Ethics Relate to (the Rest of) Philosophy?" 33, 25.

35 For a detailed treatment of the senses of objectivity and its history, see Ward, *The Invention of Journalism Ethics.*

36 Rawls, *Lectures on the History of Moral Philosophy,* 244–5.

37 Ibid.

38 Putnam, "Objectivity without Objects," 52–4.

39 Putnam, *The Collapse of the Fact-Value Dichotomy,* 33.

40 Ward, *The Invention of Journalism Ethics,* chapter 7.

41 The idea that ethical standards are absolute should be distinguished from the additional claim that we know these standards with certainty, although historically the quest for absoluteness and certainty have travelled together.

42 Scanlon, *What We Owe To Each Other,* 349.

43 Ibid., 341.

44 Richard Rorty deflates fears of relativism in "Putnam and the Relativist Menace."

45 James, "The Moral Philosopher and the Moral Life," 623.

46 Ibid., 610.

CHAPTER THREE

1 Pindar, *Nemean Odes,* VIII, 37–44, as quoted in Martha C. Nussbaum, *The* Fragility *of Goodness,* vi.

2 Rawls, *Justice as Fairness: A Restatement,* 196.

3 A detailed treatment of theory types would require another book. Here, I provide a sketch of theory options to help the reader understand my theory's features.

4 Rawls, *A Theory of Justice*, section 9.

5 The classical hedonist view, such as the epicurean view of Greek antiquity, included a rational balance and evaluation of pleasures and pains. It represents an expansion beyond simply seeking pleasures and the avoidance of pain without any guidance. Yet the addition of "reason" to the process cannot hide the fact that this hedonic theory focuses on the individualistic enjoyment of mental states. Ancient cynicism and skepticism were also hedonic since they sought mental tranquility or contentment. On these "practical" philosophies in ancient Greece, after Plato and Aristotle, see chapter 2 of my *The Invention of Journalism Ethics*.

6 Griffin, *Well Being*, 100.

7 Sen ("Capability and Well-Being," 30) describes welfarism as a theory of subjective well-being, a matter of measuring "personal utility" by focusing on pleasures, happiness, or desire fulfillment. The hope is to "aggregate" these utilities to determine public policy.

8 John Helliwell uses "individual and community level variables" to determine subjective well-being as a way to study the impact of public policies in a global world (*Globalization and Well-Being*, 47).

9 On the psychological literature, see Diener et al., "Subjective Well-Being"; Veenhoven, "Questions on Happiness"; Diener and Suh, "Measuring Subjective Well-Being to Compare the Quality of Life of Cultures"; Argyle, *The Psychology of Happiness*; Van Praag and Ferrer-I-Carbonell, *Happiness Quantified*; Layard, *Happiness*; Haidt, *The Happiness Hypothesis*; and Frey and Stutzer, *Happiness and Economics*.

10 Brandt, *A Theory of the Good and the Right*, 10.

11 Scanlon, "Value, Desire, and Quality of Life," 189.

12 Ibid., 192.

13 The discussion here reflects discussions in several books such as Kraut's *What Is Good and Why*, 130; Parfit's *Reasons and Persons*, appendix 1, 493–502; Griffin's *Well-Being*, chapters 1–3; and Geuss's "Happiness and Politics," 102–7.

14 See Berlin, *Political Ideas in the Romantic Age*, especially "The Idea of Freedom," and "Two Concepts of Freedom: Romantic and Liberal."

15 Nozick, *Anarchy, State, and Utopia*, 42–5. Also see Kraut, *What Is Good and Why*, 126n48.

16 Sen, "Capability and Well-Being," 30.

17 Nussbaum, *Frontiers of Justice*, 70.

18 The perfectionist tradition is long and varied, from Plato, Aristotle, and Aquinas to Leibniz, Kant, Bradley, Hamilton, Spinoza, Bosanquet, Hegel, Green, and Marx.

19 Hamilton, *Lectures on Metaphysics*, 14.

20 Hurka, *Perfectionism*, 3.

21 Kraut calls his flourishing theory "developmentalism" because he thinks the term "perfection" implies that the goal of ethics is a "perfect person" or one supremely perfect form of life (*What Is Good and Why*, 136).

22 On Tiny Tim mentality and well-being, see Cohen, "Equality of What?" 17. On adaptive preferences, see Elster, *Sour Grapes*, 109–40, and Nussbaum, *Women and Human Development*, 111–66.

23 For a discussion of desire theory as formal analysis, see Griffin, *Well Being*, 30–4.

24 Aristotle was one of the first philosophers to apply this biological perspective to the analysis of the good life. In modern ethical theory, the concept of flourishing received special attention from G.E.M. Anscombe in "Modern Moral Philosophy," 43–4. The concept has subsequently been used in political theory. It appears in Nussbaum's *Frontiers of Justice*, in Hursthouse's *On Virtue Ethics*, 197–231, 247–65, in Foot's *Natural Goodness*, 5, 16, 40–6, 92, 109, in Adams's *Finite and Infinite Goods*, 83–101, in Brink's *Moral Realism and the Foundations of Ethics*, 217–36, Finnis's *Natural Law and Natural Rights*, 59–99, Sen's *Development as Freedom*, 70–7, and Kraut's *What Is Good and Why*.

25 This is a modification of Kraut in *What Is Good and Why*, 5.

26 Kraut, *What Is Good and Why*, 131.

27 Etymologically, in the thirteenth century, "flourish" meant to flower or the blossom of a fruit tree, and later took on the added senses of being in one's prime, to be vigorous, to parade and swagger. "Perfect," in the thirteenth century meant to be thoroughly versed or trained, or in a complete state, and to bring to full development. In religious circles it took on the idea of being morally perfect or holy, and eventually it took on the additional senses of being in a faultless state, unqualified and unalloyed.

28 Kraut, *What Is Good and Why*, 94.

29 See Kitcher, "Biology and Ethics."

30 For ancient and modern conceptions of *eudaimonia*, see Jost and Shiner, *Eudaimonia and Well-Being*.

31 Honohan, *Civic Republicanism*, 20.

32 Kraut, *Aristotle on the Human Good*, chapter 4, "The Hierarchy of Ends," 197–266.

33 For a modern gloss on the Aristotelian idea of happiness as active achievement, involving an integration of internal and external factors in life, see Russell, *The Conquest of Happiness*, 178–9, 186–91.

34 Perfection also plays a part in religious texts, such as the Gospel of Matthew, 5:48, where the writer urges his listeners to "Be Perfect, as your heavenly Father is perfect."

35 Spinoza, *Ethics*, book 3, *Definitions of the Emotions*, 2–3.

36 Kant, *The Metaphysics of Morals*, 194.

37 Quoted in Geuss, *Public Goods, Private Goods*, 3–4.

38 Berlin, "John Stuart Mill and the Ends of Life," 184.

39 Berlin, *Four Essays on Liberty*, xlix.

40 Hobhouse, quoted in Lopston, *Theories of Human Nature*, 75–6.

41 Korsgarrd, *The Sources of Normativity*, 74.

42 Williams, *Ethics and the Limits of Philosophy*, 147, 45ff, 152–3.

43 Sen says there is a lot of agreement on what the basic needs are, as a set of minimally adequate goods without which a person is thought to be "deprived" ("Capability and Well-Being," 31). On the basic needs literature, see Streeten et al., *First Things First*.

44 My approach has been influenced by work on human goods from Rawls and Sen to Nussbaum and Held. For example, see Nussbaum's list of ten central human capabilities or entitlements, as defining a minimal level of social justice (*Frontiers of Justice*, 76–8).

45 Kraut, *What Is Good and Why*, 203.

46 Nussbaum says this intuition is close to Marx's view that humans are "in need of a totality of human life–activities" (Nussbaum, *Frontiers of Justice*, 70, 74, 278–9, 283).

47 His principles include the "equal worth and dignity" of every person, the value of active agency, and the ability to "shape human community," which connotes the capacity to "to be self-determining" (Held, "Principles of Cosmopolitan Order," 12).

48 Rawls, *Political Liberalism*, 48–54.

49 For a rebuttal of these suspicions, see Pinker, *The Blank Slate*.

50 An ethical perspective on the human species must include both an "internal" view of how it is to experience values and ethical choices *and* the third-person scientific and humanistic perspective on humans a species with distinct capacities for self-reflection and reflection self-direction.

51 A case of the human ability to change its nature is technology to alter the genetic makeup of individuals; see Habermas, "*The Future of Human Nature,*" 12–15.

52 Mill, "Autobiography," 149.

53 Singapore is an example of a society where social coordination is efficiently and forcefully maintained through strict laws backed by a non-democratic government. Rawls would not consider Singapore a well-ordered society.

54 Rawls, *A Theory of Justice*, 453.

55 Rawls sees his emphasis on the "primacy of the social" in ethics as one way in which his theory of right differs from Kant's approach, which focuses on the ethical reasoning of individuals; Rawls, "Kantian Constructionism in Ethical Theory," 553.

56 Audard, *John Rawls*, 3.

57 Rawls, *A Theory of Justice*, 4, 521.

58 On the origins of justice, Rawls is heavily influenced by Hume's discussion of "the circumstances of justice," as discussed in chapter 1. To Hume's "objective" conditions of justice, such as moderate scarcity of resources, Rawls adds the "subjective" condition of a pluralism of interests and comprehensive philosophies (Rawls, *Political Liberalism*, 66; see also *A Theory of Justice*, 520).

59 Rawls, *A Theory of Justice*, 3; *Justice as Fairness: A Restatement*, 5–8; and *Political Liberalism*, 15–28.

60 Rawls, *A Theory of Justice*, 54–90, *Justice as Fairness*, 39–79.

61 Rawls writes that the original position is "a device of representation or, alternatively, a thought-experiment for the purpose of public- and self-clarification" (*Justice as Fairness*, 17).

62 Rawls, *Political Liberalism*, 292. The terms "utilitarian" and "utilitarianism" have two sources. Bentham recounted how one night he dreamt he was the head of a "sect of utilitarians" (Postema, "Bentham's Utilitarianism," 27). Some forty years later, Mill ("Utilitarianism," 68) borrowed the term "utilitarian" from Galt's *Annals of the Parish* to designate his group of London young radicals. Mill called them "the Utilitarian Society," realizing Bentham's dream. Mill grew tired of the term, "utilitarianism" because it came to be used as a slogan for sectarian conflict.

63 Rawls, *Political Liberalism*, 291.

64 Ibid, 309.

65 Ibid., 5–6.

66 Ibid., 11; *A Theory of Justice*, 7.

67 Rawls, *Justice as Fairness*, 18–19, 20, 21.

68 Ibid., 19, 22.

69 Ibid., 22.

70 Philosophically, the distinction between the rational and reasonable goes back to Kant's distinction between agents who reason according to the hypothetical imperative (how to obtain goods) and agents who reason according to the categorical imperative, or according to what maxims could be universalized and acceptable to all rational beings. The former represents "empirical practical reason," the latter "pure practical reason." Rawls, *Political Liberalism*, 48–9n1.

71   Ibid., 49–50; Sibley, "The Rational versus the Reasonable."

72   Rawls, *Political Liberalism*, 48–9n1, 54–8.

73   Reciprocity is a Hobbesian line of thought in Rawls's writings that emphasizes real-world limits on ethics and politics; see Ward, "Thomas Hobbes:
Submission to Leviathan."

74   Philosophers have described autonomy is different ways. Locke stressed
the capacity for abstract thought and the ability to take responsibility for
one's actions. Hobbes stressed being in control of one's speech and attitudes. Kant and Mill talked about rational autonomy as a high degree of
rational self-direction. Ivison, *Rights*, 79, 207.

75   Rawls, *Political Liberalism*, 77; *A Theory of Justice*, 514–15. Rawls
explains his three-level theory of moral development in *A Theory of
Justice*, part 3, chapter 8, "The Sense of Justice," 453–512.

76   Rawls, *The Law of Peoples*, 24.

77   Rawls, *Political Liberalism*, xviii.

78   Rawls, *Justice as Fairness*, 190.

79   Rawls, *Political Liberalism*, xviii.

80   Rawls, "The Idea of Public Reason Revisited," 131.

81   Kant, "An Answer to the Question: What Is Enlightenment?" 18–20;
Critique of Practical Reason, B767–97.

82   Rawls, *Political Liberalism*, 213.

83   Ibid., 110.

84   Ibid., 114.

85   Rawls, *A Theory of Justice*, 517; *The Law of Peoples*, 56; "The Idea of
Public Reason Revisited," 137, 169.

86   Rawls, *Political Liberalism*, 119.

87   Rawls, "The Idea of Public Reason Revisited," 133–4, 143; *Political
Liberalism*, 215.

88   Rawls, "The Idea of Public Reason Revisited," 133–4. Rawls, in *Political
Liberalism*, 231–40, names the US Supreme Court of Justice as an exem-
plar in the exercise of public reason since it follows careful guidelines and
common principles to come to reasoned conclusions about the common
good.

89   Rawls says the role of the citizen is similar to the view one finds in
Rousseau's *The Social Contract*, where voting is decided by what advances
the common good (*Political Liberalism*, 219–20).

90   Rawls, "The Idea of Public Reason Revisited," 134n13.

91   This view of objectivity is close to my "pragmatic objectivity" as a
domain-specific set of agreed-upon criteria for the evaluation of fallible,
purposive inquiry in *The Invention of Journalism Ethics*, chapter 7.

92 Korsgarrd, *The Sources of Normativity*, 114.

93 I ignore virtue theories because their claim to be prior is weak. Like Kant, I take virtue to be the "moral strength" of a human being's will to do what is good or right. The exercise of virtue is prior neither logically nor epistemically. First we need to know what the good and the right require.

94 Etymologically, "prior" is Old English for "former," "elder," "superior," when used comparatively, as in the "prior" of a house of friars. By the eighteenth century, the term also meant proceeding in time, order, or importance.

95 Sandel, *Liberalism and the Limits of Justice*, xi.

96 Mill, "Utilitarianism," 96, 109, 113.

97 See Petit, "Consequentialism."

98 The priority of the right has two senses that should not be confused. One is the priority of the moral right, which is the priority of doing what is one's moral duty as determined by a self-legislative reason and the priority of the legal right, which is doing what the civil law requires for rights relations among people. In this section, I am concerned with the moral sense of right, which I regard as the basis for evaluation of the civil right.

99 For Kant's writings on the priority of the right, see *Critique of Practical Reason*, part 1, chapter 2, book 1, 17-52; *The Metaphysics of Morals*, part 1, on the doctrine of right, and 9-42; and *Groundwork of the Metaphysic of Morals*, Preface, chapters 1-2, 55-113. Ironically, the term "deontology" in ethics derives from the title of an article by Bentham, the arch-utilitarian, entitled "Deontology together with a Table of the Springs of Action and Article on Utilitarianism," which addressed matters of private, interpersonal morality; see Postema, "Bentham's Utilitarianism," 28.

100 Kant, *Critique of Practical Reason*, 65.

101 Rawls, *A Theory of Justice*, 30.

102 Sandel, *Liberalism and the Limits of Justice*, 1.

103 Rawls, *Political Liberalism*, 52.

104 For a utilitarian attempt reply to these worries, see Lyons, "Human Rights and the General Welfare."

105 Rawls, *A Theory of Justice*, 26.

106 Ibid., 28.

107 Rawls, "Kantian Constructivism in Ethical Theory," 532.

108 Rawls, *Political Liberalism*, 176.

109 Rawls, *A Theory of Justice*, 396.

110 Rawls, *Political Liberalism*, 174.

111 Rawls, *A Theory of Justice*, 566.

112 Ibid., 30.

113 Kant, "On the Common Saying," 64-5.
114 Reciprocity is one of the social origins of dignity of humans and respect. There is for Rawls an important social basis for "self-respect" closely linked to just arrangements and the opportunity to develop one's moral capacities. Reciprocity is required to ensure a stable society. It goes beyond egoism in including a reciprocal commitment to justice. Reciprocity is not just a strategic move to get what I want. In the background, is Hume's analysis of the conditions of justice, especially the limited human capacity for altruism.
115 Sullivan, "Introduction," *Immanuel Kant: The Metaphysics of Morals*, xxi.
116 Kant, *Critique of Practical Reason*, 113-15.
117 Kant, *The Metaphysics of Morals*, 151.

CHAPTER FOUR

1 On global communication, see McPhail, *Global Communication*. On global forms of journalism, see Seib, *The Global Journalist*, and de Beer and Merrill, *Global Journalism*.
2 Brock and Brighouse, *The Political Philosophy of Cosmopolitanism*, 4.
3 For Kant's cosmopolitanism, see his *Toward Perpetual Peace*.
4 See Nussbaum, *Cultivating Humanity*.
5 Brock and Brighouse, *The Political Philosophy of Cosmopolitanism*, 3.
6 Nagel, in *Equality and Partiality*, has argued that the task of constructing a society that integrates our partial and impartial perspectives is one of the greatest problems of ethical and political theory. An ethical defence of our partialities can be found in Cottingham, "Favouritism and Morality."
7 Singer, *How Are We to Live?* ix.
8 Fishkin, in his *The Limits of Obligation*, discusses how positive, general obligations of "ordinary morality" become paradoxical when extended to large numbers of people in other countries.
9 Held, in "Principles of Cosmopolitan Order," 18, argues for a "layered cosmopolitanism" that provides a framework of principles that allow for argument and negotiation of "particular spheres of value" in which national and regional affiliations are weighed. Tan argues that if we establish a just structure of global institutions, it is permissible to favour one's compatriots ("The Demands of Justice and National Allegiances," 164).
10 Pogge was one of the first philosophers to extend Rawls's theory of justice to issues of international law and justice. Pogge, *Reading Rawls*, chapters 5 and 6.
11 Christians, "Ethical Theory in a Global Setting," 5.

12 Two recent textbooks devote articles to the global context of journalism studies and media ethics. See Wahl-Jorgensen and Hanitzsch, *The Handbook of Journalism Studies*, and Wilkins and Christians, *The Handbook of Mass Media Ethics*.

13 See Ward and Wasserman, *Media Ethics without Borders*; Black and Barney, "In Search of a Global Media Ethics"; Ward, "Philosophical Foundations for Global Journalism Ethics"; and Christians and Traber, *Communication Ethics and Universal Values*.

14 Ortega y Gasset, *Meditations on Quixote*, 105.

15 For the classical roots of steadfastness, see Gadamer, *The Idea of the Good in Platonic-Aristotelian Philosophy*, 96–103.

16 See Mohammed, "Journalistic Ethics and Responsibility in Relation to Freedom of Expression" for an attempt to ground journalism ethics on Islamic principles.

17 For an exposition of a "cosmopolitan democracy," see Held, *Democracy and the Global Order*, 267–86, and "The Changing Contours of Political Community."

18 See Glasser, *The Idea of Public Journalism*.

19 In recent years, China has begun to revamp its educational system to stress not just facts but knowledge and values, in pursuit of a "harmonious" society that combines state control and free-market activities.

20 There are many views on the nature of a universal. It may be a Platonic form, a scientific law that holds of all physical objects, a belief held by all people, or a moral imperative that all rational people must hold.

21 On moral realism, see Shafer-Landau, *Moral Realism, and Brink, Moral Realism and the Foundations of Ethics*.

22 Kant, *Critique of Practical Reason*, 31.

23 For the idea of basic concepts, see Ward, *The Invention of Journalism Ethics*, chapter 7.

24 By "logical fecundity," I mean that the principle implies other principles of an ethical framework.

25 On cross-cultural values in communication, see Christians and Traber, *Communication Ethics and Universal Values*.

26 Wiredu, *Cultural Universals and Particulars*.

27 Christians, "The Ethics of Universal Being."

28 The "protonorm" approach is advanced in Christians, Rao, Ward, and Wasserman, "Toward a Global Media Ethics: Theoretical Perspectives."

29 Ivison, *Rights*, 232.

30 Nussbaum, *Frontiers of Justice*.

31 Putnam, "Are Values Made or Discovered?" 97.

32 See Young, *Post-Colonialism.*

33 Fourie, "Moral Philosophy as the Foundation of Normative Media Theory," 4.

34 In his influential book *Orientalism,* the postcolonial writer Edward Said critiqued Western culture's representation of the East by studying nineteenth-century French and British writers, travellers, and colonial administrators. More recently, geographer Derek Gregory, in *The Colonial Present,* used Said's work to analyze how media misrepresented the Iraq war and other events.

CHAPTER FIVE

1   Thomas Jefferson to Maryland Republicans, 1809. *The Writings of Thomas Jefferson,* vol. 16, 359.

2   Rawls, *A Theory of Justice,* 522.

3   Ibid., 525.

4   Ibid., 526.

5   Ibid., 527.

6   See John Dewy, *The Public and Its Problems,* especially chapter 1, "Search for the Public."

7   This does not mean that "politics" is absent from such associations, in the sense that even members of a family negotiate who in the family has certain powers or privileges. Nor does it mean that certain familial practices that are harmful to the young or to women are beyond the reach of political concern or laws.

8   Dewey, *The Public and Its Problems,* 34–5.

9   Ibid., 44.

10 Walzer, "Citizenship," 211.

11 Mansbridge, *Beyond Self-Interest,* ix.

12 Pettit, *Republicanism,* 173.

13 Riesenberg, *Citizenship in the Western Tradition,* x, xvii.

14 Geuss, *Public Goods, Private Goods,* 8–9.

15 The idea of a common good is ancient. The terms *utilitas publica* and *utilitas populi* are found in texts of Roman law. The Justianian code argued for the superiority of the common good over private good. Such notions were taken into church law as *utilitas ecclesiae,* and here again the superiority of the common good was stressed.

16 Rudd, *The Republic and The Laws,* 17, Cicero also writes (Rudd, 89): "Respect justice and do your duty. That is important in the case of one's

country. That is the way of life which leads to heaven and to the company, here, of those who have already completed their lives."

17 Held, *Models of Democracy*, 36.
18 Kempshall, The *Common Good in Late Medieval Political Thought*, 19–20.
19 Held, *The Public Interest and Individual Interests*, 19.
20 Lever, "Means, Motives, and Interests in the Law of Torts," 56.
21 Flathman, *The Public Interest*, 14.
22 See Berlin, *Political Ideas in the Romantic Age*, 51.
23 Bentham, *Principles of Morals and Legislation*, 126.
24 Rawls writes: "It is a serious error not to distinguish between the idea of a democratic political society and the idea of community" (*Justice as Fairness*, 21).
25 Dworkin, *Sovereign Virtue*, 231–3.
26 Rawls, *A Theory of Justice*, 522.
27 For an exposition of a global or "cosmopolitan democracy," see Held, *Democracy and the Global Order*, 267–86, and "The Changing Contours of Political Community."
28 Ivison, *Rights*, 200.
29 See Byers, *War Law*.
30 On the idea of global justice and democracy, see Pogge, *Reading Rawls*; Beitz, *Political Theory and International Relations*; and Held, *Democracy and the Global Order*.
31 See Murthy, *Developmental Journalism*.
32 Carey, "Some Personal Notes on US Journalism Education," 22.
33 Berger, "Grave New World?" 81.
34 Walzer, in "Deliberation, and What Else?" 58.

CHAPTER SIX

1 Tolstoy, *Writings on Civil Disobedience and Nonviolence*, 142.
2 Nussbaum, "Patriotism and Cosmopolitanism," 3–17.
3 For a history of how communal and political patriotism evolved, see Viroli's *For Love of Country* and *Republicanism*. On republicanism, see Skinner, *The Foundations of Modern Political Thought*, and Honohan, *Civic Republicanism*.
4 Fustel de Coulanges, *The Ancient City*, 264–7. Boston, MA: Lee and Shepard, 1901.
5 Cicero, *Offices*, 1.17.57.

6 Everitt, *Cicero*, 21.

7 Nussbaum, *Cultivating Humanity*, 50–84.

8 Viroli, *For Love of Country*, 48.

9 Augustine, *City of God*, esp. book 5, chapters 16 and 21, 205–16.

10 Ibid., book 19, chapters 14–27, 872–94.

11 Some of these humanists include Remigio de Girolami in the early 1300s, Lapo of Castiglionchio in the 1430s, and Matteo Palmieri, writing in the first half of the fifteenth century.

12 Cited in Viroli, *For Love of Country*, 26.

13 Cited in ibid., 27–8.

14 Cited in ibid., 32.

15 Ibid., 46.

16 Locke, *Two Treatises of Government*, 5–112.

17 Viroli, *For Love of Country*, 43.

18 Milton, *The Readie and Easie Way to Establish a Free Commonwealth*, vii, 355–6.

19 Ibid., 443.

20 Like Berlin, I see nationalism as an extension and exaggeration of a patriotic attachment to one's country. Nationalism is not simply a national sentiment but "something more definite, ideologically important and dangerous." Nationalism contains the belief in the overriding need to belong to a nation, in the organic relationships of all elements in a nation, in the value of our nation and its characteristics simply because it is *ours*, and in its supremacy to rivals. Nationalism is more than love of country. It is "collective self-worship" where nations are "centres of devotion and self-identification," and a sort of "political romanticism" driven in the belief that the nation is allowing the full perfection of its citizens. Berlin, "Nationalism: Past Neglect and Future Power," 348, 349, 352.

21 Mill, *A System of Logic*, book 6, 10.5.

22 Viroli, in *For Love of Country*, 1–3, argues that patriotism is a republican love of freedom, an openness to others, and a love of the rule of law. Nationalism is a nineteenth-century phenomena that stresses difference, intolerance of other groups, and an arrogant belief in the superiority of one's own nation.

23 Lukacs, *Democracy and Populism*, 36.

24 See Viroli, *For Love of Country*, 169–70.

25 Ibid., 173.

26 Ibid., 175.

27 Nathanson, *Patriotism, Morality and Peace*, 110

28 Ibid., 37, 38, 55.

29 See Viroli, *Republicanism.*
30 A rational love is an attachment shaped by rational deliberation on its nature and relative worth.
31 Cottingham, "Favouritism and Morality," 366–8.
32 Oldenquist, "Loyalties," 177.
33 Royce, *The Philosophy of Loyalty.*
34 See Ward, "Utility and Impartiality."
35 Cottingham, "Favouritism and Morality," 357–8.
36 Scanlon, *What We Owe to Each Other*, 20.
37 Rawls, *A Theory of Justice*, 136, 186.
38 Nathanson, *Patriotism, Morality and Peace*, 72.
39 Kant, *Groundwork of the Metaphysic of Morals*, 61–70.
40 Kant, in his later years, wrote in ways that suggests there is a corrupt part of human nature that accounts for human evil or badness. See his *Religion within the Bounds of Mere Reason*, 52–5.
41 Hartle sees a moderate patriotic view as an essential part of US political values. Hartle cites a description of US patriotism as "loyalty to national institutions and symbols because and in so far as they represent values that are the primary objects of allegiance." Hartle, *Moral Issues in Military Decision Making*, 93–4.
42 For example, in late 2005 and into 2006, the US administration characterized journalists who had exposed a secret surveillance program of the communications of US citizens, as enemies of the USA.
43 Elliott, "Terrorism, Global Journalism, and the Myth of the Nation State," 30.
44 Appiah, *In My Father's House*

Bibliography

Aboulafia, Mitchell. *The Cosmopolitan Self: George Herbert Mead and Continental Philosophy*. Urbana, IL: Illinois University Press, 2001.

Ackrill, John L. "Aristotle on Eudaimonia." In Amelie Oksenberg Rorty, ed., *Essays in Aristotle's Ethics*, 15–33. Berkeley, CA: University of California Press, 1980.

Adams, Robert. *Finite and Infinite Goods*. Oxford: Oxford University Press, 1999.

Alger, Dean. *Megamedia: How Giant Corporations Dominate Mass Media, Distort Competition and Endanger Democracy*. Lanham, MD: Rowman and Littlefield, 1998.

Altham, John E.J. and Ross Harrison, eds. *World, Mind, and Ethics: Essays on the Ethical Philosophy of Bernard Williams*. Cambridge: Cambridge University Press, 1995.

Anderson, Benedict. *Imagined Communities*. 2nd ed. London: Verso, 1991.

Anscombe, G.E.M. "Modern Moral Philosophy." In Roger Crisp and Michael Slote, eds, *Virtue Ethics*, 26–44. Oxford: Oxford University Press, 1997.

Appiah, Kwame Anthony. *In My Father's House: Africa in the Philosophies of Culture*. New York: Oxford University Press, 1991.

– "Cosmopolitan Patriots." In Joshua Cohen, ed., *For Love of Country: Debating the Limits of Patriotism: Martha C. Nussbaum with Respondents*, 21–9. Boston: Beacon Press, 1996.

– *Cosmopolitanism: Ethics in a World of Strangers*. New York: Norton, 2006.

Arendt, Hannah. *The Origins of Totalitarianism*. San Diego, CA: Harvest, 1985.

– *The Human Condition*. 2nd ed. Chicago: University of Chicago Press,
    1998.
Argyle, Michael. *The Psychology of Happiness*. London: Methuen, 1987.
Armstrong, Karen. *Buddha*. London: Penguin, 2001
Aristotle. *Aristotle's Constitution of Athens and Related Texts*. Eds K. von
    Fritz and E. Kapp. New York: Hafner, 1950.
– *The Ethics of Aristotle: The Nicomachean Ethics*. Trans. J.A.K.
    Thomson. London: Penguin, 1976.
– *De* Anima. Trans. Hugh Lawson-Tancred. London: Penguin, 1986.
– *History of Animals*. In *The Basic Works of Aristotle*. Ed. Richard
    McKeon. New York: Modern Library, 2001.
– *Nichomachean Ethics*. In *The Basic Works of Aristotle*. Ed. Richard
    McKeon. New York: Modern Library, 2001.
– *Politics*. In *The Basic Works of Aristotle*. Ed. Richard McKeon. New
    York: Modern Library, 2001.
– *Rhetoric. In 'The Basic Works of Aristotle*. Ed. Richard McKeon. New
    York: Modern Library, 2001.
Audard, Catherine. *John Rawls*. Montreal: McGill-Queen's University
    Press, 2007.
Audi, Robert. *The Good in the Right*: *A Theory of Intuition and Intrinsic
    Value*. Princeton, NJ: Princeton University Press, 2004.
– *Practical Reasoning and Ethical Decision*. London: Routledge, 2006.
Augustine, *City of God*. Trans. Henry Bettenson. London: Penguin
    Classics, 2003.
Ayer, Alfred J. *Language, Truth and Logic*. New York: Dover Publications,
    1952.
– *Philosophical Essays*. London: MacMillan, 1954.
Aylmer, George E. *The Levellers in the English Revolution*. Ithaca, NY:
    Cornell University Press, 1975.
Baier, Kurt. *The Rational and the Moral Order*. Chicago: Open Court, 1995
Baldasty, Gerald. *The Commercialization of News in the Nineteenth
    Century*. Madison, WI: University of Wisconsin Press, 1992.
Ball, Terence, James Farr, and Russell L. Hanson, eds. *Political Innovation
    and Conceptual Change*. Cambridge: Cambridge University Press, 1989.
Baron, Marcia, Philip Pettit, and Michael Slote. *Three Methods of Ethics:
    A Debate*. Malden, MA: Blackwell, 1997.
Barry, Brian. *Political Argument*. New York: Humanities Press, 1965.
Beitz, Charles. *Political Theory and International Relations*. 2nd ed.
    Princeton, NJ: Princeton University Press, 1999.

Bentham, Jeremy. *Principles of Morals and Legislation*. Oxford: Basil Blackwell, 1948.

– "Anarchical Fallacies." In John Waldron, ed., *Nonsense Upon Stilts: Bentham, Burke and Marx on the Rights of Man*. London: Methuen, 1987.

Berger, Guy. "Grave New World? Democratic Journalism Enters the Global Twenty-first Century." *Journalism Studies* 1, no. 1 (2000): 81–99.

Berlin, Isaiah. *Four Essays on Liberty*. Oxford: Oxford University Press, 1969.

– "John Stuart Mill and the Ends of Life." In *Four Essays on Liberty*, 173–206. Oxford: Oxford University Press, 1969.

– Two Concepts of Liberty." In *Four Essays on Liberty*. Oxford: Oxford University Press, 1969.

– "Nationalism: Past Neglect and Future Power." *Partisan Review* 46, no. 3 (1979): 337–58.

– *The Crooked Timber of Humanity*. London: Fontana Press, 1991.

– *The Proper Study of Mankind: An Anthology of Essays*. Eds Henry Hardy and Roger Hausheer. London: Chatto and Windus, 1997.

– *Political Ideas in the Romantic Age*. Ed. Henry Hardy. Princeton: Princeton University Press, 2006.

Black, Jay, Bob Steele, and Ralph Barney. *Doing Ethics in Journalism: A Handbook with Case Studies*. Boston: Allyn and Bacon, 1999.

Black, Jay and Ralph Barney, eds. "Search for a Global Media Ethics." (Special issue) *Journal of Mass Media Ethics* 17, no. 4 (2002).

Blackburn, Simon. "How to Be an Ethical Antirealist." In Stephen Darwall, Allan Gibbard, and Peter Railton, eds, *Moral Discourse and Practice: Some Philosophical Approaches*, 167–78. Oxford: Oxford University Press, 1997.

– *Ruling Passions*. Oxford: Clarendon Press, 1998.

– "Relativism." In Hugh LaFollett, ed., *The Blackwell Guide to Ethical Theory*, 38–52. Malden, MA: Blackwell Publishers, 2000.

– *Being Good: A Short Introduction to Ethics*. Oxford: Oxford University Press, 2002.

Bracci, Sharon L. and Clifford G. Christians, eds. *Moral Engagement in Public Life: Theorists for Contemporary Ethics*. New York: Peter Lang, 2002.

Bradley, Francis H. "The Limits of Individual and National Self-Sacrifice." In *Collected Essays*. Vol. 1. Oxford: Clarendon Press, 1935.

Brandt, Richard. *A Theory of the Good and the Right*. Oxford: Clarendon
	Press, 1979.

Braybrooke, David. "The Public Interest: The Present and Future of the
	Concept." In Carl J. Friedrich, ed., *The Public Interest*. Nomos V. New
	York: Atherton Press, 1962.

Briggs, Asa, and Peter Burke. *A Social History of the Media: From
	Gutenberg to the Internet*. Cambridge: Polity, 2002.

Brink, David O. *Moral Realism and the Foundations of Ethics*.
	Cambridge: Cambridge University Press, 1989.

Broad, C.D. *Five Types of Ethical Theory*. New York: Harcourt and Brace,
	1930.

– "Some of the Main Problems of Ethics." *Philosophy* 31 (1946): 99–117.

Brock, Gillian and Harry Brighouse, eds. *The Political Philosophy of
	Cosmopolitanism*. Cambridge: Cambridge University Press, 2005.

Brown, Donald E. *Human Universals*. New York: McGraw-Hill, 1991.

Brugger, Bill. *Republican Theory in Political Thought*. Basingstoke:
	Macmillan, 1999.

Butt, John, ed. *The Poems of Alexander Pope*. London: Methuen, 1965.

Byers, Michael. *War Law: Understanding International Law and Armed
	Conflict*. Vancouver: Douglas and McIntyre, 2005.

Campbell, W. Joseph. *Yellow Journalism: Puncturing the Myths, Defining
	the Legacies*. Westport, CT: Praeger, 2001.

Carey, James. "Some Personal Notes on US Journalism Education."
	Journalism: Theory, Practice and Criticism 1, no. 1 (2000): 12–23.

Chomsky, Noam. *Neccesary Illusions*. Don Mills, ON: Anansi, 1989.

– *Media Control: The Spectacular Achievements of Propaganda*. New
	York: Seven Stories Press, 1997.

Christians, Clifford G. "Ethical Theory in a Global Setting." In Thomas W.
	Cooper et al., eds, *Communication Ethics and Global* Change, 3–19.
	White Plains, NY: Longman, 1989.

– "Preface." In Richard Keeble, ed., *Communication Ethics Today*, ix–xiii.
	Leicester, UK: Troubador Publishing, 2005.

– "The Ethics of Universal Being." In Stephen J.A. Ward and Herman
	Wasserman, eds, *Media Ethics without Borders*. Cape Town, South
	Africa: Heinemann Publishers, 2008.

Christians, Clifford G., John P. Ferre, and Mark Fackler, eds. *Good News:
	Social Ethics and the Press*. New York: Oxford University Press, 1993.

Christians, Clifford and Kaarle Nordenstreng. "Social Responsibility
	Worldwide." *Journal of Mass Media Ethics* 19, no. 1 (2004): 3–28.

Christians, Clifford and Michael Traber. *Communication Ethics and
	Universal Values*. Thousand Oaks, CA: Sage, 1997.

Christians, Clifford G., Shakuntala Rao, Stephen J.A. Ward, and Herman Wasserman. "Toward a Global Media Ethics: Theoretical Approaches." "Target" article with invited responses. *Ecquid Novi: African Journalism Studies*, vol. 29, no. 2 (2008): 135–72.

Cicero. *Offices*. Trans. Thomas Cockman. London: J.M. Dent and Sons Ltd, 1909.

– *On the Commonwealth*. Trans George Holland Sabine and Stanley Barney Smith. Indianapolis: Bobbs-Merrill, 1976.

– *The Republic and The Laws*. Trans. Niall Rudd. Oxford: Oxford University Press, 1998.

Code, Lorraine. "Who Cares? The Poverty of Objectivism for a Moral Epistemology." In Allan Megill, ed., *Rethinking Objectivity*, 179–95. Durham and London: Duke University Press, 1994.

Cohen, Gerald A. "Equality of What? On Welfare, Goods, and Capabilities." In Martha Nussbaum and Amartya Sen, eds, *The Quality of Life*, 9–29. Oxford: Clarendon Press, 1993.

Cohen, Joshua, ed. *For Love of Country: Debating the Limits of Patriotism: Martha C. Nussbaum with Respondents*. Boston, MA: Beacon Press, 1996.

Coleman, Janet. *A History of Political Thought: From Ancient Greece to Early Christianity*. Oxford: Blackwell, 2000.

Commission on Freedom of the Press. *A Free and Responsible Press*. Chicago: University of Chicago Press, 1947.

Constant, Benjamin. "The Liberty of the Ancients Compared with that of the Moderns." In Biancamaria Fontana, ed., *Political Writings*. New York: Cambridge University Press, 1988.

Cottingham, John. "Favouritism and Morality." Philosophical Quarterly 36, no. 144 (1986): 357–73.

Couture, Jocelyne and Kim Nielsen. "Cosmopolitanism and the Compatriot Priority Principle." In Gillian Brock and Harry Brighouse, eds, *The Political Philosophy of Cosmopolitanism*, 180–95. Cambridge: Cambridge University Press, 2005.

Dahl, Robert A. *A Preface to Democratic Theory*. Chicago, IL: University of Chicago Press, 1956.

Dancy, Jonathan. *Ethics without Principles*. Oxford: Clarendon Press, 2004.

Darwall, Stephen. "How Should Ethics Relate to (the Rest of) Philosophy? Moore's Legacy." In Terry Horgan and Mark Timmons, eds, *Metaethics after Moore*, 17–37. Oxford: Oxford University Press, 2006.

–, ed. *Contractarianism/Contractualism*. Oxford: Blackwell Publishing, 2003.

Darwall, Stephen, Allan Gibbard, and Peter Railton. "Toward a *Fin de Siecle* Ethics: Some Trends." In Stephen Darwall et al, eds, *Moral Discourse and Practice: Some Philosophical Approaches*, 3–47. Oxford: Oxford University Press, 1997.

–, eds. *Moral Discourse and Practice: Some Philosophical Approaches.* Oxford: Oxford University Press, 1997.

Dawes, Robyn M., Alphons J.C. van de Kragt, and John M. Orbell. "Cooperation for the Benefit of Us – Not Me, or My Conscience." In Jane Mansbridge, ed., *Beyond Self-Interest*, 97–110. Chicago: University of Chicago, 1990.

De Beer, Arnold S. and Herman Wasserman. "A fragile affair: The Relationship between the Mainstream Media and Government in Post-Apartheid South Africa." Paper presented to University of Missouri School of Journalism, 9 April 2004, Columbia, MI.

De Beer, Arnold S. and John C. Merrill. *Global Journalism: Topical Issues and Media Systems.* 4th ed. Boston, MA: Pearson Education, 2004.

De Coulanges, Fustel. *The Ancient City.* 10th ed. Trans. Willard Small. Boston: Lee and Shepard, 1901.

Dennett, Daniel C. *The Intentional Stance.* Cambridge, MA: MIT Press, 1987.

– *Consciousness Explained.* London: Penguin, 1992.

– *Freedom Evolves.* New York, Viking, 2002.

De Waal, Frans. *Primates and Philosophers: How Morality Evolved.* Princeton, NJ: Princeton University Press, 2006.

Dewey, John. *The Public and Its Problems.* New York: Henry Holt, 1927.

– *Reconstruction in Philosophy.* Boston, MA: Beacon Press, 1948.

– *The Moral Writings of John Dewey.* Ed. James Gouinlock. Buffalo, NY: Prometheus Books, 1994.

Diamond, Jared. *The Third Chimpanzee: The Evolution and Future of the Human Animal.* New York: Harper, 2006.

Diener, Ed. "Subjective Well-Being." *Psychological Bulletin* 95 (1984): 542–75.

Diener, Ed et al. "Subjective Well-Being: Three Decades of Progress." *Psychological Bulletin* 125, no. 2 (1999): 276–302.

Diener, Ed and Eunkook M. Suh. "Measuring Subjective Well-Being to Compare the Quality of Life Cultures." In Ed Diener and Eunkook M. Suh, eds, *Culture and Subjective Well-Being*, 3–12. Cambridge, MA: MIT Press, 2000.

Dietz, Mary G. "Patriotism." In Terence Ball, James Farr, and Russell L. Hanson, eds, *Political Innovation and Conceptual Change*, 177–93. Cambridge: Cambridge University Press, 1989.

Dostoevsky, Fyodor. *Notes from Underground*. Trans. Michael R. Katz. New York: Norton, 1989.

Dworkin, Ronald. *Sovereign Virtue: The Theory and Practice of Equality*. Cambridge, MA: Harvard University Press, 2000.

Dyson, Kenneth H.F. *The State Tradition in Western Europe: A Study of an Idea and Institution*. Oxford: Martin Robertson, 1980.

Dyson, R.W., ed. *St Thomas Aquinas: Political Writings*. Cambridge: Cambridge University Press, 2002.

Ehrenberg, Victor. *The Greek State*. Oxford: Blackwell, 1960.

– *From Solon to Socrates*. 2nd ed. London: Methuen, 1973.

Elgin, Catherine Z. *Between the Absolute and the Arbitrary*. Ithica, NY: Cornell University Press, 1997.

Elliott, Deni, ed. *Responsible Journalism*. Beverly Hills, CA: Sage Publications, 1986.

– "Terrorism, Global Journalism, and the Myth of the Nation State." *Journal of Mass Media Ethics* 19, no. 1 (2004): 29–45.

Elster, Jon. *Sour Grapes: Studies in the Subversion of Rationality*. Cambridge: Cambridge University Press, 1983.

Everitt, Anthony. *Cicero: The Life and Times of Rome's Greatest Politician*. New York: Random House, 2003.

Ewen, Stuart. *PR! A Social History of Spin*. New York: Basic Books, 1996.

Fallows, James. *Breaking the News: How the Media Undermine American Democracy*. New York: Random House, 1997.

Figgis, John N. *Political Thought from Gerson to Grotius, 1414–1625*. New York, Harper: 1960.

Filler, Louis. *The Muckrakers*. Stanford, CA: Stanford University Press, 1968.

Finley, M.I. *Democracy Ancient and Modern*. New Brunswick, NJ: Rutgers University Press, 1973.

Finnis, John. *Natural Law and Natural Rights*. Oxford: Clarendon Press, 1980.

Fishkin, James. *The Limits of Obligation*. New Haven, CT: Yale University Press, 1982.

Flathman, Richard E. *The Public Interest: An Essay Concerning the Normative Discourse of Politics*. New York: Wiley and Sons, 1966.

Foot, Philippa. *Natural Goodness*. Oxford: Clarendon Press, 2001.

Fourie, Pieter. "Moral Philosophy as the Foundation of Normative Media Theory: Questioning African *Ubuntuism* as a Framework." Paper presented to the International Roundtable on Global Media Ethics, Stellenbosch, South Africa, March 2007.

Frankfurt, Harry G. *The Importance of What We Care About:
    Philosophical Essays*. Cambridge: Cambridge University Press, 1988.
– *On Truth*. New York: Knopf, 2006.
Freeman, Samuel, ed. *The Cambridge Companion to Rawls*. Cambridge:
    Cambridge University Press, 2003.
Fried, Charles. "Two Concepts of Interests: Some Reflections on the
    Supreme Court's Balancing Test." *Harvard Law Review* 76 (February
    1963): 755–78.
Friedrich, Carl J. *The Public Interest*. Nomos V. New York: Atherton
    Press, 1962.
Friend, Cecilia and Jane B. Singer. *On-Line Journalism Ethics: Traditions
    and Transitions*. Armonk, NY: M.E. Sharpe, 2007.
Frey, Bruno S. and Alois Stutzer. *Happiness and Economics: How the
    Economy and Institutions Affect Human Well-Being*. Princeton:
    Princeton University Press, 2002.
Fullerton, Romayne and Margaret Patterson. "Murder in Our Midst:
    Expanding Coverage to Include Care and Responsibility." *Journal of
    Mass Media Ethics* 21, no. 4 (2006): 304–21.
Gadamer, Hans-Georg. *The Idea of the Good in Platonic-Aristotelian
    Philosophy*. Trans. P. Christopher Smith. New Haven, CT: Yale
    University Press. 1986.
– *Truth and Method*. 2nd rev. ed. London: Continuum, 2004.
Gauthier, David P. *Practical Reasoning: The Structure and Foundation
    of Prudential and Moral Arguments and Their Exemplification in
    Discourse*. Oxford: Clarendon Press, 1963.
– *Morals by Agreement*. Oxford: Clarendon Press, 1986.
Gerson, Lloyd P. *Aristotle and Other Platonists*. Ithaca: Cornell University
    Press, 2005.
Geuss, Raymond. *Public Goods, Private Goods*. Princeton, NJ: Princeton
    University Press, 2003.
– "Happiness and Politics." In *Outside Ethics*, 97–110. Princeton:
    Princeton University Press, 2005.
Gibbard, Allan. "Wise Choices, Apt Feelings." In Stephen Darwall, Allan
    Gibbard, and Peter Railton, eds, *Moral Discourse and Practice: Some
    Philosophical Approaches*, 179–98. Oxford: Oxford University Press,
    1997.
Gilligan, Carol. *In a Different Voice: Psychological Theory and Women's
    Development*. Cambridge, MA: Harvard University Press, 1982.
Gitlin, Todd. *Media Unlimited: How the Torrent of Images and Sounds
    Overwhelms Our Lives*. New York: Metropolitan Books, 2001.

Glasser, Theodore L. *The Idea of Public Journalism*. New York: Guilford, 1999.

Goldberg, Bernard. *Bias: A CBS Insider Exposes How the Media Distorts the News*. Washington, DC: Regnery Publishers, 2003.

Grayling, A.C. *What Is Good? The Search for the Best Way to Live*. London: Phoenix, 2004.

Green, Thomas Hill. *Prolegomena to Ethics*. 5th ed. Oxford: Clarendon Press, 1907.

Gregory, Derek. *The Colonial Present: Afghanistan, Palestine, Iraq*. Malden, MA: Blackwell Publishers, 2004.

Griffin, James. *Well Being*. Oxford: Oxford University Press, 1986.

Groarke, Leo, Christopher Tindale, and Linda Fisher. *Good Reasoning Matters*. Toronto: Oxford University Press, 1997.

Gunn, John A.W. "Public Interest." In Terence Ball, James Farr, and Russell L. Hanson, eds, *Political Innovation and Conceptual Change*, 194–210. Cambridge: Cambridge University Press 1989.

Gutmann, Amy and Dennis Thompson, *Why Deliberative Democracy*. Princeton, NJ: Princeton University Press, 2004.

Habermas, Jurgen. *The Structural Transformation of the Public Sphere: An Inquiry into a Category of Bourgeois Society*. Trans. Thomas Burger with the assistance of Frederick Lawrence. Cambridge: Polity Press, 1989.

– *The Inclusion of the Other*. Cambridge, MA: MIT Press, 1999.

– "Discourse Ethics." In *Moral Consciousness and Communicative Action*, trans Christian Lenhardt and Shierry Weber Nicholsen, 43–115. Cambridge, MA: MIT Press, 2001.

– *Moral Consciousness and Communicative Action*. Trans Christian Lenhardt and Shierry Weber Nicholsen. Cambridge, MA: MIT Press. 2001.

– "Morality and Ethical Life: Does Hegel's Critique of Kant apply to Discourse Ethics?" In *Moral Consciousness and Communicative Action*, trans Christian Lenhardt and Shierry Weber Nicholsen, 195–215. Cambridge, MA: MIT Press, 2001.

– *The Future of Human Nature*. Cambridge: Polity Press, 2005.

Hachten, William. *The Troubles of Journalism: A Critical Look at What's Right and Wrong With the Press*. Mahwah, NJ: Lawrence Erlbaum Associates, 1998.

Hacking, Ian. *The Social Construction of What?* Cambridge, MA: Harvard University Press, 1999.

Haidt, Jonathan. *The Happiness Hypothesis: Finding Modern Truth in Ancient Wisdom*. New York: Basic Books, 2006.

Haller, William and Godfrey Davies, eds. *The Leveller Tracts 1647–1653.* Gloucester, MA: Peter Smith, 1964.

Hamilton, Edith and Huntington Cairns, eds. *Plato: The Collected Dialogues.* Princeton, NJ: Princeton University Press, 1973.

Hamilton, William. *Lectures on Metaphysics.* Vol. 1 of *Lectures on Metaphysics and Logic,* 2 vols. Eds H.L. Mansel and John Veitch. New York: Sheldon and Company, 1880.

Hansen, Mogens H. *The Athenian Democracy in the Age of Demosthenes.* Trans. J.A. Crook. Oxford: Blackwell, 1991.

Hanson, Russell L. "Democracy." In Terence Ball, James Farr, and Russell L. Hanson, eds, *Political Innovation and Conceptual Change,* 68–89. Cambridge: Cambridge University Press, 1989.

Hardie, William F.R. "The Final Good in Aristotle's Ethics." *Philosophy* 40 (1965), 277–95.

– *Aristotle's Ethical Theory.* Oxford, Oxford University Press, 1968.

Hare, Richard M. "Broad's Approach to Moral Philosophy." In *Essays on Philosophical Method,* 1–18. London: Macmillan, 1971.

– *The Language of Morals.* Oxford: Oxford University Press, 1978.

– "Prescriptivism." In *Objective Prescriptions and Other Essays,* 19–27. Oxford: Clarendon Press, 1999.

Hart, Herbert L.A. *The Concept of Law.* Oxford: Clarendon Press, 1965.

Hartle, Anthony. *Moral Issues in Military Decision Making.* Lawrence: University Press of Kansas, 1989.

Held, David. *Democracy and the Global Order: From the Modern State to Cosmopolitan Governance.* Cambridge: Polity Press, 1995.

– *Models of Democracy.* London: Polity Press, 1997.

– "The Changing Contours of Political Community: Rethinking Democracy in the Context of Globalization." In Barry Holden, ed., *Global Democracy: Key Debates,* 17–31. London: Routledge, 2000.

– "Principles of Cosmopolitan Order." In Gillian Brock and Harry Brighouse, eds, *The Political Philosophy of Cosmopolitanism,* 10–27. Cambridge: Cambridge University Press, 2005.

Held, Virginia, *The Public Interest and Individual Interests.* New York: Basic Books, 1970.

Helliwell, John. F. *Globalization and Well-Being.* Vancouver: UBC Press, 2002.

Herring, Pendleton. *Public Administration and the Public Interest.* New York: McGraw Hill, 1936.

Hobbes, Thomas. *Leviathan.* Ed. Richard Tuck. Cambridge: Cambridge University Press, 1991.

Honohan, Iseult. *Civic Republicanism*. London: Routledge, 2002.

Horgan, Terry and Mark Timmons, eds. *Metaethics after Moore*. Oxford: Clarendon Press, 2006.

Hudson, W.D. *Modern Moral Philosophy*. Garden City, NY: Doubleday, 1970.

Hume, David. *A Treatise of Human Nature (1739)*. 2nd ed. Oxford: Clarendon Press, 1978.

– "Of the Original Contract." In *Essays: Moral, Political and Literary*, 465–87. Indianapolis, IN: Liberty Fund, 1987.

– *An Enquiry Concerning the Principles of Morals*. Amherst, NY: Prometheus Books, 2004.

Hurka, Thomas. *Perfectionism*. New York: Oxford University Press, 1993.

– "Moore in the Middle." *Ethics*, 113 (2003): 599–628.

Hursthouse, Rosalind. *On Virtue Ethics*. Oxford: Oxford University Press, 1999.

Husserl, Edmund. "A Report on German Writings in Logic from the Years 1895–1899." In vol. 5 of *Early Writings in the Philosophy of Logic and Mathematics*, 207–24. *Collected Works of Edmund Husserl*, trans. Dallas Willard, 5 vols. Dordrecht: Kluwer Academic Publishers, 1994.

Hyde, John K. *Society and Politics in Medieval Italy: The Evolution of the Civic Life*. New York: St Martin's Press, 1973.

Ignatieff, Michael. *Isaiah Berlin: A Life*. London: Chatto and Windus, 1998.

– The Lesser Evil: Political Ethics in an Age of Terror. Toronto: Penguin, 2004.

Irwin, Terrence. *Plato's Moral Theory*. Oxford: Oxford University Press, 1977.

– "The Metaphysical and Psychological Basis of Aristotle's Ethics." In Amelie Oksenberg Rorty, ed., *Essays in Aristotle's Ethics*, 35–53. Berkeley, CA: University of California Press, 1980.

Ivison, Duncan. *Rights*. Montreal: McGill-Queen's University Press, 2008.

Jacquette, Dale. *Journalistic Ethics: Moral Responsibility in the Media*. Upper Saddle River, NJ: Pearson Prentice Hall. 2007.

Jaeger, Werner W. *Paideia: The Ideals of Greek Culture*. 2nd ed. 3 vols. New York: Oxford University Press, 1945.

James, William. "Is Life Worth Living?" In *The Will to Believe and Other Essays on Popular Philosophy*, 32–62. London: Dover, 1956.

– "The Sentiment of Rationality." In *The Will to Believe and Other Essays on Popular Philosophy*, 63–110. London: Dover, 1956.

– "The Moral Philosopher and the Moral Life." In John J. McDermott, ed., *The Writings of William James*, 610–29. Chicago: University of Chicago Press, 1977.

Jefferson, Thomas. *The Writings of Thomas Jefferson*. Memorial edition. Vol. 16 of 20 vols. Ed. Andrew A. Lipscomb. Washington, DC: Kessinger Publishing, 1985.

Johnson, Curtis. *Aristotle's Theory of the State*. London: Macmillan, 1990.

Johnstone, Christopher L. "Aristotle's Ethical Theory." In Sharon L. Bracci and Clifford G. Christians, eds, *Moral Engagement in Public Life: Theorists for Contemporary Ethics*, 16–34. New York: Peter Lang, 2002.

Jost, Lawrence J. and Roger A. Shiner. *Eudaimonia and Well-Being: Ancient and Modern Conceptions*. Kelowna, BC: Academic Printing, 2003.

Kamm, Frances M. "Nonconsequentialism." In Hugh LaFollette, ed., *The Blackwell Guide to Ethical Theory*, 205–26. Malden, MA: Blackwell Publishers, 2000.

Kant, Immanuel. *Critique of Practical Reason*. Trans. L.W. Beck. New York: Bobbs-Merrill, 1956.

– "On the Common Saying." In *Kant: Political Writings*, ed. Hans Reiss, 2nd enlarged ed., 54–60. Cambridge: Cambridge University Press, 1991.

– *The Metaphysics of Morals*. Trans Mary Gregor. Cambridge: Cambridge University Press, 1996.

– *Groundwork of the Metaphysics of Morals*. Trans. Mary Gregor. Cambridge: Cambridge University Press, 1997.

– *Religion within the Bounds of Mere Reason*. Trans A. Wood and G. Giovanni. Cambridge: Cambridge University Press, 1998.

– "An Answer to the Question: What Is Enlightenment?" In Pauline Kleingeld, ed., *Toward Perpetual Peace and Other Writings on Politics, Peace, and History*, 17–23. New Haven, CT: Yale University Press, 2006.

– *Anthropology from a Pragmatic Point of View*. Ed. Robert B. Louden. Cambridge: Cambridge University Press, 2006.

– *Toward Perpetual Peace and Other Writings on Politics, Peace, and History*. Ed. Pauline Kleingeld. New Haven, CT: Yale University Press, 2006.

Kekes, John. *Facing Evil*. Princeton, NJ: Princeton University Press, 1990.

Kempshall, Matthew S. *The Common Good in Late Medieval Political Thought*. Oxford: Clarendon Press, 1999.

Kenny, Anthony. "Happiness." In *Proceedings of the Aristotelian Society* 66 (1965–66): 93–102.

Kiefer Lewalski, Barbara, ed. *A Treatise of Civil Power*. In J. Max Patrick, ed., *The Prose of John Milton*, 439–74. New York: New York University Press, 1968.

King, Preston. *The Ideology of Order: A Comparative Analysis of Jean Bodin and Thomas Hobbes*. London: George Allan and Unwin: 1974.

Kingwell, Mark. *Better Living: In Pursuit of Happiness from Plato to Prozac*. Toronto: Penguin, 1999.

Kitcher, Philip. "Biology and Ethics" In *The Oxford Handbook of Ethical Theory*. Oxford: Oxford University Press, 2006.

Klaidman, Stephen and Tom Beauchamp. *The Virtuous Journalist*. New York: Oxford, 1987.

Korsgaard, Christine. "Commentary." In Martha Nussbaum and Amartya Sen, eds, *The Quality of Life*, 54–66. Oxford: Clarendon Press, 1993.

– *Creating the Kingdom of Ends*. Cambridge: Cambridge University Press, 1996.

– *The Sources of Normativity*. Cambridge: Cambridge University Press, 1996.

Kovach, Bill and Tom Rosenstiel. *The Elements of Journalism*. Rev. ed. New York: Three Rivers Press, 2007.

Kraut, Richard. *Aristotle on the Human Good*. Princeton, NJ: Princeton University Press, 1989.

– *What Is Good and Why: The Ethics of Well-Being*. Cambridge, MA: Harvard University Press, 2007.

Kuehn, Manfred. *Kant: A Biography*. Cambridge: Cambridge University Press, 2001.

Kukathas, Chandran, ed. *John Rawls: Critical Assessments of Leading Political Philosophers*. 4 vols. London: Routledge, 2003.

Kurka, Thomas. *Perfectionism*. Oxford: Oxford University Press, 1993.

LaFollette, Hugh. ed. *The Blackwell Guide to Ethical Theory*. Malden, MA: Blackwell Publishers, 2000.

– *Ethics in Practice*. 3rd ed. Malden, MA: Blackwell Publishing, 2007.

Land, Mitchell and Bill W. Hornaday. "Mass Media Ethics and the Point-of-Decision Pyramid." In *Contemporary Media Ethics*, 15–38. Spokane, WA: Marquette Books, 2006.

Layard, Richard. *Happiness: Lessons from a New Science*. New York: Penguin Press, 2005.

Lever, John F. "Means, Motives, and Interests in the Law of Torts." In A.G. Guest, ed., *Oxford Essays in Jurisprudence*. Oxford: Oxford University Press, 1961.

Lippmann, Walter. *Liberty and the News*. New York: Harcourt, Brace and Howe, 1920.

- *Public Opinion*. New York: Macmillan, 1922.

- *The Phantom Public*. New York: Harcourt Brace, 1925.

Locke, John. *An Essay Concerning Human Understanding*. 2 vols. New York: Dover, 1959.

- *Two Treatises of Government*. Ed. Mark Goldie. London: John Dent, 1996.

Loptson, Peter. *Theories of Human Nature*. Peterborough, ON: Broadview Press, 1995.

Lukacs, John. *Democracy and Populism*, New Haven, CT: Yale University Press. 2005.

Lukes, Steven. *Moral Relativism*. New York: Picador, 2008.

Lyons, David. "Human Rights and the General Welfar." *Philosophy and Public Affairs*, 6(2) (1977): 113–29.

Mabbott, J.D. "Is Plato's *Republic* Utilitarian?" In vol. 2 of *Plato: A Collection of Critical Essays*, 2 vols, ed. Gregory Vlastos, 57–65. New York: Anchor Books, 1971.

Machiavelli, Niccolo. *The Prince*. In vol. 1 of *Machiavelli: The Chief Works and Others*. 3 vols. Trans. Allan Gilbert. Durham, NC: Duke University Press, 1965.

- *Discourses on Livy*. Trans Harvey C. Mansfield and Nathan Tarcov. Chicago: University of Chicago Press, 1996.

Mackie, John L. *Ethics: Inventing Right and Wrong*. New York: Penguin, 1977.

MacIntyre, Alasdair. *After Virtue*. London: Duckworth, 1981.

- "Is Patriotism a Virtue?" The Lindley Lecture, University of Kansas, 1984.

- "Colors, Cultures and Practices." In *The Tasks of Philosophy, Vol. 1: Selected Essays*, 24–51. Cambridge: Cambridge University Press, 2006.

- "Epistemological Crises, Dramatic Narrative, and the Philosophy of Science." In *The Tasks of Philosophy, Vol. 1: Selected Essays*, 3–23. Cambridge: Cambridge University Press, 2006.

- "Moral Relativism, Truth and Justification." In *The Tasks of Philosophy, Vol. 1: Selected Essays*, 52–73. Cambridge: Cambridge University Press, 2006.

Madison, John. *The Federalist Papers*. New York: Doubleday, 1966.

Mansbridge, Jane, ed. *Beyond Self-Interest*. Chicago: University of Chicago, 1990.

Manville, Brook. *The Origins of Citizenship in Ancient Athens*. Princeton, NJ: Princeton University Press, 1990.

Marx, Karl. *Capital.* Vol. 1. Trans. Ben Fowkes. New York: Vintage, 1977.

– *Economic and Philosophical Manuscripts. In Karl Marx: Selected Writings.* Ed. David McLellan. Oxford: Oxford University, 1977.

Marx, Karl and Friedrich Engels. *The German Ideology. In Karl Marx: Selected Writings.* Ed. David McLellan. Oxford: Oxford University Press, 1977.

Mayer, Thomas. *Thomas Starkey and the Commonweal: Humanist Politics and Religion in the Age of Henry VIII.* Cambridge: Cambridge University Press, 2002.

Mayhew, Robert. *Aristotle's Criticism of Plato's Republic.* Lanham, MD: Rowman and Littlefield, 1997.

Maynard, Nancy. *Megamedia: How Market Forces are Transforming News.* New York: Maynard Partners, 2002.

McChesney, Robert W. *Rich Media, Poor Democracy: Communication Politics in Dubious Times.* Urbana: University of Illinois Press, 1999.

– *The Problem of the Media: US Communication Politics in the 21st Century.* New York: Monthly Review Press, 2004.

McPhail, Thomas L. *Global Communication: Theories, Stakeholders, and Trends.* Malden, MA: Blackwell Publishing, 2006.

Mendus, Susan. *Toleration and the Limits of Liberalism.* Atlantic Highlands, NJ: Humanities Press, 1989.

Mill, John Stuart. "Autobiography." In *Essential Works of John Stuart Mill.* Ed. Max Lerner. New York: Bantam Books, 1965.

– *A System of Logic.* Ed. John M. Robson. 2 vols. Toronto: University of Toronto Press, 1973–74.

– *Considerations on Representative Government.* Buffalo, NY: Prometheous Books, 1991.

– *On Liberty and the Subjection of Women.* Ed. Alan Ryan. London: Penguin Books, 2006.

– "Utilitarianism." In Henry R. West, ed., *The Blackwell Guide to Mill's Utilitarianism.* Oxford: Blackwell Publishing, 2006.

Miller, Arthur S. "The Public Interest Undefined." *Journal of Public Law*, 10 (Fall 1961).

Miller, Fred D. Jr. *Nature, Justice and Rights in Aristotle's Politics.* Oxford: Clarendon Press, 1995.

Milton, John. *The Readie and Easie way to Establish a Free Commonwealth* (1660). In *Complete Prose Work of John* Milton. Ed. Evert M. Clark. New Haven, CT: Yale University Press, 1911.

Mindich, David T.Z. *Just the Facts: How "Objectivity" Came to Define American Journalism.* New York: New York University Press, 1998.

Mohammed, Ali. "Journalistic Ethics and Responsibility in Relation to Freedom of Expression: An Islamic Perspective." In Stephen J.A. Ward and Herman Wasserman, eds, *Media Ethics Without Borders*. Cape Town: Heinemann Publishers, 2008.

Moore, George E. *Principia Ethica*. Mineola, NY: Dover Publications, 2005. (Originally published in 1903.)

Morgan, G.A. *What Nietzsche Means*. Cambridge, MA: Harvard University Press, 1941.

Murthy, D.V.R. *Developmental Journalism*. New Delhi: Dominant Publishers, 2001.

Nagel, Thomas. "Aristotle on Eudaimonia." In Amelie Oksenberg Rorty, ed., *Essays in Aristotle's Ethics*, 7–14. Berkeley, CA: University of California Press, 1980.

– *The View from Nowhere*. Oxford: Oxford University Press, 1986.

– *Equality and Partiality*. Oxford: Oxford University Press, 1991.

Nathanson, Stephen. *Patriotism, Morality and Peace*. Lanham, MD: Rowman and Littlefield, 1993.

The New Oxford Annotated Bible: New Revised Standard Version. 3rd ed. Ed. Michael D. Coogan. Oxford: Oxford University Press, 2001.

Nozick, Robert. *Anarchy, State, and Utopia*. New York: Basic Books, 1974.

Nietzsche, Friedrich. *Beyond Good and Evil*. Trans. Walter Kaufmann. New York: Vintage, 1966.

– *The Will to Power*. Trans Walter Kaufmann and R.J. Hollingdale. New York: Vintage, 1968.

Nussbaum, Martha C. *The Fragility of Goodness: Luck and Ethics in Greek Tragedy and Philosophy*. Rev. ed. Cambridge: Cambridge University Press, 1986.

– "Aristotelian Social Democracy." In R. Bruce Douglas, Gerald Mara, and Henry Richardson, eds, *Liberalism and the Good*, 203–52. New York: Routledge, 1990.

– "Non-Relative Virtues: An Aristotelian Approach." In Martha Nussbaum and Amartya Sen, eds, *The Quality of Life*, 242–69. Oxford: Clarendon Press, 1993.

– "Aristotle on Human Nature and the Foundations of Ethics." In J.E.J. Altham and Ross Harrison, eds, *World, Mind, and Ethics: Essays on the Ethical Philosophy of Bernard Williams*, 86–131. Cambridge: Cambridge University Press, 1995.

– "Patriotism and Cosmopolitanism." In Joshua Cohen, ed., *For Love of Country: Debating the Limits of Patriotism: Martha C. Nussbaum with Respondents*, 3–17. Boston, MA: Beacon Press, 1996.

- *Women and Human Development: The Capabilities Approach to Justice*. Cambridge: Cambridge University Press, 2000.
- *Cultivating Humanity: A Classical Defense of Reform in Liberal Education*. Cambridge, MA: Harvard University Press, 2003.
- *Frontiers of Justice*. Cambridge, MA: Belknap Press, 2006.

Oakshott, Michael. *On Human Conduct*. Oxford: Clarendon Press, 1975.

Oldenquist, Andrew. "Loyalties." *The Journal of Philosophy* 79, no. 4 (1982): 173–93.

O'Neill, Onora. "Introduction." In Christine Korsgaard, *The Sources of Normativity*, xi–xv. Cambridge: Cambridge University Press, 1996.
- *Towards Justice and Virtue: A Constructive Account of Practical Reasoning*. Cambridge: Cambridge University Press, 1996.

Oppenheim, Felix. "Democracy – Characteristics Included and Excluded." *The Monist* 55 (1971): 29–50.

Ortega y Gasset, José. *Meditations on Quixote*. Trans Evelyn Rugg and Diego Marin. Urbana, IL: University of Illinois Press, 2000.

Paolucci, Henry, ed. *The Political Writings of St Augustine*. Washington, DC: Regnery Publishing, 1996.

Parfit, Derek. *Reasons and Persons*. Oxford: Oxford University Press, 1984.

Patrick. J. Max, ed. *The Prose of John Milton*. New York: New York University Press, 1968.

Patterson, Philip and Lee Wilkins. *Media Ethics: Issues and Cases*. 4th ed. New York: McGraw-Hill, 2002.

Peden, Creighton and Hudson, Yeagher, eds. *Communitarianism, Liberalism and Social Responsibility*. Lewiston: E. Mellen Press, 1991.

Pennock, J. Roland and John W. Chapman, eds. *Human Nature in Politics*. Nomos XVII. New York: New York University Press, 1977.

Peterson, Theodore. "The Social Responsibility Theory of the Press." In Fredrick Siebert, Theodore Peterson, and Wilbur Schramm, *Four Theories of the Press*, 73–151. Urbana, IL: University of Illinois Press, 1956.

Pettit, Philip. "Consequentialism." In Peter Singer, ed., *A Companion to Ethics*, 230–40. Oxford: Blackwell, 1991.
- *Republicanism: A Theory of Freedom and Government*. Oxford: Clarendon Press, 1997.

Pinker, Steven. *How the Mind Works*. New York: Norton, 1997.
- *The Blank Slate: The Modern Denial of Human Nature*. New York: Penguin, 2003.

Plato. *The Republic of Plato*. Trans. Francis M. Cornford. New York: Oxford University Press, 1968.

– *The Republic of Plato*. In *The Collected Dialogues of Plato*. Eds Edith Hamilton and Huntington Cairns, 575–844. Princeton, NJ: Princeton University Press, 1973.

Pogge, Thomas. *Reading Rawls*. Ithaca, NY: Cornell University Press, 1989.

Porter, Roy. *Enlightenment: Britain and the Creation of the Modern World*. London: Penguin Books, 2001.

Post, Neal. *Amusing Ourselves to Death: Public Discourse in the Age of Show Business*. New York: Viking, 1985.

Postema, Gerald J. "Bentham's Utilitarianism." In Henry R. West, ed., *The Blackwell Guide to Mill's Utilitarianism*, 26–44. Oxford: Blackwell Publishers, 2006.

Putnam, Hilary. "A Reconsideration of Deweyan Democracy." *Renewing Philosophy*. Cambridge, MA: Harvard University Press, 1992.

– "Changing Aristotle's Mind." In James Conant, ed., *Words and Life*, 22–61. Cambridge, MA: Harvard University Press, 1994.

– "How Old Is the Mind?" In James Conant, ed., *Words and Life*, 3–21. Cambridge, MA: Harvard University Press, 1994.

– "Are Values Made or Discovered?" In *The Collapse of the Fact-Value Dichotomy*, 96–110. Cambridge, MA: Harvard University Press, 2002.

– *The Collapse of the Fact-Value Dichotomy*. Cambridge, MA: Harvard University Press, 2002.

– "Ethics without Metaphysics." In *Ethics without Ontology*, 15–32. Cambridge, MA: Harvard University Press, 2004.

– *Ethics without Ontology*. Cambridge, MA: Harvard University Press, 2004.

– "Objectivity without Objects." In *Ethics without Ontology*, 52–70. Cambridge, MA: Harvard University Press, 2004.

Quine, Willard V. *Word and Object*. Cambridge, MA: MIT Press, 1960.

– "Epistemology Naturalized." *Ontological Relativity and Other Essays*. New York: Columbia University Press, 1969.

– *Pursuit of Truth*. Cambridge, MA: Harvard University Press, 1990.

Quinton, Anthony. *Utilitarian Ethics*. London, MacMillan, 1973.

Rachels, James. "Naturalism." In Hugh LaFollette, ed., *The Blackwell Guide to Ethical Theory*, 74–91. Malden, MA: Blackwell Publishers, 2000.

Rawls, John. *A Theory of Justice* (1972). 12th impression. Oxford: Oxford University Press, 1992.

- "Kantian Constructivism in Moral Theory." *Journal of Philosophy* 77, no. 9 (September 1980): 515–72.
- *Political Liberalism.* New York: Columbia University Press, 1993.
- *Lectures on the History of Moral Philosophy.* Ed. Barbara Herman. Cambridge, MA: Harvard University Press, 2000.
- *Justice as Fairness: A Restatement.* Ed. Erin Kelly. Cambridge, MA: Harvard University Press, 2001.
- "The Idea of Public Reason Revisited." In *The Law of Peoples.* 4th printing, 131–80. Cambridge, MA: Harvard University Press, 2002.
- *The Law of Peoples.* Cambridge, MA: Harvard University Press, 2002.
- *Justice as Fairness: A Restatement.* Cambridge, MA: Harvard University Press, 2003.

Raymond, Joad. "The Newspaper, Public Opinion, and the Public Sphere." In Joad Raymond, ed., *News, Newspapers and Society in Early Modern Britain.* London: Frank Cass, 1999.

Riesenberg, Peter. *Citizenship in the Western Tradition: Plato to Rousseau.* Chapel Hill, NJ: University of North Carolina Press, 1992.

Rorty, Amelie Oksenberg, ed. *Essays in Aristotle's Ethics.* Berkeley, CA: University of California Press, 1980.

Rorty, Richard. "Putnam and the Relativist Menace." *Journal of Philosophy* 90, no. 9 (September 1993): 443–61.
- *Truth and Progress.* Vol. 3. *Philosophical Papers.* Cambridge: Cambridge University Press, 1998.

Rosen, Jay. *Getting the Connections Right: Public Journalism and the Troubles in the Press.* New York: Twentieth Century Fund Press, 1996.
- *What Are Journalists For?* New Haven, CT: Yale University Press, 1999.

Ross, W.D. *The Right and the Good.* Oxford: Clarendon Press, 1930.

Rousseau, Jean-Jacques. *The Social Contract* (1762). Trans. Maurice Cranston. London: Penguin, 1968.

Royce, Josiah. *The Philosophy of Loyalty.* New York: Macmillan, 1928.

Rudd, Niall. *The Republic and the Laws.* Oxford: Oxford University Press, 1998.

Russell, Bertrand. *The Conquest of Happiness.* New York: Norton and Company, 1996.

Said, Edward. *Orientalism (1978).* London: Penguin, 2003.

Sandel, Michael J. *Liberalism and the Limits of Justice.* 2nd ed. Cambridge: Cambridge University Press, 1998.

Scanlon, Thomas M. "Preference and Urgency." *Journal of Philosophy,* 72 (1975): 655–69.

- "Value, Desire and the Quality of life." In Martha Nussbaum and Amartya Sen, eds, *The Quality of Life*, 185–200. Oxford: Clarendon Press, 1993.
- *What We Owe to Each Other*. Cambridge, MA: Harvard University Press, 1998.

Scheffler, Samuel, ed. *Consequentialism and Its Critics*. Oxford: Oxford University Press, 1988.

Schrumpeter, John. *Capitalism, Socialism and Democracy*. London: Allen and Unwin, 1976.

Schudson, Michael. *Discovering of News: A Social History of American Newspapers*. New York: Basic Books, 1978.

Sealey, Raphael. *A History of the Greek City States, 700–338 BC*. Berkeley, CA: University of California Press, 1976.

Seib, Philip. *The Global Journalist: News and Conscience in a World of Conflict*. Lanham, MD: Rowman and Littlefield Publishers, 2002.

Sen, Amartya. "Utilitarianism and Welfarism." *Journal of Philosophy* 76, no. 9 (September 1979): 463–89.
- "Capability and Well-Being." In Martha Nussbaum and Amartya Sen, eds, *The Quality of Life*, 30–61. Oxford: Clarendon Press, 1993.
- *Development as Freedom*. New York: Alfred A. Knopf, 1999.
- *Rationality and Freedom*. Cambridge, MA: Harvard University Press, 2002.

Seters, Peter, ed. *Communitarianism in Law and Society*. Lanham, MD: Rowman and Littlefield Publishers, 2006.

Shafer-Landau, Russ. *Moral Realism: A Defence*. Oxford: Clarendon Press, 2003.

Shaver, Robert. *Rational Egoism: A Selective and Critical History*. Cambridge: Cambridge University Press, 1999.

Shorey, Paul. "Plato Ethics." In vol. 2 of *Plato: A Collection of Critical Essays*, 2 vols, ed. Gregory Vlastos, 7–34: New York: Anchor Books, 1971.

Sibley, William M. "The Rational Versus the Reasonable" *Philosophical Review* 62 (October 1953): 554–60.

Sidgwick, Henry. *The Methods of Ethics*. 7th ed. Indianapolis, IN: Hackett Publishing, 1981.

Siebert, Fredrick S. "The Libertarian Theory of the Press." In Fredrick Siebert, Theodore Peterson, and Wilbur Schramm, *Four Theories of the Press*, 39–71. Urbana, IL: University of Illinois Press.

Silverstone, Roger. *Media and Morality: On the Rise of the Mediapolis*. Cambridge: Polity Press, 2007.

Sinclair, R.K. *Democracy and Participation in Athens*. Cambridge: Cambridge University Press, 1988.

Singer, Marcus. *Generalization in Ethics*. New York, Knopf, 1961.

Singer, Peter. *How Are We To Live? Ethics in an Age of Self-Interest*. New York: Prometheus Books, 1995.

Skinner, Quentin *The Foundations of Modern Political Thought*. 2 vols. Cambridge: Cambridge University Press, 1978.

– *Machiavelli*. Oxford: Oxford University Press, 1981.

– "The Idea of Negative Liberty: Philosophical and Historical Perspectives." In Richard Rorty, J.B. Schneewind, and Quentin Skinner, eds, *Philosophy in History*, 193–221. Cambridge: Cambridge University Press, 1984.

– "The Paradoxes of Political Liberty." In Sterling M. McMurrin, ed., *The Tanner Lectures on Human Values,* vol. 7, 225–50. Salt Lake City, UT: University of Utah Press, 1986.

– "The State." In Terence Ball, James Farr, and Russell L. Hanson, eds, *Political Innovation and Conceptual Change*, 90–131. Cambridge: Cambridge University Press, 1989.

– *Liberty Before Liberalism*. Cambridge: Cambridge University Press, 1998.

Skorupski, John. "The Place of Utilitarianism in Mill's Philosophy." In Henry West, ed., *The Blackwell Guide to Mill's Utilitarianism*, 45–59. Oxford: Blackwell, 2006.

Skyrms, Brian. *The Evolution of the Social Contract*. New York: Cambridge University Press, 1996.

Slote, Michael. *From Morality to Virtue*. New York: Oxford University Press, 1992.

– *Morals from Motives*. Oxford: Oxford University Press, 2001.

Slote, Michael and Roger Crisp, eds. *Virtue Ethics*. Oxford: Oxford University Press, 1997.

Smith, Michael. *The Moral Problem*. Malden, MA: Blackwell Publishing, 1994.

Sober, Elliott and David Sloan Wilson. *Unto Others: The Evolution and Psychology of Unselfish Behavior*. Cambridge, MA: Harvard University Press, 1998.

Spencer, David R. *The Yellow Press: The Press and America's Emergence as a World Power*. Evanston, IL: Northwestern University Press, 2007.

Spinoza. *Ethics*. In *Complete Works of Spinoza*. Ed. Michael L. Morgan. Indianapolis: Hackett Publishing, 2002.

Steiner, Linda and Chad M. Okrusch. "Care as a Virtue for Journalists." *Journal of Mass Media Ethics* 21, nos 2–3 (2006): 102–22.

Stevenson, Charles L. *Ethics and Language*. New Haven, CT: Yale University Press, 1944.

Strack, Fritz, Michael Argyle, and Nobert Schwarz. *Subjective Well-Being*, 7–26. Oxford: Pergamon Press, 1991.

Strauss, Leo and Joseph Cropsey. "Marsilius of Padua." In *History of Political Thought*. 2nd ed., 251–70. Chicago: Rand McNally, 1972.

Streeten, Paul et al. *First Things First: Meeting Basic Needs in Developing Countries*. New York: Oxford University Press, 1981.

Sullivan, Roger J. "Introduction." In *Immanuel Kant: The Metaphysics of Morals*, trans. Mary Gregor, vii–xxvi. Cambridge: Cambridge University Press, 1996.

Sunstein, Cass R. *Democracy and the Problem of Free Speech*. New York: Free Press, 1993.

Tan, Kok-Chor. "The Demands of Justice and National Allegiances." In Gillian Brock and Harry Brighouse, eds, *The Political Philosophy of Cosmopolitanism*, 164–79. Cambridge: Cambridge University Press, 2005.

Taylor, Charles. *Philosophical Papers*. Cambridge: Cambridge University Press, 1985.

– *Sources of the Self: The Making of the Modern Identity*. Cambridge: Cambridge University Press, 1992.

– "A Most Peculiar Institution." In J.E.J. Altham and Ross Harrison, eds, *World, Mind, and Ethics: Essays on the Ethical Philosophy of Bernard Williams*, 132–55. Cambridge: Cambridge University Press, 1995.

– *Philosophical Arguments*. Cambridge, MA: Harvard University Press, 1995.

Thagard, Paul. *Conceptual Revolutions*. Princeton, NJ: Princeton University Press, 1992.

Thomson, Judith Jarvis. "A Defence of Abortion." *Philosophy and Public Affairs* 1 (1971).

Thucydides. *History of the Peloponnesian War*. 14 vols. Cambridge, MA: Harvard University Press, 1919–56.

Tolstoy, Leo. *Writings on Civil Disobedience and Nonviolence*. Philadelphia: New Society, 1987.

Toulin, Stephen. *Human Understanding: The Collective Use and Evolution of Concepts*. Princeton, NJ: Princeton University Press, 1972.

Tuck, Richard. *Natural Rights Theories: Their Origin and Development*. Cambridge: Cambridge University Press, 1981.

Unamuno, Miguel de. *The Tragic Sense of Life in Men and Nations*. Trans. Anthony Kerrigan. In *Selected Works of Miguel de Unamuno*, vol. 4. London: Routledge and Kegan, 1972.

Van Evra, Judith. *Television and Child Development*. 3rd ed. Mahwah,
    NJ: Lawrence Erlbaum Associates, 2004.
Van Gelderen, Martin and Quentin Skinner. *Republicanism: A Shared
    European Heritage*. 2 vols. Cambridge: Cambridge University Press,
    2002.
Van Praag, Bernard and Ada Ferrer-i-Carbonell. *Happiness Quantified: A
    Satisfaction Calculus Approach*. Oxford: Oxford University Press, 2004.
Veenhoven, Ruut. "Questions on Happiness: Classical Topics, Modern
    Answers, Blind Spots." In Fritz Strack et al., *Subjective Well-Being*,
    7–26. Oxford: Pergamon Press, 1991.
Venturi, Franco. *Utopia and Reform in the Enlightenment*. Cambridge:
    Cambridge University Press, 1971.
Viroli, Maurizio. *From Politics to Reason of State: The Acquisition and
    Transformation of the Language of Politics 1250–1600*. Cambridge:
    Cambridge University Press, 1992.
– *For Love of Country: An Essay on Patriotism and Nationalism*. Oxford:
    Clarendon Press, 1996.
– *Republicanism*. Trans. Antony Shugaar. New York: Hill and Wang,
    2002.
Vlastos, Gregory, "Justice and Happiness in the Republic." In vol. 2 of
    Plato: A Collection of Critical Essays, 2 vols. Ed. Gregory Vlastos,
    66–95. New York: Anchor Books, 1971.
Wahl-Jorgensen, Karin and Thomas Hanitzsch. *The Handbook of
    Journalism Studies*. New York: Routledge, 2009.
Waley, Daniel. *The Italian City-Republics*. 2nd ed. London: Longmans,
    1978.
Walzer, Michael. "Citizenship." In Terence Ball, James Farr, and Russell
    L. Hanson, eds, *Political Innovation and Conceptual Change*, 211–19.
    Cambridge: Cambridge University Press, 1989.
– "Deliberation, and What Else." In Stephen Macedo, ed., *Essays on
    Democracy and Disagreement*. Oxford: Oxford University Press, 1999.
Ward, Stephen J.A. *The Invention of Journalism Ethics: The Path to
    Objectivity and Beyond*. Montreal: McGill-Queen's University Press,
    2005.
– "Philosophical Foundations for Global Journalism Ethics." *Journal of
    Mass Media Ethics* 20, no. 1 (2005): 3–21.
– "Utility and Impartiality: Being Impartial in a Partial World." *Journal of
    Mass Media Ethics* 22, nos 2–3 (2007): 151–67.
– "Thomas Hobbes: Submission to Leviathan." In Clifford Christians
    and John Merrill, eds, *Ethical Communication: Five Moral Stances in
    Human Dialogue*. Columbia: University of Missouri Press, 2008.

Ward, Stephen J.A. and Herman Wasserman, eds. *Media Ethics Without Borders*. Cape Town: Heinemann Publishers, 2008.

Watson, Harry. "Free Agency." *Journal of Philosophy* 72 (1975), 205–20.

Wilkes, Kathleen V. "The Good Man and the Good for Man in Aristotle's Ethics." In Amelie Oksenberg Rorty, ed., *Essays in Aristotle's Ethics*, 341–57. Berkeley, CA: University of California Press, 1980.

Wilkins, Lee and Clifford G. Christians. *The Handbook of Mass Media Ethics*. New York: Routledge, 2009.

Wilkins, Lee and Renita Coleman. *The Moral Media: How Journalists Reason about Ethics*. Mahwah, NJ: Lawrence Erlbaum Associates, 2005.

Williams, Bernard. *Morality: An Introduction to Ethics*. New York: Harper and Row, 1972.

– *Ethics and the Limits of Philosophy*. Cambridge, MA: Harvard University Press, 1985.

– *Truth and Truthfulness: An Essay in Genealogy*. Princeton, NJ: Princeton University Press, 2002.

– *The Sense of the Past*. Princeton, NJ: Princeton University Press, 2006.

Wiredu, Kwasi. *Cultural Universals and Particulars: An African Perspective*. Bloomington, IN: Indiana University Press, 1996.

Wootton David, ed. Republicanism, *Liberty and Commercial Society, 1649–1776*. Stanford, CA: Stanford University Press, 1994.

Worden, Blair. "Marchamont Nedham and the Beginnings of English Republicanism, 1649–1656." In David Wootton, ed., *Republicanism, Liberty and Commercial* Society, 45–81. Stanford, CA: Stanford University Press, 1994.

Wright, Robert. *The Moral Animal: Evolutionary Psychology and Everyday Life*. New York: Vintage Books, 1994.

Young, Robert J.C. *Post-Colonialism*. Oxford: Oxford University Press, 2003.

Index

180–1, 205; in journalism ethics,
44, 47–8; methodological, 90–1;
and moderate relativism, 96–7;
ontological, 90; pragmatic,
92–3, 248n91; questioning
of, 49; relativity and, 93–102;
traditional, 93
Oldenquist, Andrew, 226, 229
On Liberty (Mill), 143
Orientalism (Said), 252n34
Ortega y Gasset, José, 165
overlapping consensus, 133–4

Paine, Tom, 49
parochial journalism, 159–60, 236
partialities, 226–8, 229
passivism, 99–100
patria, 217–18, 220, 221
Patriarca (Filmer), 220–1
patriotism: of Athenian city-state,
217; as attitude, 223; authoritarian, 216; and citizenship,
215, 227; communal, 216–22,
229; constitutional, 222;
cosmopolitanism and, 161, 233;
cosmopolitan journalism and,
162, 165; and cultural identity,
222; democratic (*see* democratic
patriotism); developmental
journalism and, 206; domestic
vs global, 233–4; ethical theory
of, 223; evaluation of claims of,
225–30, 232–3; extreme, 223,
231; feudal, 219; genuine, 229;
global, 214–15, 232–3, 234;
global journalism ethics and,
213; group loyalty and, 223,
233; humanists and, 219–20;
of humanity, 233–4; and
imperialism, 222; journalism
and, 213–14, 230–1, 232;

journalism ethics and, 214, 215,
227–8; language of, 220–1,
222; and liberty, 220; medieval,
218–19; moderate, 223–4, 225,
228–30, 231; modern nation-
state and, 221; and nationalism,
222; nation-based, 232, 234;
natural, 220; political, 216–22,
229–30; and racial superiority,
222; religion and, 218–19;
Renaissance, 219–20; republican,
216–17, 219–20; requirements
of, 215–16; Roman, 217–18;
romantic, 221–2; royalist, 220–1;
structure of, 223–5
perfectionism, 110, 116–17
Petit, Phillip, 141, 144
philosophical ethics, 23, 24–5;
applied ethics vs, 59–60;
normative ethics and, 88–9. *See
also* metaethics
phronesis, 65
physical goods, 118, 120, 122
Plato, 173
pluralism/plurality: absolutism
and, 98; of beliefs/values, 85,
95; and eclecticism, 64–5; and
ethical thinking, 15; and ethics,
22; free press and, 45; and global
journalism ethics, 159; holism
and, 85; reasonable, 132–5;
and relativism, 95–6; and social
bridging, 170; of values, 68, 85,
179–80; of views of good,
143
Pogge, Thomas, 250n10
political association(s), 186–9;
citizens in, 192; liberal democracy and, 192, 201; public and,
189–90; and social unions,
188

radical skepticism, 21
rational and moral capacities, 169–70
rational and moral goods, 118–19,
120
rational autonomy, 131, 148
rationality, 46, 130–1, 169–71, 205
rational universals, 174
Rawls, John: on Ancient Greek
ethics as naturalistic, 28; and
citizenship, 190–1; on concepts
vs conceptions, 105–6; on
consequentialism, 146–7; on
contractual process, 71, 127,
143; on "decent" society, 203;
and ethics as agreement, 34;
on five forms of good, 146; on
global basic structure, 203; on
good judged against rational
plan for life, 107; on humans
in society, 186; on justice and
social institutions, 127; on
justice as fairness (see under
justice); on justice vs self-
interest, 142; on Kant's view
of constructivism and moral
objectivity, 34; on Kant's view of
ethical objectivity, 91, 247n55;
on moral reasonableness, 119;
and naturalistic ethics, 31; on
objectivity, 136–8; Political
Liberalism, 75, 133–4, 136;
on political liberalism, 133–4,
143; on political vs ethical
identity, 129–30; and primacy
of the social, 247n55; on
primary goods, 169; principles
of justice, 58, 127–8, 133–4,
142–3, 175; and problems within
liberalism, 126–7; on public
reason, 133, 135–8; and rational
vs unreasonable, 130–1; and

reflective equilibrium, 75; and
right vs good, 141–2, 145, 147;
and self-respect, 250n114; on
social union, 186–7; A Theory of
Justice, 75, 127, 133, 134, 136,
228, 242n23; and well-ordered
society, 125–7
realism: objective, 98–9;
procedural, 35, 91; substantive,
35–6, 94
reason: "fact of," 174, 175; of state,
220
reasonableness, 130–1; journalism
and, 205; promotion of, 169,
171–3; and public reason, 185
reasonable pluralism, 132–5
reciprocity, 130–1, 250n114
reflection, 53
reflective engagement, 53–4; in
journalism ethics, 167; universals
and, 175–6
reflective equilibrium, 63, 69, 74–7,
89, 149; in journalism ethics, 166,
167; and theory of good, 105
relativism: absolutism and,
93–5, 99; consensus and, 96;
constructivism and, 96; ethical
plurality and, 95–6; extreme,
98–100; moderate, 95, 96–7, 98,
99, 100; moral, 24; naturalism
and, 96; objective, 94; radical,
95; and ultimate ethical
principles, 95
religion: and common good, 197;
and journalism ethics, 51; and
patriotism, 218–19
representation: of non-dominant
groups, 172; of others, 182
republicanism, 197–8
republican patriotism, 216–17,
219–20, 224

res publica, 195, 217
Riesenberg, Peter, 192
right(s): congruence with
  flourishing, 148; congruence
  with good, 145–7, 172;
  deontology and, 141–2; ethical
  flourishing and, 125, 172;
  good in, 138–49; and justice,
  140–1, 142–3; for liberal society,
  125; moral vs legal, 249n98;
  normative democratic theory
  and, 184; priority of, 140–5;
  relations, 184; and well-ordered
  society, 144
Rinuccini, Alamanno, Dialogue on
  Liberty, 219
romantic patriotism, 221–2
Ross, W.D., 65; Foundations of
  Ethics, 30
Rousseau, Jean-Jacques, Social
  Contract, 248n89
Royce, Josiah, 226
Rusconi, Gian Enrico, 222

Said, Edward, Orientalism, 252n34
Sandel, Michael J., 142
Saussure, Ferdinand de, 82–3
Scanlon, Thomas, 17, 18, 34, 35,
  108, 227
science: absolutism and, 100–1;
  construction of ethics for, 38;
  holism and, 83; hypotheses in,
  37; naturalism and, 27, 29, 41–2;
  normative and factual premises
  in, 240n43; philosophy and, 31
self-actualization, 109, 117
self-government, 191, 192, 194
self-interest, 131, 142, 199
self-realization, 172
Sen, Amartya, 109–10, 246n43
Seneca, 218

Sidgwick, Henry, 84, 141; Methods
  of Ethics, 30
Singer, Marcus, 239n8
Singer, Peter, 156
Smith, Adam, 35
social contract: of global
  journalism, 162–5; of journalism,
  206–7; journalism ethics as, 72;
  between journalists and public,
  50; multisociety, 165
Social Contract (Rousseau),
  248n89
social contract(s), 36, 51, 71
social goods, 118, 119, 120–1;
  journalism and, 207; and
  physical goods, 122–3. See also
  common goods
social institutions. See institutions
social justice, 184, 205, 208
social sciences: and ethics, 41; and
  naturalism, 27
society, 186; democratic, 184, 201;
  global, 204; humans in, 186;
  modern, 200–1; private, 202;
  social unions within, 186–7
Society of Professional Journalists
  (SPJ), 49–50, 67, 77
Spinoza, Benedict de, 116
Steele, Bob, Doing Ethics in
  Journalism, 67
Stevenson, Charles, 30, 59
Summa Theologia (Aquinas), 219

Tan, Kok-Chor, 250n9
Taylor, Charles, 73
theories: building of, 232; desire,
  106, 107; development, 109–10;
  expanionist, 107–10; expanionist
  vs non-expansionist, 106;
  hedonic, 106; non-expansionist,
  106–7; as philosophical